Exam Preparatory Manual of

Forensic Medicine and Toxicology

Questions and Answers

Including Solved Last 5 Years Professional and Supplementary Examination Question Papers of More than 20 Universities

Exam Preparatory Manual of Forensic Medicine and Toxicology

Questions and Answers

Gautam Biswas
MD (Forensic Medicine)
Professor and Head
Department of Forensic Medicine and Toxicology
Dayanand Medical College and Hospital
Ludhiana, Punjab

Tejpreet Singh
MBBS
Junior Resident
Department of Forensic Medicine and Toxicology
Dayanand Medical College and Hospital
Ludhiana, Punjab

CBSPD

CBS Publishers & Distributors Pvt Ltd

New Delhi • Bengaluru • Chennai • Kochi • Kolkata • Lucknow • Mumbai
Gujarat • Hyderabad • Jharkhand • Nagpur • Patna • Pune • Uttarakhand

Exam Preparatory Manual of
Forensic Medicine and Toxicology
Questions and Answers

ISBN: 978-93-90709-15-1

First Edition: 2021
Reprint: 2025, 26

Published by **Satish Kumar Jain** and produced by **Varun Jain** for

CBS Publishers & Distributors Pvt Ltd
4819/XI Prahlad Street, 24 Ansari Road, Daryaganj, New Delhi 110 002, India
Ph: 011-23289259, 23266838 Website: www.cbspd.com
e-mail: delhi@cbspd.com

Corporate Office: 204 FIE, Industrial Area, Patparganj, Delhi 110 092, India
Ph: 011-4934 4934 Fax: 011-4934 4935 e-mail: publishing@cbspd.com; publicity@cbspd.com

Branches

- **Bengaluru:** Seema House 2975, 17th Cross, K.R. Road, Banasankari 2nd Stage, Bengaluru 560 070, Karnataka
  Ph: +91-80-26771678/79 Fax: +91-80-26771680 e-mail: bangalore@cbspd.com
- **Chennai:** 18/8B, Subbarayan Street, Shenoy Nagar, Chennai 600 030, Tamil Nadu, India
  Ph: +91-44-42032115, 26681266 e-mail: chennai@cbspd.com
- **Kochi:** 42/1325, 1326, Power House Road, Opp KSEB Power House, Ernakulam 682 018, Kochi, Kerala
  Ph: +91-484-4059061–65, 67 Fax: +91-484-4059065 e-mail: kochi@cbspd.com
- **Kolkata:** 147, Hind Ceramics Compound, 1st Floor, Nilgunj Road, Belghoria, Kolkata 700 056, West Bengal, India
  Ph: +91-33-25633055/56 e-mail: kolkata@cbspd.com
- **Lucknow:** Basement, Khushnuma Complex, 7 Meerabai Marg(behind Jawahar Bhawan), Lucknow 226 001, UP, India
  Ph: +91-522-4000032 e-mail: tiwari.lucknow@cbspd.com
- **Mumbai:** PWD Shed, Gala No. 25/26, Ramchandra Bhatt Marg, Next JJ Hospital Gate No. 2, Opp. Union Bank of India, Noorbaug, Mumbai 400 009, Maharashtra, India
  Ph: +91-22-66661880/89 e-mail: mumbai@cbspd.com

Representatives

- **Gujarat** 0-9879558667
- **Hyderabad** 0-9885175004
- **Jharkhand** 0-9811541605
- **Nagpur** 0-8692091830
- **Patna** 0-9334159340
- **Pune** 0-9664372571
- **Uttarakhand** 0-9716462459

Printed at: HT Media Ltd, Greater Noida, UP, India

Preface

This book is meant for the last minute revision before the examination. It will be helpful to the students in their professional examinations as well as the semester or terminal examinations and class tests.

The academic year 2020-21 has been an exception as many students were unable to cope up their studies due to the current pandemic situation of COVID-19. Most of the colleges were having online classes and it was not possible to address the difficulties faced by the students. There must have been many queries which the students wanted to ask, but it was not possible since the physical classes were not held. It has taken a toll on most of the students and some of them were not able to study the subjects properly.

This book will help the students to quickly revise the important questions and their answers that were asked in the last 5 years in various universities in India. The students need to have gone through the textbooks earlier for retaining the information given in this book. They can cover the important questions in 1–2 days. It will help them to sail through their professional examination and even score good marks in their theory paper. This book is not meant to cover the whole syllabus and will not solve the purpose of a textbook.

The answers have been written based on an examiner's expectation from the students and will fetch them a decent score. There may be some unexpected questions too, which is the norm in some of the universities.

Best wishes...

Gautam Biswas
Tejpreet Singh

Acknowledgements

We are thankful to the following faculty (in a random order) and students for their help in preparing this book:

Dr Parmod Goyal
Dr Murugesa Bharati
Dr Pramod Tiwari
Dr Chandresh Tailor
Dr Vijay Kumar
Dr Jagadeesh Narayanareddy
Dr Soumeek Chowdhuri
Dr Amarjyoti Patwory
Dr Vijay Pal Khanagwal
Dr Binay Kumar
Dr Uzma Waseem Bachh
Dr Somshekhar Sharma
Dr Anil Kohli
Dr Viswaskanth B
Dr Tapas Kumar Bose
Dr Aditya Sharma
Dr Swapnil S Agarwal
Dr Pradeep Kumar MV
Dr Lalit Kumar Varshney
Dr SK Dhattarwal
Dr Jitender Kumar Jakhar
Dr Vivek Kumar
Dr Sudha R
Tejasvi Jhamb (Final year student)

Dr Virendar Pal Singh, Professor, Department of Forensic Medicine and Toxicology (FMT), Dayanand Medical College and Hospital (DMCH), deserves special appreciation for providing positive feedback and valuable suggestions. Special thanks go to Mr Kuljeet Singh, Mr Amit Kumar and Mr Luv Sharma for their help in typing the manuscript without any complaints.

Sincere thanks and gratitude go to Shri Prem Kumar Gupta, Secretary, Managing Society, DMCH, and Dr Sandeep Puri, Principal, DMCH, for their continuous support, motivation, encouragement and invaluable suggestions.

Last but not least, admiration and appreciation to the whole team of CBS Publishers & Distributors, especially to Mr SK Jain (CMD), Mr Varun Jain (Director), Mr YN Arjuna (Senior Vice President—Publishing, Editorial and Publicity), Ms Ritu Chawla (General Manager), Mr Sumit Behl (Asst. Marketing Manager), Mr Neeraj Prasad and Ms Baljeet Kaur (Graphic Designers), Mr Parmod Rajput and Ms Jyoti Kaur (DTP Operators) and Mr Prasenjit Paul (Copy Editor) for their patience, encouragement and professionalism during the entire process.

Gautam Biswas
Tejpreet Singh

Exam Guidelines

1. Read the question paper properly and thoroughly. Spend 5–7 minutes and think as to how to approach the paper before you start answering.
2. If some question is out of syllabus or you have not covered it before the examination or you have forgotten it, try to use common sense and read the question a few more times. The answer may be there within the question itself.
3. Your answer should be to the point. Do not write what you have not been asked. It will be unnecessary wastage of time.
4. Since the examiner usually spends on an average 7–12 minutes on theory paper, it is advisable that:
   a. Long questions should be in detail, at least 3–4 pages along with flowcharts and line diagrams wherever possible.
   b. Short notes should touch all the important points. It should be in structured form with headings, subheadings and diagrams.
   c. Differentiation should be in tabulated form, mention the important differentiating features on the left side column.
5. Write the dosages for the drugs that you mention in treating a person in case of poisoning.
6. Add MLI wherever possible/needed.

Students may scan and send their University Question Papers either to *forensicdmc@gmail.com* or WhatsApp at 8699511456. It will be duly acknowledged.

Contents

Preface v

Exam Guidelines ix

1. Medical Jurisprudence, Acts and Legal Procedure 1
2. Autopsy and Thanatology 26
3. Identification 46
4. Asphyxial Deaths 63
5. Injury 81
6. Sexual Jurisprudence and Infanticide 122
7. Forensic Psychiatry 150
8. Toxicology 161

CHAPTER 1

Medical Jurisprudence, Acts and Legal Procedure

LONG QUESTIONS

1. Define professional negligence along with its various components and types. What are the normal defences against negligence? (Sher-i-Kashmir Institute, Srinagar Supple 2019) (North Eastern Hill University Shillong 2018, Gujarat Supple 2017)

Define negligence. Name the different types of negligence. Discuss medical negligence. (North Eastern Hill University, Shillong Supple 2019) (VNS, Gujarat 2017)

Ans:

Definition of Professional Negligence

It is defined as lack of reasonable care and skills on part of a doctor that resulted in injury/death of the patient.

Components of Medical Negligence (4D's)

1. **Duty** of doctor
2. **Dereliction** of duty
3. **Damage** to patient
4. **Direct** causation

   For a case of medical negligence to be established, all four conditions must be present.

Types of Negligence

1. Civil negligence
2. Criminal negligence

Civil negligence	Criminal negligence
Injury or damage is mild	More serious than civil negligence as injury is very serious
The patient goes to civil court or consumer court to ask for the compensation as the injury or damage suffered by him can be compensated by money	The patient/ family reports the matter to the police Gross negligence on part of doctor leads to serious injury/death of the patient
Punishment—in form of fine, no imprisonment for doctor	Sec. 304 A IPC deals with criminal negligence—punishment of 2 years of imprisonment and fine
E.g. Failure to take consent for blood transfusion	E.g. Operation on wrong limb

Civil and Criminal Negligence

When patient goes to the civil court or consumer court and also reports the matter to police. In this case, medical negligence can be fought in both civil and criminal courts simultaneously.

For examples of medical negligence—Refer to long question no. 2.

Defences against Negligence

1. **No duty owed to patient:** The doctor did not treat the patient, so no duty exists.
2. **Res judicata:** The things have already been decided by the court, it cannot be tried again by the same court.
3. **Contributory negligence:** Not only doctor, even patient is also found to be negligent. So, doctor can take this as a defence.
4. **Therapeutic misadventure**
   - Occurrence of damage or mishap with the patient due to some drug or procedure.
   - Doctor is not liable
   - *For example:* Hypersensitivity to penicillin, fatal complications with blood transfusion
5. **Limitation:** The case against the negligence of doctor should be filed within 2 years from the date of alleged negligence.
6. **Error of judgement:** It has been recognized by the courts and law. Since a doctor's decision turned out to be wrong, he cannot be liable for medical negligence.
7. **Products liability:** When a manufacturer supplies defective drug/instrument which was prescribed by the doctor to the patient and the patient sustains injury. In this case, the manufacturer is held responsible for the injury.
8. **Informed consent for the act:** The patient was duly informed of the consequences.

2. Define professional negligence. What are the various instances wherein a registered medical practitioner can be held guilty of professional negligence? What will be the punishment, if he/she is found guilty? (Sardar Patel University, Gujarat 2020, Supple 2018) (Delhi University 2015)

Ans:

Definition of Professional Negligence

Refer to long question no. 1.

Various Examples of Medical Negligence

1. **General examination**
   - Failure to examine the patient himself/herself.
   - Failure to attend a patient with consequent damage.
   - Failure to obtain informed consent for any procedure.
   - Making a wrong diagnosis in the absence of skill and knowledge.
2. **Surgery**
   - Delayed diagnosis of acute abdominal lesions (e.g. appendicitis).
   - Retention of instruments, sponges, swabs, etc in operation sites.
   - Operating on the wrong patient, wrong limb/organ, etc.

3. **Emergency medicine**
   - Missing fractures
   - Overtight or prolonged use of plaster casts
   - Inadequately treated hand injuries
   - Undiagnosed intracranial hemorrhage
4. **Obs-Gynae**
   - Performing abortion without indication
   - Mismanagement of delivery (under influence of alcohol/drug)
   - Unwanted pregnancy due to failed tubal ligation
5. **Medicine:** Failure to diagnose MI

Punishment for Professional Negligence

1. Fine
2. Imprisonment
3. Warning
4. Penal erasure

Sec. 304-A IPC deals with criminal negligence where the doctor may be punished with imprisonment for 2 years and fine.

Penal erasure: It is the removal of the name of a doctor from the State Medical Register as a penalty which can be temporary or permanent.

- Temporary erasure—the doctor is not allowed to practise his medical profession for a specified period (may be days, weeks, months or years) in which his name remains removed from the register.
- Permanent erasure of name—is also known as **professional death sentence.**

But the doctor can appeal to Central Health Ministry/Central Government (within 30 days of the decision) which forwards to NMC and the decision is given.

3. Define professional misconduct. Illustrate with suitable examples. What is the action taken against the guilty doctor and by whom? (Adesh, Bathinda 2018) (AIIMS Patna 2019, 2017) (Rajiv Gandhi University, Bengaluru 2015) (Sai Tirupati University, Rajasthan 2019)

Define professional misconduct. Describe various instances wherein a registered medical practitioner can be held guilty of professional misconduct. Differentiate professional misconduct with professional negligence. (Sardar Patel University, Gujarat 2019, 2018) (AIIMS Patna 2017)

Ans:

Definition of Professional Misconduct

Any conduct on part of doctor which is considered disgraceful or dishonourable as judged by professional men of good repute and competence.

Some Examples of Professional Misconduct (6A's)

1. **Adultery:** Voluntary sexual intercourse between a man (married or unmarried, does not matter) and a married woman.

2. **Advertisement:** A physician should not overadvertise himself. He should not
   a. Affix a signboard on a chemist shop
   b. Use touts or agents to procure patients
   c. Advertise himself through manufacturing firms directly or indirectly.
3. **Association with unqualified persons**
4. **Addiction:** To drugs, e.g. cocaine, LSD, etc.
5. **Alcoholism:** The doctor should not practise under the influence of alcohol which interferes with proper practice of medicine.
6. **Abortion:** Doctor performing an illegal abortion is against the medical ethics.
7. **Dichotomy:** (Fee-splitting or fee sharing). It is giving or receiving commission from fellow doctors, manufacturers or chemists.
8. **Issuing a false certificate:** In connection with sickness, insurance, passport, public services, attendance in court
9. **Sex determination test** with an intention of female foeticide.
10. If a doctor does not maintain the **medical records** of indoor patients for a period of 3 years.

Punishment

1. Warning	2. For serious professional misconduct—penal erasure
• Disciplinary action is taken by the Medical Council • Which is issued to the doctor who is guilty of the professional misconduct	• It is the removal of the name of a doctor from the State Medical Register as a penalty • Which can be temporary or permanent • In temporary erasure—the doctor is not allowed to practise his medical profession for a specified period in which his name remains removed from the register. • In permanent erasure—also known as **professional death sentence.** • But the doctor can appeal to Central Health Ministry/ Central Government (within 30 days of the decision) which forwards to NMC and then decision is given

Difference Between Professional Misconduct and Professional Negligence

Refer to difference no. 4.

4. A young man of 25 years allegedly assaulted by some persons brought to the emergency in unconscious state. On examination, there is bleeding scalp wound on the right-side scalp. Just during CT scan within half an hour, the man regained consciousness and wanted to tell something.
a. How will you proceed to record the dying declaration?
b. Duties of emergency medical officer in management of this case.
c. In case of death what is the probable autopsy findings determining the cause of death? (West Bengal Supple 2019)

Ans:

a. Steps in recording of dying declaration
   1. Ideally, Magistrate should be informed to record the dying declaration in presence of witness. But in case the person is about to die, then statement should be recorded by the doctor in presence of two or more witnesses.

2. The preliminary particulars of the patient is noted—name, age, sex, address, Reg. No., MLC No., police station, date and time of admission, location of patient (ward, hospital), ID marks, etc.
3. The doctor should certify that the patient is conscious and fit for giving statement (i.e. compos mentis)—orientation to time, place and person, GCS, BP, pulse, respiratory rate, temperature, ability to speak.
4. Oath is not required (as it is believed that dying person speaks the truth)
5. Statement should be recorded in simple narrative without any alterations, in patient's own words. Date and time of commencement of recording and completion of statement, mode of statement (writing/speech/gesture).
6. If possible, the written statement should be read over to the patient so that it can be rechecked.
7. After taking the dying declaration, it should be signed by the doctor (along with registration no.) and witness.
8. Declaration is sealed and handed over to concerned police officer along with the receipt.

   MLI: If the declarant survives, the declaration is not admitted, but has corroborative value.

b. The emergency medical officer should maintain the ABC of the patient. He should make a quick examination and try to settle the patient.
   - Any bleeding should be dressed and fractures stabilized with temporary splint.
   - He should be sent for CT scan head and X-rays of any suspected fracture.
   - A neurosurgery consult should be arranged immediately.

c. The patient must have had extradural hemorrhage (EDH). Since the initial injury was concussion, subsequently middle meningeal bleed caused the ensuing decompensation from the expanding blood collection leading to coma.

Autopsy Findings

1. Laceration on right side temporal scalp.
2. Hematoma in the epidural space on removal of the skull cap.
3. There may be fissure fracture of the temporal bone.
4. Diffuse brain swelling and cerebral contusions may be seen.
5. Subfalcine herniation extending from the side of the hematoma to the opposite side.
6. Swelling of the cerebral hemisphere under the hematoma with smooth appearance of the brain.

5. What do you mean by evidence? Write the procedure of recording of evidence of a witness in a court of law. (North Eastern Hill University, Shillong, 2017)

Ans:

Definition of Evidence

It is defined as legal means to prove or disprove any medico-legal fact under inquiry.

Procedure of Recording of Evidence

1. **Oath**	• The witness has to take oath that whatever he will say, he will speak the truth, whole truth and nothing but the truth. • **MLI-Perjury:** When person gives false evidence under oath, he is punishable under Section **193 IPC.**
2. **Examination-in-chief**	• **Definition**: It is the examination of witness by the party who calls him or by the prosecution lawyer (in case of criminal cases). • **Main purpose**: To place all the facts known by the witness in front of court· *Leading questions* are not asked in examination-in-chief except when witness is declared hostile by the court.
3. **Cross-examination**	• **Definition:** It is the examination of the witness by the opposite party or the lawyer of the accused party. • **Main purpose** 1. To elicit facts favourable to the case. 2. To test the accuracy of the statements of the witness 3. To modify victim's statements 4. To give a new look to the case • Leading questions are **allowed** in cross-examination. • Witnesses must be very careful while answering the questions in cross-examination as defence lawyer will try to weaken the evidence of witness. There is **no time limit** for cross-examination.
4. **Re-examination**	• **Definition:** It is the examination of a witness subsequent to the cross-examination by the party who called him/ prosecutor lawyer. • **Main purpose** 1. To clarify the doubts that has been raised. 2. To explain some facts more deeply, to avoid misinterpretations • New points are not discussed.
5. **Court questions**	• Judge can ask any question at any stage of examination.

6. What is a summon? How is it served? Briefly describe the different steps of recording of evidence of a witness in the court of law. (North Eastern Hill University, Shillong Supple 2018)

Ans:

Definition of Summon

It is a written document issued by the court, which compels the attendance of the witness in the court of law, on a particular day, at a particular date and time, under penalty.

- It is also known as 'subpoena' and Section **61–69 CrPC** deals with summon.
- It is issued by the court in writing, in duplicate signed by the Magistrate and bears the seal of the court.
- It is delivered to the witness through a police officer or an officer from the court.
- On getting the summons, the witness keeps a copy and signs on the back of the other copy of summon.

- The witness must appear before the court on the specified date and time with proper records.
- A witness must attend the court unless there are valid and urgent reasons for not attending.

A. If a Doctor Gets More than one Summon on the Same Date

But from two different courts	Then he should attend the: 1. Criminal court (given priority over civil court) 2. Higher court
Same type of court	Should attend the court from which he received the summons first and should inform the other court.

B. In Case Witness Fails to Attend the Court

1. With valid reason (like illness)	2. Without any valid reason
Then message must be conveyed to the court, so that a new date of hearing will be issued to him	• Civil cases—liable to pay damages • Criminal court—court may issue notice and asks the reason for nonattendance. In case of no justification, he may be imposed a **fine or/and imprisonment** and **warrant** may be issued against him

Recording of Evidence in Court

Refer to long question no. 5

7. Write in detail about medical evidence and its types. (Pondicherry 2015) (VNS, Gujarat 2017)

Ans:

Definition of Evidence

It is defined as legal means to prove or disprove any medico-legal fact under inquiry.

Types

1. Oral evidence
2. Documentary evidence

1. Oral Evidence

It means all statements (oral or verbal) which the court permits or requires to be made before it by witnesses, in relation to matters of fact under inquiry.

Types of oral evidence

1. Direct evidence
2. Hearsay evidence/indirect evidence

MLI: Oral evidence is more important than documentary evidence, as it permits cross-examination.

Documentary evidence is accepted by the court only after oral testimony by the person concerned.

Exceptions to it are:

1. Dying declaration
2. Matter written in the books
3. Evidence given by witness in lower court
4. Reports of certain scientific experts. (ballistic expert, fingerprint expert, DNA fingerprint expert)
5. Public records
6. Hospital records, etc

2. Documentary Evidence

All the documents (written or printed) that are produced for the inspection of the court.

Different Types of Documentary Evidence are

1. **Medical certificates**	These are issued by Registered Medical Officer, e.g. • Fitness Certificate • Illness Certificate • Birth Certificate • Death Certificate • Disability Certificate • Mental illness Certificate Doctors must retain one duplicate copy of these certificates
2. **Medico-legal certificates**	• Reports prepared by a doctor at the request of the investigating officer/victim, usually in criminal cases, e.g. a. Injury report b. Wound certificate c. Post-mortem report d. Report after examination of victim of sexual assault These reports do not serve as evidence, until the doctor attends the court and testifies to the facts under oath.
3. **Dying declaration**	**Definition:** It is written or oral statement which is made by the dying person as a result of unlawful act, leading to his or her death. Section **32 IEA** deals with dying declaration.
4. **Dying deposition**	1. It can only be recorded by the magistrate. 2. In the presence of accused party/lawyer. 3. Oath is taken. 4. Cross examination is permitted. **MLI** • Has more legal value as acts as bedside court • Not followed in India

8. Define evidence. Discuss documentary evidence. (Sher-i-Kashmir Institute, Srinagar Supple 2017)

Ans: Refer to long question no. 7.

9. Discuss briefly the duties of a doctor in court while giving evidence. (Adesh, Bathinda supple 2018)

Ans:

The Duties of a Doctor in Court While Giving Evidence are:

1. He should attend the court punctually
2. He should be well prepared before entering the witness box
3. Take all records and relevant reports as required by court
4. He should be well dressed
5. He should switch off the mobile or keep the mobile in silent mode
6. He should not discuss the case with anyone in the court except prosecutor lawyer
7. He should speak slowly, distinctly and audibly and should use simple language (not technical language)
8. He should address the Judge by his proper title such as 'Sir' or 'Your honor'
9. If a question is not understood, he can ask the lawyer to explain it better
10. He should be pleasant, polite and courteous in the court
11. He should not lose temper
12. He should not volunteer any information beyond what is asked until or unless he feels that his answer to a particular question does not reflect the whole truth.
13. If he does not wish to make any statement, he can say 'no opinion' or 'no comments.'
14. He should avoid speaking on a subject in which he has little or no practical experience.

10. A surgeon attends a late night new year party where he consumes substantial amount of alcohol. While returning home, he receives an emergency call for appendicitis surgery of a young patient. He goes to the hospital and undertakes the surgery. During surgery, the small intestine sustains cuts by the surgeon which remains unnoticed. The patient reports back with complications for which another surgery was done. Three months later patient files the case of negligence against the doctor. (Rajasthan University 2017)

a. Does the case fulfil the criteria for criminal negligence when the second surgery is successful and does not leave any complications? Give reasons for your answer.

b. Does the surgeon's behavior amount to unethical practice and why?

c. What should the surgeon have done on receiving the emergency call while returning home?

Ans:

a. Yes, the case fulfils the criteria for criminal negligence. During surgery small intestine sustained cuts by the surgeon leading to an injury which resulted in complications to the patient (damage). Any damage suffered is negligence. Successful second surgery does not vitiate (annul) the wrongdoing done in the first surgery.

   Sec. 304-A IPC deals with criminal negligence where the doctor may be punished with imprisonment up to 2 years and fine.

b. Yes, the surgeon's behavior amounts to unethical practice. It is considered 'professional misconduct" as per the **Indian Medical Council (Professional Conduct, Etiquette and Ethics) Regulations.** He should not "be **drunk and disorderly** so as to interfere with proper practice of medicine."

c. He should have informed that he had alcohol and not in a position to operate when he received the call. He should have delegated this duty one of his colleagues and should not have established therapeutic relationship with the patient.

11. A patient had undergone laparotomy for acute abdomen. He died after 14 days of operation. During the postoperative period, he constantly complained of abdominal pain which was treated symptomatically by the surgeon. Alleging negligence in treatment, the relatives asked for a postmortem examination. At autopsy, two gauze pieces were recovered from the peritoneal cavity and cause of death was found to be septic shock following peritonitis. With reference to the case, answer the following questions: (Sardar Patel University, Gujarat 2016)

a. In the terminology of medical negligence, what does findings of gauze piece amount to?

b. Who all can be held liable for the negligence act and why?

c. What all punishments would each of the guilty are liable to be awarded? Explain with reasons.

Ans:

a. In the terminology of medical negligence, finding of gauze pieces amounts to gross negligence and comes under **"Doctrine of Res ipsa loquitur"** which means thing/ fact speaks for itself. The negligence is so gross and obvious that patient does not need to prove any negligence (which is required in other cases).

For application of this rule, three conditions which must be fulfilled are very clear:

i. **In the absence of negligence, the injury would not have occurred**—it occurred due to negligence of surgeon; the surgeon should have been more careful in instructing his staff to get the gauze pieces counted before closing the abdomen.

ii. **The doctor had a full control over the treatment resulting in injury the patent**—the surgeon operated on the patient.

iii. **Patient is not guilty of contributory negligence**—which is obvious, as this happened postoperative and was under the care of surgeon.

b. The surgeon along with the support staff will be held responsible as they were responsible for the well-being of the patient. There was dereliction of duty on the part of surgeon which resulted in damage (death) of the patient and he was directly involved in the causation.

c. The surgeon will be tried under **Sec. 304-A IPC** which is death due to rash and negligent act (criminal negligence) and the doctor may be punished with imprisonment up to 2 years and fine. There may be penal erasure by the State Medical Council.

12. Define inquest. What are the types of inquest? Describe various types of inquest in brief. (AIIMS Patna 2015)

Ans:

Definition of inquest

It is an inquiry or investigation by legal authorities into the cause of death where death is due to unnatural means.

Types of Inquest	Conducted by
Police inquest	Police
Magistrate inquest	Magistrate
Coroner's inquest	Coroner
Medical examiner system	Medical examiner

1. Police Inquest: Section 174 CrPC

- **Definition:** The investigation or inquiry by the police into the cause of death is called police inquest.
- **Most common** type of inquest in India.
- Which is held routinely
- Investigation is done by the police officer/investigation officer not below the cadre of **Senior Head Constable.**

Purpose of police inquest

To find out the

- Identity of the deceased
- Place of death
- Time of death
- Cause of death

Procedure

1. Information of death is given to the police
2. Police officer informs the nearest Executive Magistrate in order to proceed with the inquest
3. Preparation of Panchnama
    - Investigating officer holds an inquiry into the matter, in the presence of two witnesses (neighbours of that locality—panchas)
    - Statements are also recorded from the family members
    - Finally, inquest report is prepared which is called **panchnama**
    - It is then signed by the investigating officer himself and by the **panchas**
4. In case of foul play/when unnatural death is suspected: Investigating officer forwards the body for postmortem examination with the copy of inquest papers
5. Then, report is finally forwarded to the magistrate.

2. Magistrate Inquest: Section 176 CrPC

- **Definition:** The inquiry into the case of death conducted by magistrate is called Magistrate Inquest.
- It may be conduct by executive magistrate or judicial magistrate.

Magistrate inquest is conducted in:

1. Death of person in prison
2. Death in police custody
3. Death of person due to police firing
4. Rape in police custody
5. Dowry death
6. Exhumation

   In India, only Police and Magistrate Inquest is allowed

3. Coroner's Inquest

Definition: It is the inquiry into the cause of death conducted by coroner.

- Coroner is a person with medical and legal knowledge of the rank of first-class judicial Magistrate, appointed by State Government.
- It was followed earlier in Kolkata and Mumbai but was abolished subsequently.
- At present, it is followed in countries such as UK, USA, etc.
- It is similar to magistrate inquest in quality.
- Coroner is authorised only to conduct inquest; he is not authorised to conduct trial.

4. Medical Examiner System

- This type of inquest is conducted in the USA.
- It has a Board Certified Forensic Pathologist who visits the crime scene, gather evidence and interviews the people to gather information and even conducts autopsy
- Best system for inquest.

13. Define 'consent'. What is informed consent? Discuss about the privileged communications with suitable examples. (Pondicherry 2017)

Describe rules of consent in brief. (AIIMS Patna 2016)

Ans:

Definition of Consent

It means voluntary agreement, compliance or permission for some act.

Types of Consent

1. **Implied consent**
   - When a patient comes to the doctor for his medical examination and treatment
   - It neither expressed in words nor in written form
   - It is basically limited to inspection, palpation, percussion and auscultation
2. **Expressed consent:** It is the consent which is specifically expressed by the patient

Oral consent	Written consent
Obtained for minor procedures	Obtained for: 1. All major diagnostic/ therapeutic procedures 2. General anaesthesia

Informed Consent

Also called *Doctrine of Informed Consent*
The doctor should explain

- The condition or nature of illness
- The need for diagnostic tests to be done
- All the treatment options
- And the alternative procedures
- Risk benefit ratio of the procedures
- Associated complications or consequences
- Prognosis of the treatment
- Duration and treatment cost

It should be in simple and proper language so that patient can decide if he/she wants to undergo the treatment or not.

Exceptions to informed consent:

1. In case of **emergency—**as per Section **92 IPC**
2. **Therapeutic privilege:** If doctor feels that full disclosure to patient can cause anxiety, then doctor can disclose full information to any of the family members. For example, cancer report
3. **Therapeutic waiver:** The patient having full faith in the doctor may waiver his/her rights of informed consent
4. **Prisoners:** Convicted person has no right as any other citizen
5. Medical examination requested by the police officer of an arrested accused—under Sec. **53 (1) CrPC**
6. Treatment of notifiable diseases for community interest
7. **Medico-legal postmortem**—as per Section **174 CrPC.**

RULES OF CONSENT

1. Should be free, voluntary, cleared, informed and there should not be any undue influence, fraud, misinterpretation of facts.
2. All the procedures beyond routine physical examination requires expressed consent.
3. When written consent is obtained, it should also be signed by some other witness.
4. In case of children less than 12 years of age and in case of insane person, the consent comes from the parent or guardian.
5. As per Section **90 IPC**—consent given by an insane or intoxicated person, is not valid.
6. As per Section **92 IPC**—in case of emergency, if a patient is unconscious and no guardian is available to give consent, then doctor can perform emergency procedure/surgery without the consent, if it is essential to save the life of the patient.
7. Any person of more than 18 years of age can give valid consent.

8. Consent given for a diagnostic procedure cannot be considered as consent for therapeutic treatment or for some other procedure.
9. No consent is required in case of medico-legal autopsies.
10. Consent of both partners (husband and wife) is required for contraceptive sterilisation and artificial insemination.
11. Pregnant female (>18 years) alone can give consent for termination of pregnancy
12. Husband or wife has no right to deny the treatment for his or her spouse.
13. For examination of victim of a criminal case (e.g. rape), consent is mandatory.

PRIVILEGED COMMUNICATION

Definition of Privileged Communication

Disclosure of confidential information by the doctor to the concerned public authority due to his legal, moral and social duty to protect the interest of the community.

- It is an exception to professional secrecy.
- The doctor has the moral duty to keep the information about the illness of his patient secret or confidential. But he also has a moral duty to protect the interests of the community. So here, privileged communication plays an important role.
- The doctor will not be liable to damage because it is in the interest of the community.

Some Examples of Privileged Communication are:

1. **Court of law:** In court of law, doctor cannot claim professional secrecy concerning the facts about illness of his patient.
2. **Civic benefit:** In case drivers are suffering from epilepsy, alcoholism, drug addiction, color blindness, the doctor should advise him to change the employment because of the dangers of his present occupation both to himself and to the public. If he refuses, then doctor can disclose this information to the concerned authority.
3. **Venereal disease:** If the person is suffering from syphilis or HIV infection and is going to marry, it is the duty of the treating doctor to advise him not to marry till he is cured. If patient refuses, doctor can disclose the details of the disease to the other party.
4. **Suspected crime:** If the physician comes across any suspected crime, such as assault, traffic offence or homicidal poisoning while treating the patient, he should inform police (Sec. **39 CrPC**).
5. **Notifiable clauses:** It is the duty of the doctor to notify births, deaths, stillbirths, infectious diseases, epidemic and food poisoning to public health authorities.
6. **In patient's interest:** Doctor may disclose patient's condition to his relatives in case person is suffering from certain symptoms like suicidal tendencies, so that he can be treated properly.

SHORT NOTES

1. Functions of State Medical Council. (Adesh, Bathinda supple 2020) (KHMS 2016) (Rajasthan University 2016) (Rajiv Gandhi University, Bengaluru 2015)

1. Maintaining the medical register	• Maintains a register of medical practitioners within its jurisdiction • After passing the medical degree, provisional registration is done, and after completing the internship, permanent registration is given
2. Renewal of registration	• Permanent registration certificate has to be renewed after every 5 years • For renewal, it is mandatory for doctor to show certificate of participation in CME programmes for at least 30 hrs
3. Disciplinary control	• State Medical Council has the power of taking disciplinary control over the doctor found indulging in unethical practice by: 1. Issuing warning 2. Suspension 3. Penal erasure (temporary/ permanent)

2. Consent (BFUHS, Punjab supple 2020, 2017, 2016) (Andhra Pradesh 2016, supple 2016) (VNS, Gujarat supple 2018) (JIPMER supple 2018)

Ans: Refer to long question no. 13.

3. Implied consent (Uttarakhand University 2015)

Implied consent is one which is not expressly granted by a person (verbally or written), but rather implicitly granted by a person's actions and the facts and circumstances of a particular situation (or in some cases, by a person's silence or inaction).

Implied consent can be:

a. When a patient comes to the doctor's clinic for medical examination and treatment. It is basically limited to inspection, palpation, percussion and auscultation.
b. Medical treatment given to an unconscious patient is implied, despite the unconscious person being unable to expressly grant consent for that treatment.

4. Defences available to registered medical officer against alleged medical negligence (Sardar Patel University, Gujarat 2015) (AIIMS, Patna 2016)

Ans: Refer to long question no. 1.

5. Contributory negligence (BFUHS, Punjab supple 2020) (North Eastern Hill University, Shillong supple 2020)

Ans:

Definition of Contribution Negligence

Any unreasonable conduct from the part of the patient/attendant which combined with the doctor's negligence contributed to the injury complained of, as a direct cause and without which the injury would not have occurred.

Patient contributes to his negligence when he:

- Fails to follow doctor's instructions regarding medicines
- Fails to give proper medical history to the doctor (not informing about the drug allergies)
- Fails to follow up (in spite of doctor's suggestion)

Example: Doctor applied a tight plaster cast on the patient's hand (doctor's negligence) As a result, the patient developed numbness in his fingers, but he did not inform the doctor (patient's negligence). Consequently, the patient had suffered permanent injury as it is resulted to the formation of gangrene.

Limitations to Contributory Negligence

1. Last clear chance doctrine
2. Avoidable consequences rule

MLI:

1. Acts as a good defence for the doctor in civil cases but burden of proof lies with the doctor
2. Not act as defence in case of criminal cases

6. Professional negligence. (Rajiv Gandhi University, Bengaluru 2020) (Uttarakhand University 2017) (KHMS, Tamil Nadu 2018, 2017, 2016) (North Eastern Hill University, Shillong 2017) (Himachal Pradesh 2017) (Sher-i-Kashmir, Srinagar supple 2015) (JIPMER 2016)

Ans: Refer to long question no. 1.

7. Documentary evidence. (Andhra Pradesh supple 2015) (Pondicherry, 2019)

Ans: Refer to long question no. 7.

8. Perjury (Rajiv Gandhi University, Bengaluru 2020, 2015) (KHMS, Tamil Nadu 2018) (Andhra Pradesh 2015)

Ans:

Definition	As per Sec. **191 IPC,** it is defined as wilfully giving false evidence under oath.
Punishment for perjury	As per Sec. **193 IPC,** imprisonment up to 7 years and fine.
Reasons behind perjury	a. Witness may have taken bribe b. He may be under threat c. He may have personal bias towards one party

9. Doctrine of Calculated Risk. (Adesh, Bathinda supple 2019)

Ans:

Definition: Every procedure has an inherent risk, which unavoidable in spite of providing a reasonable care.

- It means doctor is not liable if he has provided reasonable care and taken calculated risk to save the life of a patient but during the process, the patient suffered damage.
- An exception to Doctrine of Res ipsa loquitur
- And acts as a good defence to any doctor.
- For example—a patient undergoing CABG dies during the surgery, will not amount to negligence rather it becomes a case of professional accident as there is a calculated risk of danger.

10. Res ipsa loquitur (Rajiv Gandhi University, Bengaluru 2020, 2015) (AIIMS, Patna 2019, 2017, 2015) (Pondicherry 2019, 2017) (North Eastern Hill University, Shillong 2018) (Adesh, Bathinda Supple 2017) (Rajasthan University 2016) (Uttarakhand University Supple 2017, 2016) (BFUHS, Punjab 2015) (VNS, Gujarat 2018, supple 2019) (Sai Tirupati University, Rajasthan 2018)

Ans:

1. Doctrine of Res ipsa loquitur means "thing/facts speaks for itself".
2. Normally, in case of professional negligence of doctor, burden of proof lies with the patient.
3. But in some cases where rule of "Res ipsa loquitur" applies, the negligence is so gross and obvious that patient does not need to prove any negligence.
4. For application of this rule, three conditions must be fulfilled:
   i. In the absence of negligence, the injury would not have occurred.
   ii. The doctor had a full control over the treatment/instrument resulting in injury the patient
   iii. Patient is not guilty of contributory negligence.
5. **Examples**
   a. Operating on a wrong patient or wrong part of the body. For example, instead of operating on right leg, doctor operates on the left leg.
   b. Leaving surgical instruments in abdomen after surgery.
   c. Blood transfusions mismatch hazard.

11. Consumer court/Consumer Protection Act (AIIMS, Patna 2019, 2017) (SGRD, Amritsar 2019) (VNS, Gujarat supple 2018)

Ans:

1. In 1986, Consumer Protection Act was introduced to protect the interest of the consumer and for the settlement of consumer disputes.
2. In 1992, medical services were also covered under Consumer Protection Act.
3. The Consumer Protection Act, 2019 replaced the more than three decades old Consumer Protection Act, 1986.
4. **E-filing of complaints:** The consumer can file complaints with the jurisdictional consumer forum located at the place of residence/work of the consumer. It also enables the consumer to file complaints electronically and for hearing and/or examining parties through video-conferencing.
5. **Mediation:** There is a provision for settlement of disputes by way of mediation at the stage of complaint or at any later stage, if acceptable to both parties. In the event of failure to settle the dispute, the respective commissions shall continue to adjudicate the dispute.
6. **Products liability:** Consumers have the right to seek compensation for any harm caused.
7. **Advantages of consumer court**
   a. They provide speedy and simple solutions to the consumer disputes (A/k/a fast-track courts)
   b. Do not require any lawyer
   c. No court fee is taken
8. **Limitation period:** The complaint has to be lodged within **2 years** from the date of cause of action.

Consumer Disputes Redressal Agencies

	District Commission	State Commission	National Commission
Level	At District level	At State level	At National level
Headed by	District Judge	Judge of High Court	Judge of Supreme Court
Jurisdiction	Up to ₹ 1 crore	₹ 1 crore to 10 crores	More than ₹ 10 crores

Medical Services

In 1995, it was decided to cover Medical Services under Consumer Protection Act, and hospitals were divided into 3 categories:

Category 1: Government hospitals, dispensaries, non-government hospitals or nursing home where services are provided for free (i.e., no charge is taken from the patient). Do not fall under Consumer Protection Act

Category 2: Hospitals or nursing homes where some patients (who are not able to pay for treatment) are given services for free while others those who can afford are given services on payment basis. Fall under Consumer Protection Act

Category 3: Medical services provided on Payment Basis. Fall under Consumer Protection Act

12. Privileged communication. (BFUHS, Punjab supple 2019, supple 2016) (Uttarakhand University Supple 2018) (Delhi University 2015) (VNS, Gujarat 2018)

Ans:

Refer to long question no. 13.

13. Inquest. (West Bengal University supple 2019) (Rajasthan University 2018) (BFUHS, Punjab 2017)

Ans:

Refer to long question no. 12.

14. Section 53 CrPC (Pondicherry 2016) (JIPMER 2016)

Sec. 53 CrPC deals with examination of accused by medical practitioner at the request of police officer.

1. When a person is arrested on a charge of committing an offence and there are reasonable grounds for believing that an examination of his person will afford evidence as to the commission of the offence, it shall be lawful for a doctor, to make an examination of the person arrested as is necessary in order to obtain evidence, even by using reasonable force if requested by a police officer not below the rank of sub-inspector.

   This includes examination of blood, bloodstains, semen, swabs in cases of sexual offences, sputum and sweat, hair samples and fingernail clippings using modern and scientific techniques including DNA profiling.
2. Whenever a female accused is to be examined under this section, the examination shall be made only by, or under the supervision of, a female doctor. Such an examination by a male doctor must not be carried out even in the presence of a female nurse.

15. Vicarious liability/Doctrine of 'Respondent Superior'. (BFUHS, Punjab 2019, Supple 2019) (Rajiv Gandhi University, Bengaluru 2019) (Delhi University 2018) (West Bengal University 2017) (Himachal Pradesh 2017) (Jammu and Kashmir 2017) (Uttarakhand University 2016) (Sardar Patel University, Gujarat 2015) (KHMS, Tamil Nadu 2015) (VNS, Gujarat 2016)

Ans:

Definition: An employer will be held responsible for any negligent act done by his employees.

- The term means "let the master answer".
- It is also called "Captain of ship doctrine": Chief surgeon, will be answerable for his subordinate's negligence. Doctor (employer) will be held responsible for the mistake of the nursing staff (employee).
- Under this, the hospital is responsible for all the negligence of his employees who are acting under its supervision and control.

- For application of this principle, following conditions must be fulfilled:
  1. Employee–employer relationship.
  2. The employee's conduct should be within the scope of employment.
  3. The act should have occurred while on the job.

Examples:

a. Hospital management is held responsible for the mistakes committed by the residents and interns in training but a physician will be held responsible for the acts of interns and residents carried out under his direct supervision and control.
b. Hospital management is not held responsible for the mistakes committed by the senior medical staff.
c. If a doctor after operating the patient, leaves a swab or instrument inside the patient's body, he will be held responsible. The anesthetist will not be held responsible.

16. Subpoena/ Summon. (Sardar Patel University, Gujarat 2020, 2019, 2018, supple 2019) (Adesh, Bathinda 2018) (Sher-i-Kashmir, Srinagar Supple 2018) (North Eastern Hill University, Shillong 2016) (AIIMS, Patna 2015) (VNS, Gujarat 2018, supple 2017)

Ans: Refer to long question no. 6.

17. Cross examination. (Adesh, Bathinda supple 2018) (Delhi University 2017) (Uttarakhand University 2016, supple 2017)

Ans: Refer to long question no. 5.

18. Novus actus interveniens. (Adesh, Bathinda Supple 2018)

Ans:

- Novus actus interveniens ('new intervening act') is an independent event which, after the accused's act has been concluded either caused or contributed to the consequence concerned.
- This new act breaks the causal chain between the accused's action and the liability that is implicated to him as a result thereof.
- As a novus actus is an 'independent' intervening act, it can be caused by anyone or anything other than the accused. This general category also includes the injured party himself, doctor or even an act of God.
- Novus actus is a defense for the accused who wish to prove that his liability is limited or non-existent and should be attributed on another party.
- **Example:** When a patient is hospitalized with head injury due to an assault, sustains fracture of femur in hospital due to fall on wet floors.

19. Powers of judicial magistrates. (AIIMS, Patna 2018) (Sai Tirupati University, Rajasthan 2018)

Ans:

Magistrate	Imprisonment (up to)	Fine
1. Chief Judicial Magistrate	7 years	Unlimited
2. Judicial 1st Class Magistrate	3 years	₹ 10,000/–
3. Judicial 2nd Class Magistrate	1 year	₹ 5000/–

20. Various courts and their powers (Sardar Patel University, Gujarat June 2016) (Pondicherry 2016) (VNS, Gujarat supple 2018) (JIPMER 2016)

Ans:

Criminal courts	Punishment	Fine
1. Supreme Court (**Highest court** in country)	Can pass **any sentence** including death sentence	Unlimited
2. High Court • Highest Court in State • Death sentence given by sessions court is confirmed by High Court.	Can pass **any sentence** including death sentence	Unlimited
3. Sessions Court • Highest Court in district	Can pass **any sentence** including death sentence (but forwarded to High Court for confirmation.)	Unlimited
4. Magistrate Court		
Chief Judicial Magistrate	Up to 7 years of imprisonment	Unlimited
Judicial 1st Class Magistrate	Up to 3 years of imprisonment	₹ 10,000/–
Judicial 2nd Class Magistrate	1 year of imprisonment	₹ 5000/–

21. Schedule of MCI. (AIIMS, Patna 2018, 2016)

Ans:

1st Schedule	All the recognised medical qualifications granted by medical universities in India
2nd Schedule	It comprises all the medical qualification granted by medical universities that are located outside India
Part: 1 of 3rd Schedule	Comprises qualification granted by medical institutions not included in first schedule
Part: 2 of 3rd Schedule	Comprises medical qualification granted medical institutions outside India but not included in second schedule

22. Dying declaration. (North Eastern Hill University, Shillong supple 2020) (BFUHS,Punjab 2019, 2017, 2015) (SGRD, Amritsar 2019) (West Bengal University 2019) (Sardar Patel University, Gujarat 2015) (Uttarakhand University 2016, 2015)

Ans: Refer to long question no. 4.

23. Dying deposition. (BFUHS, Punjab Supple 2018) (AIIMS, Patna 2016)

Ans: Refer to long question no. 7.

24. Penal erasure. (BFUHS, Punjab Supple 2018) (Rajiv Gandhi University, Bengaluru 2015) (VNS, Gujarat 2019, supple 2019)

Ans:

Definition of Penal Erasure

It is the removal of the name of a doctor from the State Medical Register as a penalty. Penal erasure can be temporary or permanent.

Temporary Erasure of name	Permanent Erasure of name (also called professional death sentence)
The doctor is not allowed to practise his medical profession for a specific period of time (like weeks/months/years) in which his name remains removed from the register	• It is the permanent removal of name of the doctor from the State Medical Register • After removal of the name permanently, the doctor is not allowed to practise his medical profession for his whole life

But if the doctor is not satisfied with the decision of State Medical Council, he can appeal to Central Health Ministry (within 30 days of the decision) which forwards to NMC, and the decision is given.

25. Professional misconduct/Infamous conduct. (West Bengal University 2018, supple 2019) (North Eastern Hill University, Shillong 2016, 2015, Supple 2018) (Sardar Patel University, Gujarat 2017, 2015, supple 2015) (KHMS, Tamil Nadu 2015) (GMC, Chandigarh 2015) (GMC, Chamba 2019)

Ans: Refer to long question no. 3.

26. Leading questions (North Eastern Hill University, Shillong 2018)

Ans:

Definition of Leading Question

Any question suggesting the answer, which the person putting it wishes or expects to receive.
Answer for leading questions is either Yes/No.

Examples:

- Was the injury caused by knife?
- Was kerosene used to burn her?

1. Leading questions are not allowed in Examination-in-Chief and Re-Examination.

2. But leading questions may be asked in Examination-in-Chief under two conditions.
   - When the witness is declared hostile by the court
   - When court give permission to ask leading questions
3. Leading questions are allowed in cross-examination.

27. Conduct money (Rajiv Gandhi University, Bengaluru 2015) (GMC, Chamba 2019)

Ans:

Definition of Conduct Money

It is the fee paid to a witness in **civil cases** at the time of serving the summons to meet the expenses for attending the court.

- If the conduct money is not sufficient or not paid, then it can be brought into the notice of court before giving evidence and court will decide the amount.
- In **criminal cases**—no conduct money is paid at the time of serving the summon. The witness must attend the court in interest of State or justice. However, Government usually pays TA and DA allowances.

28. Professional death sentence. (Rajiv Gandhi University, Bengaluru 2018) (Rajasthan University 2018)

Ans:

Definition of Professional Death Sentence

It is defined as the permanent removal of name of the doctor from the State Medical Register (penal erasure).

- This punishment is given to a medical practitioner when he is found guilty of the serious professional misconduct, like
  1. Adultery
  2. Addiction to drugs
  3. Alcoholism
  4. Criminal abortion
  5. Female feticide
- After removal of the name permanently, the doctor is not allowed to practise his medical profession for his whole life.

29. Conduct of a doctor in witness box. (Rajasthan University 2018) (Pondicherry, 2017)

Ans: Refer to long question no. 9.

30. Informed consent (SGRD, Amritsar 2019) (Sardar Patel University, Gujarat Supple 2018) (Adesh, Bathinda supple 2018, 2016) (Rajasthan University 2018, 2016) (North Eastern Hill University, Shillong 2016)

Ans: Refer to long question no. 13.

31. Police inquest (KHMS, Tamil Nadu 2016)

Describe the procedure of police inquest. (Rajiv Gandhi University 2015)

Ans:
Refer to long question no. 12.

32. Magistrate's inquest/Section 176 CrPC (Uttarakhand University 2017) (KHMS, Tamil Nadu 2015) (Delhi University Supple 2016) (Himachal Pradesh 2017) (Rajiv Gandhi University, Bengaluru 2015)

Ans: Refer to long question no. 12.

33. Expert witness (Sai Tirupati University, Rajasthan 2019)

Ans:
Definition: An expert witness is a person who is skilled in a particular field (law, science or art).

Legally Defined Under Sec. 45 IEA.

- He can draw conclusions on facts observed by him or by others.
- He can express an opinion on observations made by others.
- He can volunteer information, and highly responsible for his/her comments.

DIFFERENTIATIONS

1. Examination-in-Chief and cross-examination (BFUHS, Punjab Supple 2020)

	Examination-in-Chief	Cross-examination
Definition	The first statement which is recorded by the prosecution lawyer/the party who calls him	The statement which is recorded by the lawyer of the accused party
Leading questions	Not allowed	Allowed
Order of sequence	Oath is followed by Examination-in-Chief	Examination-in-Chief is followed by cross-examination
Objectives	To place before the court all the facts that bear on the case	To elicit facts favorable to his case; test the accuracy of the statements, and to discredit the witness

2. Dying Declaration and Dying Deposition (University of Health Sciences, Rohtak 2019, 2017, supple 2020) (GMC, Chandigarh 2015) (Rajasthan University 2017, 2016) (North Eastern Hill University, Shillong supple 2016) (VNS, Gujarat 2018)

	Dying declaration	Dying deposition
Oath	Not required	Must
Recorded	By anyone (magistrate/doctor/police officer)	Only by magistrate
Accused party	Not allowed	Allowed
Cross-examination	Not allowed	Allowed
Followed in India	Yes	No
If person survives	Loses its value, but has corroborative value	Value is retained
Legal value	Less	More
Type of evidence	Documentary	Oral
Role of doctor	Assess compos mentis and record the statement in absence of magistrate, but in presence of witnesses	Assess compos mentis only

3. Civil negligence and criminal negligence (University of Health Sciences, Rohtak 2019, 2017, supple 2020) (Adesh, Bathinda 2019, 2017) (BFUHS, Punjab 2019, supple 2019) (Delhi University 2017) (GMC, Chandigarh 2016) (North Eastern Hill University, Shillong Supple 2016)

	Civil negligence	Criminal negligence
Trial by	Civil court/consumer court	Criminal court
Negligence	Simple absence of care and skill	Gross negligence
Punishment	Monetary compensation	Imprisonment, fine or both
Evidence	Strong evidence is sufficient	Guilt should be proved beyond reasonable doubt
Complainant	Sufferer party	Public prosecutor on behalf of the State
Contributory negligence	Act as defense for doctor	Not a defense for doctor
Consent for act	—do—	—do—
Litigation	Between two parties	State vs doctor

4. Professional misconduct and professional negligence (Sher-i-Kashmir, Srinagar 2020, supple 2017) (West Bengal University 2017) (Sardar Patel University, Gujarat supple 2016) (Delhi University Supple 2016) (Uttarakhand University 2015)

	Professional misconduct	Professional negligence
Definition	Conduct which is considered disgraceful and dishonorable by professional colleagues of good repute	Lack of reasonable care and skills that resulted in damage /death of the patient
Offence	Violation of Code of Medical Ethics	Absence of care and skill
Duty of care	Need not be present	Should be present
Damage to person	—do—	—do—
Trial by	State Medical Council	Courts- civil/ criminal
Punishment	Warning or erasure of name	Fine, imprisonment or both
Appeal	To NMC or central government	Higher court

CHAPTER

2

Autopsy and Thanatology

LONG QUESTIONS

1. Classify the changes occurring in the body after death. Discuss their role in the determination of 'Time Since Death'. (BFUHS, Punjab 2019, 2015, supple 2018) (North Eastern Hill University, Shillong 2018, 2017, supple 2017) (VNS, Gujarat supple 2018, supple 2019) (Sai Tirupati University, Rajasthan 2018)

What are the early signs of death? How may the TSD be estimated from the postmortem changes? (North Eastern Hill University, Shillong supple 2016, supple 2019)

Ans: Classification of changes occurring after death.

Changes after Death

Immediate changes	Early changes	Late changes
1. Irreversible cessation of the function of: a. Brain b. Respiration c. Circulation	1. Facial pallor 2. Changes in the eye 3. Algor mortis 4. Livor mortis (PM staining) 5. Rigor mortis 6. Primary flaccidity of muscles 7. Loss of elasticity of skin	1. Decomposition/putrefaction 2. Adipocere 3. Mummification (Mnemonic: **MAD**)

Role in Determination of Time Since Death (TSD)

1. **Changes in eye**
   1. Eyeball—becomes flaccid due to fall in IOP (from 10 to 0 mmHg) within 4–6 hrs after death
   2. Sclera
      Tache noire
      - Deposition of dust particles over sclera giving dark brown-black color, triangular in appearance with apex towards canthus and base at limbus
      - Occurs within 3–6 hrs after death
   3. Cornea—hazy and opaque 6–8 hrs after death
2. **PM staining**

Mottled patches	30 min–1 hour after death
Coalesce	4–6 hours after death
PM fixation	8–12 hours after death

3. Algor mortis: Not a reliable method; the body attains environmental temperature in about 16–20 hours after death.

4. Rigor mortis

Starts	Within 1–2 hours after death
Appearance of rigor mortis	Takes 12 hours to develop
Persistence of rigor mortis	Persists for next 12 hours
Vanishes off	In next 12 hours

5. Putrefaction

Greenish discolouration of right iliac fossa	12–24 hours after death
Marbling	36–48 hours after death
Skin slippage	36–48 hours after death
Peeling of skin	48–72 hours after death
Loosening of hair	>72 hours after death

6. Adipocere: Starts 3 days after death

7. Mummification: 3 months–6 months after death

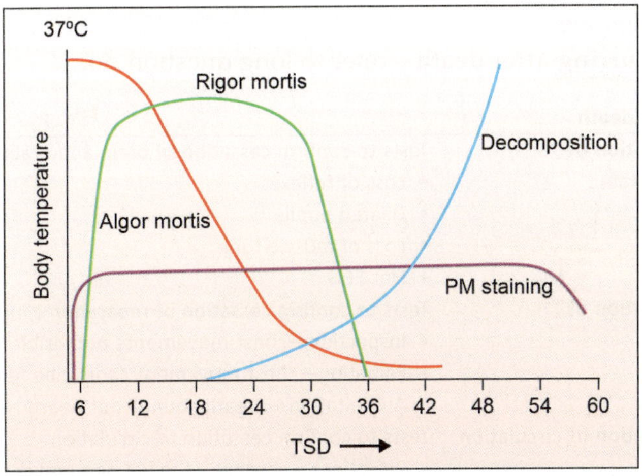

Other Changes which are Used in Determining TSD

1. **Insect activity:** By 18–36 h, flies lay their eggs. The eggs hatch into maggots or larvae in about 12–24 h. In 4–5 days, maggots develop into pupae, and by 8–12 days pupae into adult flies. Lice usually dies within 3–6 days after death.
2. **Stomach contents:** From the state of digestion and quantity of food in the stomach, TSD can be estimated. If the quality, quantity and the time of last meal taken can be known, the TSD can be estimated. If the stomach is full and contains undigested food, then death occurred within 2–4 h of eating of the last meal.
3. **Intestinal contents:** From the content of the pelvic colon and rectum, it can be said if the person attended the nature's call within last few hours or not. If it contains feces, death may have occurred in the night and if empty, sometime after evacuation in the morning (depending upon the person's habit).

4. **Contents of urinary bladder:** The amount of urine in the bladder may give some idea of TSD. If a body is found in the morning with the bladder full, then he might have died before the usual time of leaving his bed.
5. **Biochemical and enzymatic changes**
   - *Blood*: Potassium and magnesium rise, whereas sodium and chloride fall after death.
   - CSF: Potassium, creatine and uric acid increase, and glucose values decrease after death.
   - *Vitreous humor*: Potassium, magnesium, urea and creatinine increase after death.
6. **Facial hair growth:** If the time of his last shave is known, then survival time can be calculated, and the TSD can be estimated indirectly.
7. **Circumstantial evidences:** Pocket articles, mobile, diary, cinema tickets, etc. may indicate the date and time up to which the person survived.

2. Define somatic death. Enumerate usual PM changes occurring after death. Describe immediate signs of death. (AIIMS, Patna 2015) (VNS, Gujarat 2017)

Ans: Definition of somatic death: It is defined as complete and irreversible cessation of brainstem functions.

PM changes occurring after death—refer to long question no. 1.

Immediate signs of death	
1. **Irreversible cessation of the function of brain**	Tests to confirm cessation of brain and brainstem • Loss of reflexes • Dilated pupils • Loss of muscle tone • Flat EEG
2. **Irreversible cessation of respiration**	Tests to confirm cessation of reparation clinical examination • Inspection—chest movements not visible • Palpation—chest movement cannot be felt • Auscultation—breath sounds not heard
3. **Irreversible cessation of circulation**	Tests to confirm cessation of circulation • Pulsations—absence of radial, femoral and carotid pulses • Absence of the heart beat on auscultation • Flat ECG for 5 min

3. Define rigor mortis. Describe in brief its mechanism of formation. Discuss the other conditions mimic rigor mortis. (West Bengal University, 2017) (University of Health Sciences, Rohtak 2017) (Rajasthan University, 2016) (Sai Tirupati University, Rajasthan 2019)

Ans: Definition of rigor mortis: It is defined as stiffening of muscles of body after death.

Mechanism of Rigor Mortis

- It involves both voluntary and involuntary muscles
- Seen after primary flaccidity
- It is based on the concept of actin-myosin complex

- In relaxed position—interdigitation of actin-myosin filaments is seen to a small extent
- After death—ATP generation stops but consumption continues. So, depletion of ATP occurs leading to a permanent link in actin-myosin complex giving rise to stiffening of muscles

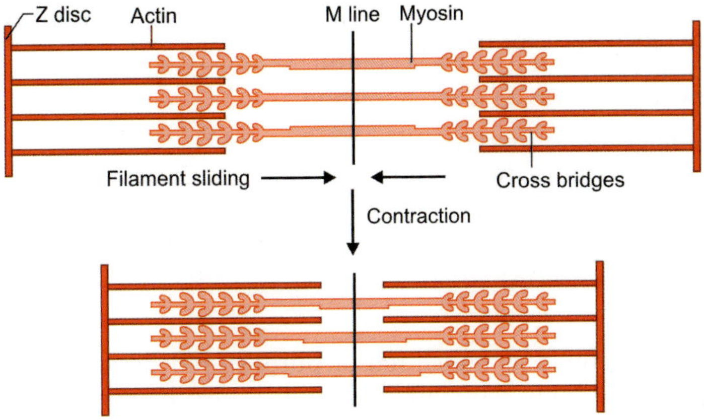

Conditions Simulating Rigor Mortis

1. Heat stiffening—refer to short question no. 19
2. Cold stiffening—refer to short question no. 14
3. Cadaveric spasm—refer to short question no. 20
4. Gas stiffening

4. Define death. Enumerate usual PM changes occurring after death. Discuss changes occurring in muscles after death (Sher-I-Kashmir Institute, Srinagar supple 2018) (Sardar Patel University, Gujarat 2017) (VNS, Gujarat 2016) (Sai Tirupati University, Rajasthan 2019)

Ans: Definition of death: The word 'death' denotes the death of a human being, unless contrary appears from the context **(Sec. 46 IPC)**. It is defined as permanent and irreversible cessation of functions of brainstem.

Enumerate PM changes after death—refer to long question no 1.

For changes in muscles after death—refer to long question no 3.

5. Define rigor mortis. Describe in brief regarding mechanism and time of development of rigor mortis. How will you differentiate Rigor Mortis and cadaveric spasm? (AIIMS Patna, 2016)

Ans: Definition and mechanism of rigor mortis—refer to long question no. 3.

Time of development of rigor mortis—refer to short question no. 17.

For difference **rigor mortis and cadaveric spasm**—refer to difference no. 1.

6. Define and classify types of death. Discuss different modification to the process of decomposition. (BFUHS, Punjab 2020)

Ans: Definition of death—refer to long question no. 4.

Types of Death

1. ***Somatic death:*** It is defined as complete and irreversible cessation of brainstem functions.
2. ***Molecular death:*** It is defined as progressive disintegration of body cells and tissues which occurs after somatic death.
   Refer to difference no. 2 for more details.

Modification of the Process of Decomposition

1. Adipocere—refer to the short question no. 3.
2. Mummification—refer to the short question no. 10.

7. Describe in brief about PM hypostasis. (AIIMS, Patna 2019, 2017) (Sai Tirupati University, Rajasthan 2018)

Ans: Hypostasis

1. **Definition:** It is defined as bluish-red or purplish-red discolouration of the skin over the dependant body parts after death. It is also known as livor mortis, PM staining, PM lividity.
2. **Mechanism:** After death, blood stops flowing and due to force of gravitation gets collected in vessels and capillaries of dependant body parts resulting in PM staining.
3. **Fixation of PM staining:** Time taken for fixation—8 hrs
   If position of body is changed before fixation—position of lividity also changes

Staining fixed	TSD >8 hrs
Staining not fixed	TSD <6 hrs

4. **Testing for fixation**
   - Firmly press the area with thumb for 30–45 seconds
   - If hypostasis disappear—PM staining not fixed
   - If hypostasis remains—PM staining fixed
5. **Development of PM staining**

Onset	30 min
Well developed	4 hrs
Completely develops	6 hrs

6. **Areas of contact pallor:** PM staining is not seen in areas which are in direct contact with the ground, i.e. PM staining is not seen over pressure areas. For example, in case of supine position—pressure points are at back of head, shoulder blade, gluteal region, back of foot.
7. **Distribution and extent of PM staining**

Supine position	Back of head, chest and legs, except areas of contact pallor
Prone position	On front of face, chest and abdomen
Hanging	Lower parts of forearm and legs (glove and stocking distribution)
Drowning	In stagnant water—found on face, upper part of chest, hands and legs
	In moving water—PM staining not seen as body moves continuously

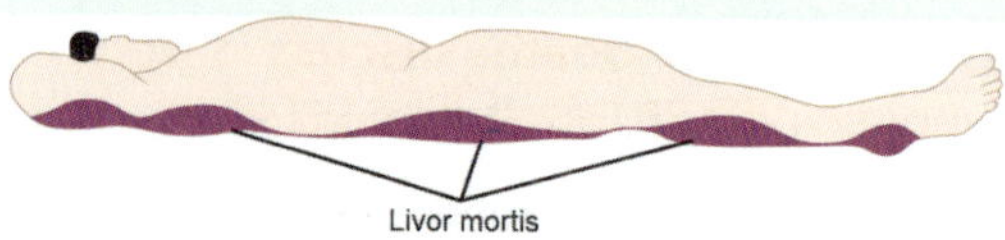

8. **Color of PM staining**

Color of PM staining	Cause of death
Bluish-purple	Normal
Cherry red	Carbon monoxide
Bluish-green	Hydrogen sulphide
Black	Opiates
Brick red	Cyanide poisoning

9. **MLI**
   i. It is a sign of death
   ii. It helps in estimation of TSD
   iii. Helps in determining position of body after death
   iv. Determination of cause of death
   v. Mistaken for bruise

8. Discuss algor mortis. (Sher-i-Kashmir Institute, Srinagar supple 2017)

Ans: Algor Mortis

Definition: It is the cooling of body after death.

- It is usually the first sign of death.
- Fall in body temperature is not uniform from the moment of death onwards. Therefore, it follows a Sigmoid shape curve.

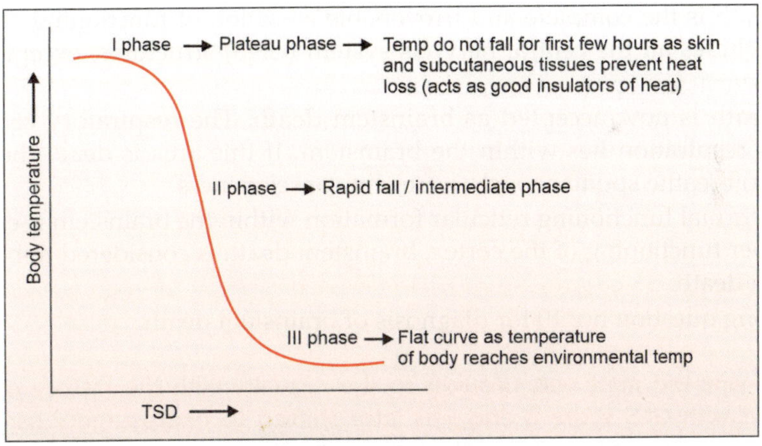

Average rate of fall of body temperature is 0.4°–0.7°C/hour and attains environmental temperature in 15–18 hrs after death

$$TSD = \frac{\text{Normal body temperature} - \text{Rectal temperature}}{\text{Rate of cooling per hour}}$$

Recording of Temperature after Death

Site	Method
• Rectum	Thermocouple
• Subhepatic space	Thanatometer—25 cm long
• External auditory canal	

Factors affecting Algor Mortis

Environmental temperature	**Most important factors** Rate of fall of body temperature is directly proportional to the difference between the temperature of the dead body and the environmental temperature.
Humidity	Cooling is rapid in humid environment
Movement of air	Body in open air cools faster than that in closed room
Clothing	As clothes do not allow dissipation of heat therefore, body cools slowly

MLI

i. Helps in estimation of TSD
ii. It is a sign of death
iii. Rapid cooling of a dead body delays the processes of rigor mortis and decomposition.

9. What do understand by the legal concept of death? Discuss in detail about the diagnosis of brainstem death. (North Eastern Hill University, Shillong 2019) (Sai Tirupati University, Rajasthan 2018)

Ans: The legal concept of death is "brainstem death".

1. The traditional cardiopulmonary standard (cessation of heart beat and breathing) is not considered currently, since circulation and respiration could be maintained by means of a mechanical respirator, despite loss of all brain functions.
2. Brain death is the complete and irreversible cessation of functioning of the brain. Brain includes all the central nervous system (CNS) structures, except the spinal cord.
3. Brain death is now accepted as brainstem death. The respiratory center which controls respiration lies within the brainstem. If this area is dead, the person is unable to breathe spontaneously or regain consciousness.
4. Since a normal functioning reticular formation within the brainstem is essential for the proper functioning of the cortex, brainstem death is considered to be sufficient for brain death.

Refer to long question no. 10 for diagnosis of brainstem death.

10. A 25-year-old male was brought to the casualty with the history of fall from height with GCS score 3 and was later shifted to neurosurgery care. On day two of the treatment, the treating physician suspected brainstem death of the patient. (Pondicherry 2019)

a. Mention the criteria to pronounce brainstem death.

b. Who are the members of the brainstem death declaration committee and what are the procedures followed by them to declare the same?

c. What are the different types of donors for organ transplantation?

Ans: The two essential requirements for the diagnosis of brain death are:

1. **Establishment of cessation of all brain functions**, i.e. cerebral and mainly brainstem functions—determined clinically and confirmed by laboratory tests which include EEG (flat isoelectric EEG).

2. **Demonstration that cessation of these functions is irreversible:**
   Irreversibility is established by:
   a. Determination of the cause of loss of brain function.
   b. Exclusion of reversible conditions like hypothermia, electrolyte imbalance, drug intoxication, shock, hypotension, etc.

Brainstem Death Certification

a. Two medical practitioners of which one should be neurologist or neurosurgeon must perform the brainstem death tests.
b. Patient's attending physician should participate in determination of death.
c. Such tests *should not be performed* by transplant surgeons or any doctor in the transplant team.

The three important findings seen in brain death are coma, absence of brainstem reflexes and apnea

1. **Coma** or unresponsiveness: No cerebral motor response to pain in all extremities
2. **Absence of brainstem reflexes**
   a. Absent pupillary response to bright light.
   b. No oculocephalic reflex or absent oculovestibular reflex.
   c. No corneal reflex to touch with a cotton swab or no grimacing to deep pressure on nail bed, supraorbital ridge.
   d. No gag reflex or cough response to bronchial suction.
3. **Apnea test:** It is based on the fact that loss of brainstem function results in loss of centrally controlled breathing, with resultant apnea.

Types of Donor for Transplants

1. **Autograft:** Tissue transplanted from one part of the body to another in the same individual—*autotransplant or homologous transplantation*.
2. **Allograft:** Organ or tissue transplanted from one individual to another of the same species with a different genotype—*homograft*.
3. **Isograft:** Organs or tissues are transplanted from a donor to a genetically identical recipient.
4. **Xenograft:** Organs or tissue transplanted from one species to another, e.g., grafting of animal tissue into humans.
5. **Split transplants:** Deceased-donor organ (e.g. liver) may be divided between two recipients.

11. What is medico-legal autopsy? What are the objectives of medico-legal autopsy? Describe the type of skin incisions for opening scalp, chest, and abdomen. (North Eastern Hill University, Shillong 2016)

Ans: Medico-legal autopsy: It is a type of scientific examination of a dead body carried out in case of sudden, suspicious, obscure, unnatural, litigious or criminal deaths in order to establish the cause and manner of death and time since death.

- A complete autopsy should be done (all the body cavities should be opened and every organ must be examined)
- It should be done by the doctor himself and not by any attendant

Objectives of Medicolegal Autopsy

1. To find out the cause of death
2. To find out time since death, mode of death and place of death
3. To find out manner of death (accidental, homicidal or suicidal)
4. To establish identity of deceased when not known/not identifiable
5. To identify if injuries are AM or PM in nature
6. In case of newborns, to determine the question of live birth and viability of the baby

Types of Skin Incisions

Skin incisions are of following types:

1. **I-shaped or standard midline incision:** *Most common method.* It extends from the chin down to the symphysis pubis and avoiding the umbilicus.
2. **Y-shaped incision:** The straight line of Y corresponding to the xiphisternum to pubis incision of I-shaped incision. The forks of Y run down medially to the chest and extending towards the acromion process.
3. **Modified Y-shaped incision:** It is used to study the neck, like in hanging or strangulation. An incision is made in midline from suprasternal notch to symphysis pubis. The incision extends from suprasternal notch over the clavicle to its center on both sides and then passes upwards towards mastoid process.

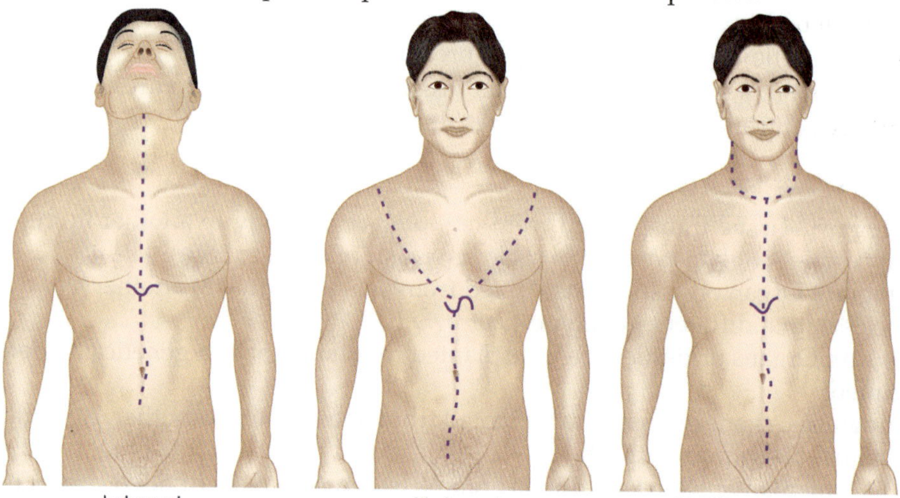

I-shaped Y-shaped Modified Y-shaped

1. Scalp

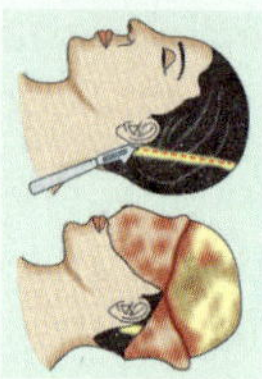

1. An ear-to-ear bone deep incision is made along the vertex of the scalp.
2. The scalp is reflected forwards to the superciliary ridges, and backwards to a point just below the occipital protuberance.
3. Look for hematoma, edema or any fracture.
4. Sawing of skull is done by making a saw-line in slightly V-shaped direction (angle of 120°).
5. Skull cap is removed and dura is exposed which is examined from outside for EDH, then dura is cut from periphery and then falx cerebri, and examined for SDH and SAH.

2. Chest

1. The skin and muscles of the chest are dissected sidewise and carried back to the midaxillary line, down to the costal margin and up over the clavicles.
2. Examine the ribs and sternum for fractures.

	3. Open the chest by cutting the costal cartilages from second rib onwards close to the costochondral junctions with help of cartilage knife. 4. Sternoclavicular joints are finally disarticulated on both sides. 5. Sternum is removed. Pleural cavity is examined for presence of any blood, pus, adhesions.
3. Abdomen	1. An incision to rectus abdominis till 5 cm above pubis symphysis. 2. A small nick is made in the fascia to admit the left index and middle fingers with palmar surfaces up. 3. Peritoneum is cut up to the xiphoid and abdominal cavity is looked for presence of any blood, pus, fluid or perforation. 4. Finally, evisceration of the organs is done.

SHORT NOTES

1. Negative autopsy. (Rajiv Gandhi University, Bengaluru 2020) (Rajasthan University, 2016)

Ans: Definition of negative autopsy: An autopsy in which cause of death cannot be found even after with gross, microscopic, radiological and toxicological analysis.

- For example, SIDS can be considered as 'negative autopsy'.

Incidence: 4–6% of all autopsies are found to be negative autopsy.

Reasons

i. Inadequate history about signs and symptoms prior to death
ii. Lack of experience on part of doctor
iii. Inadequate examination of external injuries—e.g., needle marks in case of drug addicts, entry wound in case of electrocution
iv. Inadequate examination of internal injuries—e.g., air embolism and pneumothorax are often missed.
v. Inappropriate methods for collection and preservation of samples

2. Postmortem caloricity. (AIIMS, Patna 2019, 2018, 2017) (Adesh, Bathinda Supple 2018, 2017) (North Eastern Hill University, Shillong Supple 2018)

Ans:

Definition of postmortem caloricity—the initial rise of body temperature for first two hours after death.

Causes of PM Caloricity

Causes of PM caloricity	Mechanism
1. Infectious diseases/septicemia	Due to increased bacterial activity
2. Hot temperature (tropical countries)	As dead body absorbs heat from the environmental temperature
3. Convulsions (tetanus, strychnine poisoning)	Due to increased muscular contractions
4. Pontine hemorrhage	Due to loss of heat regulation centre

MLI—PM caloricity leads to wrong estimation of TSD.

3. Adipocere formation (Rajiv Gandhi University, Bengaluru, 2018)

Ans:

a. **Definition of adipocere:** It is a modification of putrefaction in which putrefaction is arrested and body fat is changed into fatty acids and wax-like substance called adipocere.

b. **Formation**

Unsaturated fats
(on breast, face, subcutaneous tissue)

↓ Hydrolysis and hydrogenation of fats

Saturated fatty acids
(main constituent—palmitic acid)

↓ Ca^{++} ion

Soap leading to saponification

c. **Sites of adipocere formation:** Fat rich tissues (breast, cheeks, face, abdomen, buttocks) due to presence of abundant subcutaneous tissue.

d. **Factors favouring adipocere formation**
   i. Warm and moist environment
   ii. Presence of bacteria esp. *Clostridium welchi*
   iii. Abundance of fatty tissues, therefore, adipocere is formed quickly in obese people
   iv. Dead bodies placed in airtight coffins

e. **MLI**
   i. It gives a rough estimate of TSD.
   ii. The features are well-preserved, which helps in identification.
   iii. The cause of death can be determined, since injuries are recognizable.
   iv. Some idea about the place of disposal of the body can be made; adipocere requires a warm and humid place or presence of water.

4. Suspended animation/apparent death (Rajasthan University, 2018) (Uttarakhand University 2018) (Adesh, Bathinda Supple 2017) (Rajiv Gandhi University, Bengaluru 2015) (North Eastern Hill University, Shillong 2015) (Andhra Pradesh Supple 2016)

Ans: Definition of suspended animation: It is a condition in which vital signs of life (like heart beat and respiration) cannot be detected by routine clinical methods, as the functions are reduced to a minimum.

Mechanism: BMR is greatly reduced so that the requirement of the oxygen decreases but dissolved oxygen in body fluids is enough to satisfy the demands of the body.

Types

1. Voluntary	Seen in yoga practitioners
2. Involuntary (Mnemonic—**DENTIST**)	**D**rowning, **E**lectrocution, **N**ewborn, **T**yphoid, **I**nsanity, **S**unstroke, **TB**

MLI

- The patient can be resuscitated by cardiac massage and artificial respiration.
- Before certifying death, ECG or EEG should be done to rule out suspended animation

5. Postmortem findings in starvation death. (Rajasthan University, 2018) (Uttarakhand University 2018) (Pondicherry Supple 2017) (Pondicherry 2016) (JIPMER 2016)

Ans: PM findings in starvation death

General	Emaciation with loss of body weight, sunken eyes and pronounced rib cage.
Subcutaneous tissue	Complete loss of fat in subcutaneous tissue, loss of adipose tissue of mesentery
Muscles	Atrophy of skeletal muscles
GIT	Mucosal atrophy and atrophy of GIT walls (thin paper like)
Stomach and intestines	Empty with dry stools in colon
Liver	Centrilobular necrosis due to protein deficiency
Gall bladder	Distended with bile, bigger in size
Urinary bladder	Empty
Brain	Normal, no atrophy

6. Brain death. (Rajasthan University, 2018) (BFUHS, Punjab 2016) (Rajiv Gandhi University, Bengaluru 2019)

Ans: Refer to long question no. 10.

7. Tests to be performed to diagnose brainstem death (Sardar Patel University, Gujarat 2019)

Ans: Refer to long question no. 10.

8. Describe marbling and its medico-legal importance. (Rajiv Gandhi University, Bengaluru, 2019)

Ans: Marbling

1. **Definition of marbling:** It is the greenish discoloration of superficial vessels over the skin due to formation of sulfmethemoglobin.
   - It is a sign of putrefaction.
2. **Mechanism of formation**
3. **Onset:** 36–48 hours after death
4. **Sites of appearance:** Marbling first appears on neck, chest, shoulders and upper aspects of limbs
5. **MLI**
   i. It helps in estimation of TSD.
   ii. Indicates initiation of putrefactive changes.

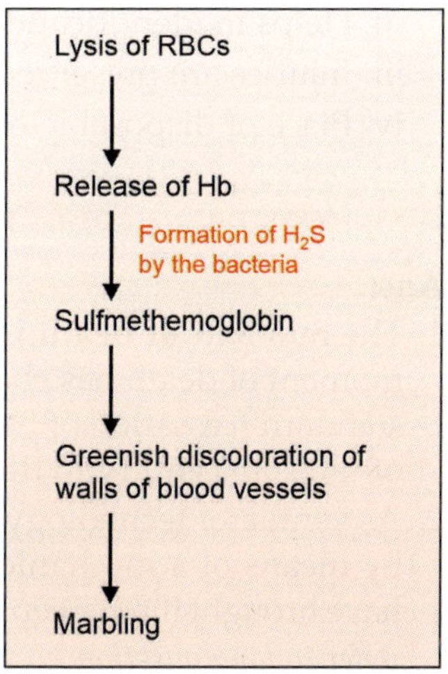

9. Rigor mortis. (BFUHS, Punjab 2017) (Sardar Patel University, Gujarat Supple 2015) (Rajiv Gandhi University, Bengaluru 2015) (Rajasthan University 2017)

Postmortem rigidity. (University of Health Science, Rohtak Supple 2020)

Ans: Refer to long question no. 3.

10. Mummification. (Uttarakhand University 2017, 2016) (Rajiv Gandhi University, Bengaluru 2020) (GMC, Chandigarh 2015)

Ans: Mummification

1. **Definition:** It is the rapid dehydration and shrivelling of the dead body due to evaporation of water from the body.
   - It is a modification of putrefaction (dry decomposition)
2. **Features of mummification**
   - Mummified bodies are colorless, odorless.
   - The entire body loses weight and becomes thin and brittle.
   - Internal organs become shrunken, hard or unidentifiable.
   - It begins in the exposed parts of the body (face, hands, feet) and extends to entire body.
   - Skin is stretched tightly across anatomical prominences, such as the cheek bones, chin, costal margins and hips, adheres closely to the bones, and often covered with fungal growths.
3. **Time taken for development of mummification**: 3 months to 1 year.
4. **Conditions required for mummification**

Hot environment	Like desert
Poisoning	Arsenic poisoning favours mummification
Free air movement	Favours mummification
Dry atmosphere	Mummification does not occur in humid conditions

5. **MLI**
   i. TSD can be estimated.
   ii. Helps in identification as the features are well-preserved.
   iii. Injuries are preserved and cause of death can be established.
   iv. Place of disposable of body can be obtained—requires hot, dry environment.

11. Modern concept of moment of death (Delhi University 2017)

Ans:

1. The **moment of death** is the exact time when the person dies. The concept of the moment of death has changed through the years. The traditional cardiopulmonary standard (cessation of heartbeat and breathing) was the measure used during most of the 20th century to determine the presence of life.
2. As ventilator technology advanced, circulation and respiration could be maintained by means of a mechanical respirator, despite loss of all brain functions, and thus have brought the concept of **brain death**, i.e., irreversible loss of cerebral functioning. *Refer to long question no. 9 also.*

12. Time since death. (West Bengal Supple 2017)

Ans: Refer to long question no. 1

13. Cold stiffening (AIIMS, Patna 2016)

Ans: Cold Stiffening

1. It occurs when a body is exposed to freezing temperature (below–3.5°C) for a long period, the tissues becoming frozen and stiff, simulating rigor.
2. On forcibly flexing the joints, crackling sounds of ice crystals can be felt.
3. **Reason for occurrence**
    - Freezing of body fluids at the tissue level and in the synovial sacs of the joints
    - Hardening of the subcutaneous fatty tissue.
4. **MLI:** If body is exposed to warm temperature, the stiffness disappears and normal rigor mortis occurs.

14. Changes in the eyes after death. (BFUHS, Punjab Supple 2016) (SGRD, Amritsar 2019)

Ans:

1. Loss of corneal reflex	Not a reliable sign
2. Cornea	Become hazy and opaque 6–8 hrs after death
3. Pupils	Become dilated and fixed
4. Eyeball	Becomes flaccid due to fall in IOP (from 10 mmHg to 0 mmHg) within 4–6 hrs after death
5. Sclera	**Tache noire** • Deposition of dust particles over sclera giving dark brown-black color, triangular in appearance with apex towards canthus and base at limbus • Occurs within 3–6 hrs after death
6. Retina	**Kevorkian sign/trucking of blood vessels** • Segmentation of retinal blood vessels • Occurs immediately after death • Seen with ophthalmoscope 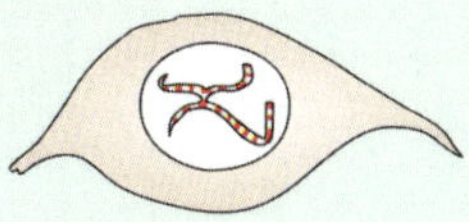
7. Vitreous humor	Increase in—K^+, hypoxanthine Decrease in—Na^+, Cl^-, Glucose

15. Mode of death. (GMC, Chandigarh 2016)

Ans: Definition of mode of death: It is an abnormal physiological state existing at the time of death, e.g. coma, congestive cardiac failure, cardio-respiratory failure, cardiac arrest or pulmonary edema. There are three modes of death depending upon the system most obviously affected are:

1. Coma
2. Syncope
3. Asphyxia

Coma	Syncope	Asphyxia
Definition: State of deep unconsciousness from which a person cannot be roused, with minimal or no detectable responsiveness to stimuli.	**Definition:** Death from failure of the function of the heart resulting in hypoxia and hypo-perfusion of the brain.	**Definition:** Death due to failure of functioning of lungs
Seen in cases of • Disease of the brain • Systemic disorders—diabetic ketoacidosis, uremia, eclampsia • Intoxication—alcohol, opium	**Seen in cases of** • Heart disease • Hemorrhage • Vagal inhibition • Poisoning like digitalis, aconite, etc.	**Seen in cases of** • Hanging • Strangulation • Throttling

16. Rule of 12 (Andhra Pradesh Supple, 2016) (VNS, Gujarat 2019)

Ans:

1st phase	Appearance of rigor mortis	Takes 12 hrs but involves only proximal parts
2nd phase	Persistence of rigor mortis	Next 12 hrs (12–24 hrs), rigor mortis present at distal parts
3rd phase	Passing off rigor mortis	Takes another 12 hrs (24–36 hrs)

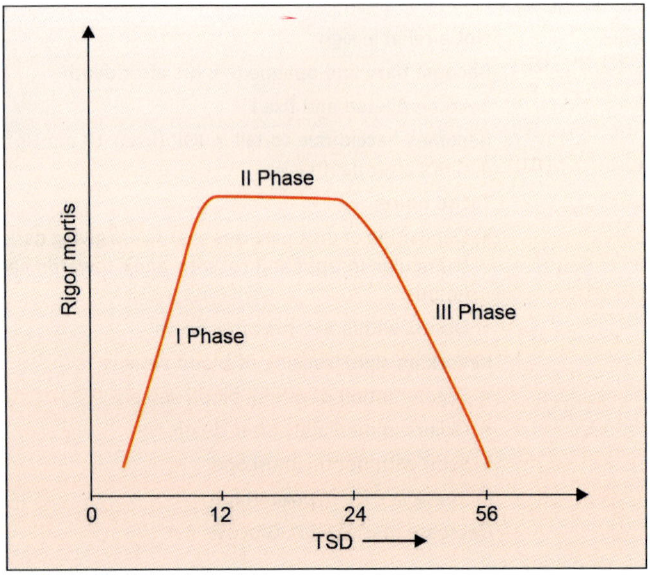

17. Postmortem hypostasis (Uttarakhand University 2016) (JIPMER supple 2018)

Ans: Refer to long question no. 7.

18. Heat stiffening. (AIIMS, Patna 2015)

Ans: Heat Stiffening

1. When the body is exposed to a temperature of >65°C, coagulation of muscle protein occurs leading to rigidity.

2. Usually, flexors are affected and muscles are contracted giving rise to a condition called **pugilistic attitude**.
3. Rigidity of muscles is more in heat stiffening than that in rigor mortis
4. **MLI**
   i. It remains until decomposition occurs leading to softening of muscles and ligaments
   ii. Rigor mortis is absent
   iii. Seen in death due to burns

19. Cadaveric spasm. (Andhra Pradesh, 2015)

Ans: Cadaveric Spasm

1. **Definition of cadaveric spasm:** It is a condition in which the muscles of the body that were in state of contraction at the time of death continue to be in contracted state even after death without passing through the stage of primary relaxation.
2. The other muscles of the body are in stage of primary relaxation.
3. **Involvement of muscles**

Spasm of voluntary group of muscles	Involvement of whole body (rare)
• Presence of grass and weeds in hands—in case of drowning • Weapon clenched in hands—in case of suicides	For example: Soldiers shot in battle

4. **Mechanism of development:** Depletion of ATP in affected muscles with persistence of contraction even after death leading to the failure of muscle relaxation during molecular death and impairment in ATP resynthesis
5. Cadaveric spasm continues till rigor mortis appears, then vanishes off with rigor mortis
6. **MLI**
   i. Indicates **sudden death** with great emotional stress (excitement, exhaustion, fear, fatigue)
   ii. It suggests **manner of death**
      - Suicidal death—weapon/pistol held clenched tightly in hand
      - Homicidal death—clothings, hair or buttons of assailant may be held firmly in hand
   iii. It suggests **antemortem death**
      In case of drowning—presence of weed, grass and mud clenched in hands

20. Causes of sudden natural death. (Rajiv Gandhi University, Bengaluru 2015)

Ans: Definition of sudden death: Death occurring instantaneously or within 1 h of the onset of morbid symptoms (as per WHO, within 24 hrs).

- It is the sudden and unexpected death of a person, who prior to death was not suffering from any dangerous disease, poisoning or injury.

1. **Cardiovascular diseases** (MC cause of sudden death)	• Myocardial infarction • Coronary artery disease • Congenital heart disease

	• Valvular heart disease • Cardiomyopathies • Aortic aneurysm
2. **Respiratory system**	• Pneumothorax • Acute epiglottitis • Air embolism • Pulmonary embolism • Obstruction of respiratory passage by foreign body
3. **GIT**	• Appendicitis • Pancreatitis • Strangulated hernia • Peritonitis • Massive GIT hemorrhage
4. **CNS**	• SAH • Intracerebral hemorrhage • Stroke • Brain tumor • Meningitis
5. **Genitourinary and reproductive system**	• Ruptured ectopic • Uterine hemorrhage • Tumors of bladder and kidney • Chronic nephritis
6. **Endocrine causes**	• Diabetic coma • Pheochromocytoma • Adrenal insufficiency
7. **Miscellaneous**	• Anaphylaxis • Drug abuse • Mismatched blood transfusion

21. Objectives of medico-legal autopsy. (Rajiv Gandhi University, Bengaluru, 2015) (Rajasthan University 2018) (KHMS, Tamil Nadu 2016) (VNS, Gujarat supple 2019)

Ans: Objectives of medico-legal autopsy

1. To find out the cause of death (natural or unnatural)
2. To find out time since death, mode of death and place of death
3. To find out manner of death (accidental, suicidal or homicidal)
4. To establish identity of deceased when not known/not identifiable
5. To identify if the injuries are antemortem or postmortem in nature
6. In case of newborns, to determine the question of live birth and viability of the baby.
7. To find out if any treatment was given to deceased before death.
8. To investigate into the case so that, it can help in identifying the criminal (e.g., foreign materials, fingerprints)

22. Algor mortis (KHMS, Tamil Nadu Supple 2019) (Pondicherry 2015) (VNS, Gujarat 2017, 2019)

Ans: Refer to long question no. 8.

23. Casper's dictum (SGRD, Amirtsar 2019)

Ans:

1. Casper's dictum is related to **rate of putrefaction.**
2. One week of putrefaction in air is equivalent to two weeks in water, which is equivalent to eight weeks buried in soil, given the same environmental temperature.
3. The rate of decomposition in air, water and deep burial is **1: 2: 8.**

	Decomposition
Air	1
Water	2 (2 times slower)
Deep burial	8 (8 times slower)

4. Therefore, the deeper is the burial of the body, better will be the preservation for a period of time.
5. The process of decomposition in water is slow due to:
   i. Absence of air
   ii. Clothing provides protection
   iii. Early cooling of the body.
6. **MLI**
   i. After removal of body from water—rate of decomposition is rapid due to imbibition of water and optimum temperature for the growth of microorganisms.
   ii. In submerged dead bodies—decomposition starts early in the head and face.

24. Exhumation (AIIMS, Patna 2019, 2017, 2015) (Delhi University supple 2016) (Rajiv Gandhi University, Bengaluru 2015) (BFUHS, Punjab 2016) (VNS, Gujarat 2019) (JIPMER supple 2018)

Ans:

Definition of exhumation: It is the lawful digging out of an already buried body from the grave for postmortem examination.

- It is not frequent in India because mostly the bodies are cremated. But there is no time limit for exhumation.
- **Authorization:** Exhumation orders are only given by the magistrate.

Purpose for Exhumation

1. For identification of the diseased
2. To determine the cause of death, time since death and manner of death
3. For doing autopsy for the second time when the first autopsy was not done
4. To retrieve some vital objects (bullets) from the body
5. When the body has been disposed of without conducting any autopsy and later on foul play is suspected.

Procedure

1. It should be done in daylight, under the supervision of magistrate, doctor and police officer.
2. The area should be properly screened off from the public.

3. Before digging out grave, burial spot should be identified.
4. Photographs should be clicked and samples of the soil from above, below and sides of the grave are taken.
5. The body is taken out and identification marks are noted.
6. Autopsy is conducted, and in case of suspected poisoning, viscera may be preserved for chemical analysis.

DIFFERENTIATIONS

1. Cadaveric spasm and rigor mortis (Jammu and Kashmir 2017) (Himachal Pradesh University 2017) (Adesh, Bathinda supple 2017) (Pondicherry 2016) (Rajasthan University, 2015) (GMC, Chandigarh 2015)

Ans:

	Cadaveric spasm	Rigor mortis
Onset	Instantaneous	Within 2 hrs after death
Muscles involved	Voluntary muscles	All the muscles (voluntary and involuntary)
Molecular death	Does not occur	Occurs
Response to electrical stimulus	Yes	No
Primary flaccidity	Not seen	Occurs before rigor mortis
Mechanism	Not known	Breakdown of ATP below critical level
Predisposing factors	Excitement, extreme exhaustion	No
Other methods of producing	No other method	By freezing By exposing to temp >65°C
Intensity	Very strong	Comparatively moderate
MLI	Suggests manner of death	Time since death can be estimated

2. Somatic death and Molecular death. (Delhi University 2018) (KHMS, Tamil Nadu 2016)

Ans:

	Somatic death	Molecular death
Definition	Complete and irreversible cessation of brainstem functions	Progressive disintegration of body cells
Occurs	Before molecular death	After somatic death
Cells	Alive	Dead
Response to external stimulus	Present	Absent
Conditions simulating	Suspended animation	No condition resembles it
Confirmed by	Flat ECG and EEG, absent pulse and absent breath sounds	Rigor mortis, algor mortis, PM staining

3. Rigor mortis and pugilistic attitude (KHMS, Tamil Nadu 2018)

Ans:

	Rigor mortis	Pugilistic attitude
Mechanism	Breakdown of ATP of muscles	Due to coagulation of muscle proteins
Type of phenomenon	Postmortem phenomenon	Can be antemortem or postmortem
Degree of stiffness	Moderate	High
Onset	In sequence	Diffuse
Disappearance	In sequence	Uniform
External characteristics	Not specific	Signs of exposure to heat (blisters, singeing, burning)

4. Medicolegal autopsy and Pathological autopsy (Sher-i-Kashmir Institute, Srinagar Supple 2019) (KHMS, Tamil Nadu 2015) (West Bengal University 2017)

Ans:

	Medicolegal autopsy	Pathological/clinical autopsy
Done in	Unnatural deaths	Natural deaths
Purpose	Cause of death and TSD	To know pathophysiology of disease causing death
Done by	Forensic medicine experts	Pathologists
Consent	From State	From relatives
Body handed over to	Investigating officer	Relatives

CHAPTER 3

Identification

LONG QUESTIONS

1. **Define identification. Enumerate various data of identification. Describe the surest data of identification.** (North Eastern Hill University, Shillong 2015) (Sai Tirupati University, Rajasthan, 2019)

What is the dactylography? Briefly describe the different types of dactylographs. What is the medicolegal importance of dactylography? (AIIMS Patna 2019, 2017) (North Eastern Hill University, Shillong 2016) (VNS, Gujarat 2017)

What are the parameters that help in identifying the individuals? Describe the role of fingerprints in personal identification. (Rajiv Gandhi University, Bengaluru Supple 2015)

Ans:

Definition of Identification

Determination of the individuality of a person by recognizing certain characteristics that are unique to that person.

Types

1. Complete/absolute identification: Dactylography
2. Incomplete/partial identification: Race, age, sex, height

Data of Identification

General	Miscellaneous	Forensic study
Age	Anthropometry	Dactylography
Sex	Superimposition	DNA fingerprinting
Race	Marks	Hair
Religion	• Tattoo marks	
Stature	• Scars	
Bones		
Teeth		

The Surest Method of Identification is Dactylography

Definition of Dactylography

- It is the study of fingerprints as method of identification.
- Fingerprints appear by 12 weeks of IUL, completely formed by 20 weeks of IUL
- It is the surest data of identification/most reliable method of identification as
  a. Patterns are not inherited
  b. Different even in identical twins

Definition of Fingerprints

Impression of the patterns as a result of secretion of oils from the glands in the skin

History

- First person to use fingerprinting—William Hershel
- Systemised by—Sir Francis Galton
- Improved by—Sir Henry, hence called **Henry and Galton System**

Classification of Fingerprints

Loops (most common)	70%
Whorls	25%
Arches	5%
Composite (least common)	1%

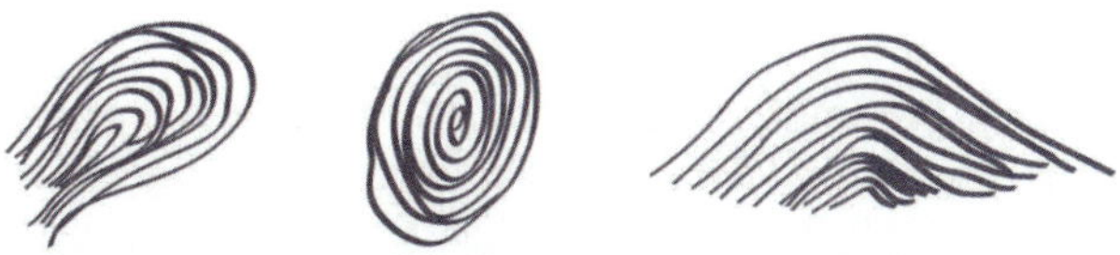

Loops Whorls Arches

Locard's Principle of Exchange

When two objects come into contact with each other, there is always some transfer of material from one to the other. Latent prints are example of this principle.

Types of Fingerprints

1. Visible print—seen with naked eye. For example, fingerprints made from grease, blood
2. Latent print—not visible to naked eye, therefore, needs developing to make it visible
3. Plastic print—impressions over soft materials like soap, cheese

Recording of Fingerprints

Before recording the fingerprints, hands are washed, cleaned and dried and then fingerprint is taken using Printer's ink on an unglazed paper.

It is done by two methods

1. **Plain impression**—by gently pressing the inked surface on tip of finger on paper
2. **Rolled impression**—by rolling thumb/finger from side to side.
   It is customary to take LTI in males and RTI in females.

Removal of Fingerprinting

1. Fingerprints can be erased permanently and deliberately by criminals to reduce their chance of conviction.
2. Alteration of fingerprints are seen in eczema, celiac disease
3. Permanent impairment of fingerprints are seen in leprosy, electric injury, radiation

Medico-legal Importance

1. Identification of criminals
2. Identification in case of accidental exchange of newborn infants.
3. Identification of victims of mass disaster
4. Bank forgeries
5. Properties and legal documents
6. Identification in mummified bodies
7. Electronic fingerprints for security applications
8. Identification of licensing procedure
9. *Sex determination:* The amino acid content in fingerprints can be used to determine sex.
10. *Drug use:* The secretions in fingerprint contain residues of various chemicals and their metabolites, which can be detected.

2. Enumerate various parameters to establish identity of an individual. Describe various intersex disorders. Write about medico-legal significance of age 14, 18 and 21 years. (Sardar Patel University, Gujarat 2018) (VNS, Gujarat 2016) (JIPMER supple 2018)

Ans:

Definition of Intersex

These are individuals in which male and female characters, like gonads, physical features and sexual behavior co-exist in varying proportions in the same individual.

Types

They were classified into four groups:

a. Gonadal agenesis
b. Gonadal dysgenesis
c. True hermaphroditism
d. Pseudo-hermaphroditism

Currently they are considered under **disorders of sexual development** (DSD) to substitute the obsolete nomenclature of 'intersex', 'hermaphroditism' and 'pseudo-hermaphroditism'.

1. **Gonadal agenesis:** Sex organs (testes and ovaries) never develop. The individuals are chromatin negative. This is determined very early in fetal life.
2. **Gonadal dysgenesis:** In these individuals, external sexual structures are present, but the testes or ovaries fail to develop at puberty. Most common examples are Klinefelter and Turner syndrome.
3. **True hermaphroditism:** The external genitalia may be of both sexes and the internal genitalia may consist of either ovaries or testes. Rare condition, nuclear sex is usually female but can be male.
4. **Pseudo-hermaphroditism:** In these individuals, there is lack of differentiation of external genitalia while the internal genitalia are of only one sex (testes or ovary). They are classified as male (testes present; nuclear sex XY) or female (ovaries present; nuclear sex XX), independent of anomalies of external genitalia which is opposite of normal.

MLI: Marriage, inheritance and civil rights

AGE	MLI
14 years	Cannot be employed in a factory before 14 yrs of age, according to Factory Act.
18 years	1. **Minimum age of consent for** • Sexual intercourse (considered **statutory rape** even if intercourse was done with her consent below this age) • Major procedure/surgery • Medical termination of pregnancy (under MTP Act) • Removal/donation of body organ for therapeutic purpose (Transplantation of Human Organs Act) 2. Age of **majority** 3. Age for **marriage (girls)** 4. Can cast **vote** 5. Can be employed in a factory 6. Mentally sound person can make a **valid will (testamentary capacity)** 7. Age for **permanent license** to drive a private motor vehicle 8. **Abetment to suicide** of a person below this age is punished severely 9. Taking away a girl without consent of parent/ guardian is **kidnapping** 10. Minimum age for entering a government service
21 years	1. Age for **marriage (males)**. 2. Importation of girl of age <21 yrs from foreign country for the purpose of illicit intercourse is punishable 3. Age of **majority** when individual is under guardianship of court or ward.

3. What is criminal responsibility of an individual? Discuss in brief the various IPC sections defining it. (Adesh, Bathinda supple 2016)

Ans:

In law, criminal responsibility means liability to punishment.

IPC Section	Deals with
82	Child under 7 years of age is not liable for any criminal act
83	Child of 7–12 years is liable and presumed to be capable of committing an offence, if has attained sufficient mental maturity to judge the nature and consequences of the act
84	A person of unsound mind is not liable for act **(McNaughten's Rule)**
85	A person under involuntary (fraudulently) intoxication is not liable for act
86	A person under voluntary intoxication is liable for his act
87	A child under 12 yrs cannot give valid consent to suffer any harm which can occur from an act done in good faith and for his benefit
89	A person under 18 yrs of age cannot give valid consent to suffer any harm which may result from act not intended or not known to cause death or grievous hurt

4. Police has recovered a bundle of bones and submitted for medico-legal examination. Discuss what medico-legal information can be provided to derive scientific conclusion. (Delhi University Supple 2016)

Ans:

1. **To determine whether it's a bone or not?**
   Forensic expert with his anatomical background can differentiate a bone from the substances that may look like bone, e.g., wood, plastic.
2. **If it is a bone, does it belong to human or animal?**

Fragmented bones	
1. Old/ burnt/cremated bones	a. Gross anatomical characteristics
	b. Microscopic characteristics (Haversian system)
	c. Chemical analysis of bone ash may be done
2. Fresh/ones which still has some blood constituents	Serological test (precipitin test) can be done

   But it's very easy to identify the species if whole skeleton is available.

3. **Whether the bones belong to one individual or not?**

Bones available are placed in anatomical position of articulation	
• If all the available separate parts fit to each other and • If age, sex and race of all the bones are same	} It belongs to the single individual

4. **Determining the stature of individual**
   Hepburn's osteometric board is used to measure length of the long bones
   Best bone to determine stature—femur
   Methods: Regression formula
   Percentile formula
   Karl Pearson's formula is used for Americans.

5. **Determining the race of the individual**

   Race can be determined from the **cephalic index.**

$$CI = \frac{\text{Maximum transverse breadth of skull} \times 100}{\text{Maximum AP length of skull}}$$

   The Indian skull is Caucasian with few Negroid characters, and the value is 75–79.9.

6. **Determining the age of the individual**
   a. Dentition and mandible
   b. Ossification centres of bones (studied by means of X-rays)
   c. Closure of cranial sutures (—do—)
   d. Symphyseal surfaces of pubic bone.
7. **Determining sex of the individual:** Sex is determined from skeleton based on sexual characteristic of skull, pelvis, mandible, sacrum and long bones (seen after puberty).

   Krogman's degree of accuracy in sex determination from bones:

Whole skeleton	100%
Pelvis + Skull	98%
Pelvis	95%
Skull	92%
Long bones	80%

8. **Identification of the individual:** It can be determined from:
   - DNA analysis
   - Teeth: Extractions, artificial dentures
   - Superimposition
   - Neutron activation analysis
   - Radiological investigations
9. **Determining cause of death**
   a. Fractures of bones
   b. Foreign body (bullet)
   c. Chemical analysis for detection of metallic poison
10. **Determining time of death:** It may be determined from the condition of parts and decomposition changes.
11. **Determining type of weapon:** From antemortem injuries it may be possible to determine whether a hard blunt weapon, a light or heavy sharp cutting weapon, a pointed weapon or a firearm was used.

SHORT NOTES

1. Gustafson's method (Sher-i-Kashmir Institute, Srinagar 2020) (Rajiv Gandhi University, Bengaluru 2019) (Adesh, Bathinda supple 2018) (Rajasthan University 2018) (Pondicherry Supple 2017) (Andhra Pradesh 2016)

Ans:

- It is a method used for age estimation in dead
- To access the pathological changes—longitudinal section of the tooth is taken
- Best teeth for study—anterior teeth (incisors/canines)
- Estimates age between 25 and 60 years
- It is based on the criteria given below:

Criteria
1. **A**ttrition
2. **S**econdary dentin
3. **P**eridontosis
4. **R**oot resorption
5. **T**ransparency of root: *Most reliable criteria*
6. **C**ementum apposition

(Mnemonic—**AS PRTC**)

Limitation

Useful only in dead (as teeth have to be extracted for examination)

2. Turner syndrome (Adesh, Bathinda 2019)

- Most common sex chromosome disorder associated with female hypogonadism
- Most common cause of primary amenorrhea
- Chromosomal abnormality—mosaic karyotype (45XO/46XX)
- Barr body—false negative
- Anatomically—female

Clinical Features

External	Internal
1. Short stature	1. CVS anomalies: Bicuspid aortic valve > Coarctation of aorta
2. Webbed neck	2. Renal abnormalities: Horseshoe kidney, hypertension.
3. Low hairline	3. Streak ovaries (ovarian dysgenesis), uterus hypoplasia
4. Ptosis with low-set ears	
5. Widely spaced nipples	
6. Cubitus valgus	
7. Short fourth metacarpals	
8. Lymphedema of hands and feet	

Diagnosis

- Decreased estrogen levels lead to raised LH, raised FSH (hypergonadotropic hypogonadism)
- Karyotype showing 45XO chromosomes

3. Klinefelter's syndrome (Adesh, Bathinda Supple 2019)(North Eastern Hill University, Shillong Supple 2019)

- Most common sex chromosome disorder associated with male hypogonadism
- Chromosomal abnormality: 46XXY
- Anatomically: Male
- Barr body: False positive

Clinical Features Due to

Low testosterone levels	Raised estrogen levels	Other features
1. Delay in onset of puberty 2. Axillary and pubic hair are absent 3. Hair on chest and chin are reduced 4. Azoospermia	Gynecomastia at puberty	1. Tall stature (height greater than arm span) 2. Testes: Firm, fibrotic small, non-tender 3. IQ—low

Diagnosis

- Karyotyping (46XXY)
- Serum testosterone is low, leading to raised LH, FSH and estrogen levels.

4. Locard's principle of exchange (BFUHS, Punjab 2019, 2015) (Rajiv Gandhi University, Bengaluru 2015) (Andhra Pradesh 2016) (VNS, Gujarat 2017)

1. Dr Edmond Locard formulated the Locard's principle of exchange: "When two objects come into contact with each other, there is always some transfer of material from one to the other".
2. Once this transfer is detected and the substance classified and/or individualized, the forensic specialist will have a clue as to what may have occurred at the scene. The forensic scientist's job is to uncover and reconstruct how the evidence fits into the investigation of a crime.
3. For example, fingerprints left behind on a knife in crime scene or semen deposited in vagina in sexual assaults.

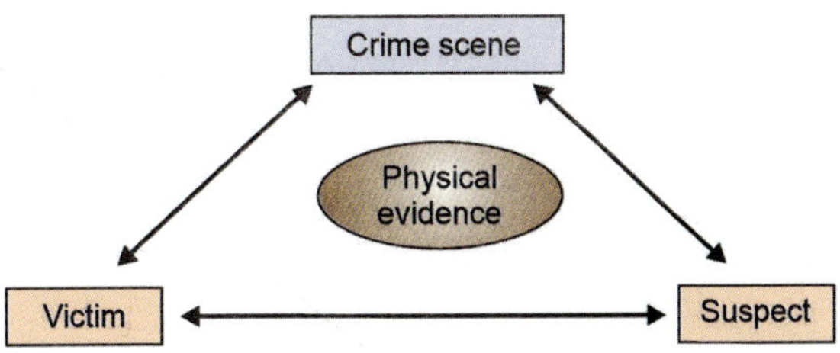

5. Sequence of appearance of permanent teeth (BFUHS, Punjab 2019) (VNS, Gujarat 2019) (Sai Tirupati University, Rajasthan, 2019)

Ans:

Mnemonic	Tooth	Eruption (yrs)
Mummy	1. First **m**olar	6–7
Is	2. Central **i**ncisor	6–8
In	3. Lateral **i**ncisor	7–9
Pain	4. First **p**remolar	9–11
Papa	5. Second **p**remolar	10–12
Can	6. **C**anine	11–12
Make	7. Second **m**olar	12–14
Medicine	8. Third **m**olar	17–25

Successional Teeth

- 20 in number
- Comes in place of temporary teeth

Superadded Teeth

- 12 in number
- All permanent molars belong to this category

6. Temporary dentition (KHMS, Tamil Nadu Supple 2020)

Ans:

20 in number with dental formula 2-1-0-2 (2 incisors, 1 canine, no premolars, 2 molars)

Tooth	Eruption (months)
Central Incisors	
• Lower	6
• Upper	7
Lateral Incisors	
• Upper lateral	9
• Lower lateral	10
1st **M**olar	12
Canines	18
2nd **M**olar	24

(Mnemonic—**I'm CM**)

7. Poroscopy and cheiloscopy (Rajiv Gandhi University, Bengaluru 2018)

Ans:

Poroscopy

- **Definition:** It is a method of identification by comparing the impressions of sweat pores found on the papillary ridges of the fingers.
- Discovered by Dr Edmond Locard.

- Just like the ridges, the pores are also permanent, immutable and individualistic, and these are useful to establish the identity of individuals.
- **MLI**
  1. Helpful in identification of an individual from a group of suspected individuals.
  2. Useful when only the fragments of fingerprints are available.

Cheiloscopy

Definition: The impressions produced by the wrinkles and grooves of the lips is known as lip prints.The study of these lip prints is called cheiloscopy.

Classification: Suzuki classified lip prints into 4 types.

Type I	**Complete** longitudinal fissures
Type I'	**Partial** longitudinal fissures
Type II	**Branched** grooves
Type III	**Intersected** grooves
Type IV	**Reticular** grooves
Type V	**Undetermined** pattern

MLI

1. Sex can be determined as type I, I′, II is more common in females but type III, IV more common in males
2. Useful for personal identification.

8. Tattoo marks (Adesh, Punjab 2017) (KHMS, Tamil Nadu 2015)

Ans:

Definition: These are patterns made in the skin by multiple small puncture wounds with needles or an electric vibrator dipped in colouring matter (e.g. pigment or dye)

Dyes used: Indian ink, indigo, cobalt, carbon black, Prussian blue, etc.

Classification: Traumatic tattoos, amateur tattoos, professional tattoos, cosmetic tattoos, medical tattoos.

Fading of Tattoo

Tattoos may fade if:

- Pigments are not introduced deep into the skin
- On exposed parts of body
- Parts which undergo constant friction
  That is why tattoos on the hands disappear early due to constant friction.

Associated risk: Infection, hepatitis B, AIDS, syphilis, sepsis, etc.

Removal of tattoos

1. Dermabrasion using dermabraders or laser therapy: Q switched Nd:YAG laser
2. Surgical methods
   - Complete excision and skin grafting
   - Burning by means of red-hot iron
   - Scarification
3. Electrolysis.

MLI

1. Identification: Tattoo marks give information about the person that helps identification of both living and dead, for e.g. in Sydney shark case
2. Providing information about race, religion and nationality
3. Political connections
4. Profession/occupation
5. May provide information about personal details, e.g. date of birth
6. In decomposed dead bodies, tattoo pigments can be found in the regional lymph nodes.

9. Cephalic Index (Uttarakhand University 2017, 2016) (Rajiv Gandhi University, Bengaluru 2015) (GMC, Chamba 2019)

Ans:

$$\text{Cephalic index} = \frac{\text{Max transverse breadth of skull}}{\text{Max AP length of skull}} \times 100$$

Skull can be classified into three types based on cephalic index (CI)—

	Skull type	Cephalic index	Race	
D	Dolichocephalic (long-headed)	70–75	Aryans, Negroes	AN
N=M	Mesaticephalic (medium-headed)	75–80	Europeans, Chinese	Exam
B	Brachycephalic (short-headed)	80–85	Mongolian	Medicos

(Mnemonic—DNB AN Exam for Medicos)

10. Age with reference to kidnapping from lawful guardianship (Rajiv Gandhi University, Bengaluru 2015)

Ans:

- Taking out or enticement of a male under 16 years or a girl below 18 years of age, or any person of unsound mind from custody of her lawful guardian without the consent of such guardian amounts to **kidnapping (Sec. 361 IPC)**.
- Lawful guardian includes any person lawfully entrusted with the care or custody of such minor or other person.
- If a girl below 21 years of age is 'imported' to India from foreign country for the purpose of illicit intercourse, the act amounts to **kidnapping (Sec. 366 B IPC)**.

11. Latent fingerprint (West Bengal University 2017)

Ans:

- Latent fingerprints are friction skin impression made of moisture, eccrine gland secretions and sebaceous oils.
- They are generally not visible to the unaided eye.
- Latent prints are the most prominent example of Locard's principle of exchange.
- Most crime scene fingerprint impressions are commonly latent prints.

- **Composition:** Sodium and potassium chlorides, amino acids, urea, lactic acid, free fatty acids, triglycerides and wax esters.
- Most methods for the development of latent prints were developed on the basis of knowledge about the latent print residue composition.
- Latent print requires additional processing to be rendered visible and suitable for comparison. Processing of latent prints to render them visible and suitable for comparison is called *development, enhancement* or *visualization*.

12. Changes in symphyseal surface of pubis with age (West Bengal University Supple 2017)

Ans:

Age (in years)	Features on symphyseal surface
Around 20	Uneven surface with transverse ridges across articular surface
25–40	Granular appearance of surface and ridges gradually disappear
40–50	Oval smooth surface with raised ends
50–60	Erosion of surface and breakdown of ventral margins
>60	Irregular erosions of surface

13. Medico-legal importance of scar (BFUHS, Punjab Supple 2016)

Ans:
1. Identification of the individual.
2. Disfigurement of face by scar due to assault/vitriolage is considered grievous hurt under Sec. 320 of IPC.
3. Linear needle scars indicate an IV drug abuser.
4. Shape of scar may indicate the nature of weapon or agent that caused injury.
5. Age of scar indicates time of infliction of injury.
6. Scars on wrist or throat may indicate previous attempts at suicide.
7. A person may allege scar due to disease as those of wound caused in an assault.

14. Four applications of DNA fingerprinting (North Eastern Hill University, Shillong 2016)

Ans:
1. To solve paternity and maternity disputes.
2. In case of sexual offences like rape, sodomy.
3. In case of accidents/mass disaster for identification of skeletal remains/mutilated bodies.
4. Diagnosis of inherited disorders in adults, children, newborn and prenatal babies. Like thalassemia, sickle cell anaemia, cystic fibrosis.
5. Developing cures for inherited disorders by studying the DNA fingerprints of relatives who have a history of some particular disorder.
6. Used to link suspects to evidence found at the crime scene like blood, hair or clothing.

15. Medico-legal importance of 16 years of age (Andhra Pradesh 2016)

Ans:

1. Taking away a male of age <16 years of age without consent of guardian amounts to kidnapping.
2. Learner license to drive a vehicle of 50 cc engine and without any gear.
3. If a person of >16 years but below 18 years of age commits a crime, he will be tried as an adult for the following three types of offences:

Offence	Punishment
Heinous offence	>7 yrs imprisonment
Serious offence	3–7 yrs imprisonment
Petty offence	<3 yrs imprisonment

16. Superimposition (Rajiv Gandhi University, Bengaluru 2015)

Ans:

- **Definition:** It is a technique of identification in which an unknown recovered skull can be matched with the available photograph (of face) of a suspected person.
- The complete skull along with mandible is required to obtain positive identification.

Technique (Photographic Method)

- The negatives are prepared, one from the original photograph (of face) and another from the skull recovered.
- Appropriate magnification is done.
- The two negatives are then superimposed by keeping one over the other and examined to judge whether or not the unknown recovered skull is of the presumed person as interpupillary distance of a person never changes regardless of his age.

Limitation

This technique is criticised because the photographs of different persons can be fitted in the photographs of skull.

Advancement in Technology

1. Computer-assisted superimposition system which has improved accuracy and identification of the person takes very less time.
2. Video super-imposition

Test is of a more negative value, because it can be *definitely be stated* that the skull and photograph are not those of the same person.

17. Bitemarks and its medico-legal importance (Rajiv Gandhi University, Bengaluru 2019) (North Eastern Hill University, Shillong 2019)

1. Bitemarks is semicircular or crescentic caused by the front teeth (incisors and canines) with a gap on either side due to separation of upper and lower jaw.
2. There may be abrasions, bruises and lacerations or a combination of all these.

3. **MLI:** Bitemarks are commonly seen in cases of:
   i. *Sexual assault*: Marks are usually seen on breasts, neck, shoulders, thighs, abdomen, pubis or vulva.
   ii. *Child abuse*: Marks are seen anywhere on the body, such as arms, hands, shoulders, cheeks, buttocks and trunk.
   iii. Bitemarks on foodstuffs (apples, cheese or chocolate), leather (key rings or belts) and wood (pencils) in cases where a perpetrator might have taken a bite out of something in the victim's home and left it behind.
   iv. Police officers may be bitten by the resisting offenders.
   v. In sporting events, such as football, rugby or wrestling.
   vi. In assaults, where marks may be found anywhere on the body.
      1. *Self-inflicted bitemarks* are present on accessible parts of the body, e.g., shoulders or arms; seen in psychiatric patients or teenage girls.
      2. *In sexual assault*, sucking action during bites produces multiple petechial hemorrhages due to rupture of small capillaries and venules.
      3. *Accidental marks* resulting from falls on to the face and during fits, biting of tongue and lips may also be there.

18. Corpus delicti. (BFUHS, Punjab Supple 2018) (VNS, Gujarat 2019)

Ans:

a. **Definition of corpus delicti:** It means that it must be proved that crime has occurred before a person is convicted for committing that crime.
b. It includes dead body and also other documents (like photographs, bullet, marks of weapon, cartridges) which should be identified.
c. Most important of these is the identification of the dead body for the establishment of crime.
d. If victim's identity cannot be identified, then it becomes very difficult for the investigating team to prove the crime.
e. MLI: In murder cases, before passing a sentence, it is essential to identify dead body and to prove corpus delicti.

19. Dactylography (BFUHS, Punjab 2020, 2016) (North Eastern Hill University, Shillong Supple 2020) (Rajiv Gandhi University, Bengaluru 2020) (West Bengal University Supple 2019) (Rajasthan University 2018, 2015) (KHMS, Tamil Nadu 2016) (GMC, Chandigarh 2015)

Ans: Refer to long question no. 1.

20. Types of fingerprints (GMC, Chandigarh 2016)

Ans: Refer to long question no. 1.

21. Intersex states (Adesh, Bathinda Supple 2020) (North Eastern Hill University, Shillong 2018)

Ans: Refer to long question no. 2.

22. Write medico-legal importance of age 21 years. (West Bengal University 2019)

Ans: Refer to long question no. 2.

23. Medico-legal importance of age 18 years (BFUHS, Punjab Supple 2019)

Ans: Refer to long question no. 2.

DIFFERENTIATIONS

1. Human hair and animal hair (Adesh, Bathinda supple 2020) (West Bengal University 2018) (North Eastern Hill University, Shillong supple 2017)

	Human hair	Animal hair
Texture	Thin and fine	Thick and coarse
Root	Bulb-shaped	Brush like
Cortex	Broader	Narrow
Medulla	Narrow/ noncontinuous/ fragmented	Broad/continuous
Medullary index	<1/3	>1/3
Tip	Cut/ frayed	Tapered
Pigment granules	Uniformly distributed	Mostly present around the medulla

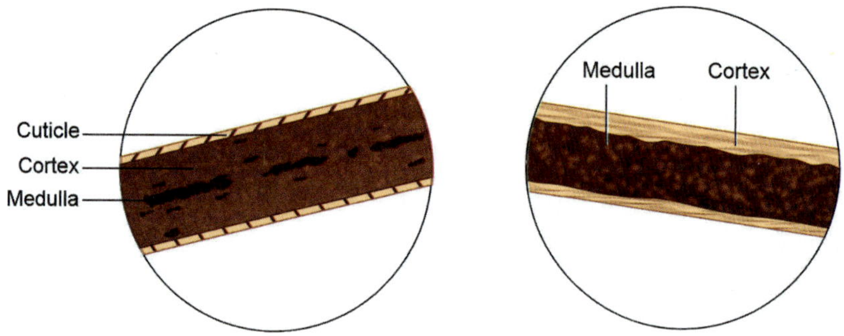

2. Male and female pelvis (Delhi University 2018, 2017) (Rajasthan University 2017, 2016)

	Male pelvis	Female pelvis
Pre-auricular sulcus	Narrow, shallow	Broad, deep
Subpubic angle	V-shaped (70°–75°)	U-shaped (90°–100°)
Sciatic notch	Small, narrow, deep	Large, wide, shallow
Pubis body	Narrow and triangular	Broad and square
Ischial spines	More prominent	Less prominent
Ischial tuberosity	Inverted	Everted
Obturator foramen	Oval	Triangular, apex forwards
Pelvic inlet	Heart-shaped	Circular / elliptical
Pelvic cavity	Funnel-shaped	Broad
Pelvic outlet	Smaller	Larger
Sacroiliac joint surface	Large, less angulated	Small and L-shaped

3. Male and female mandible (Delhi University supple 2016)

	Male mandible	Female mandible
Chin	Square	Rounded
Body height	Greater	Smaller
Ascending ramus	Greater breadth	Smaller breadth
Angle of mandible	Everted	Inverted
Angle of body with ramus	Less obtuse	More obtuse
Condyles	Large	Small
Ramus flexure	Rearward angulation of posterior border	Straight ramus
Muscular markings	Prominent	Not prominent

4. Male and female skull (Delhi University 2015)

	Male skull	Female skull
Forehead	Sloping/receding	Vertical
Glabella and supraorbital margins	More prominent	Less prominent
Orbits	Square–shaped and small	Round-shaped and large
Mastoid process	Large, round and blunt	Small and pointed
Frontonasal junction	Presence of angulation	Smoothly curved
Zygomatic arch	More prominent	Less prominent
External occipital protuberance	—do—	—do—
Partial eminence	Less prominent	More prominent
Frontal eminence	—do—	—do—
Palate	U-shaped	Parabola-shaped
Suprameatal crest	Present	Absent

5. Male and female femur (University of Health Sciences, Rohtak 2019, supple 2020)

	Male femur	Female femur
General	Heavy and rough	Light and smooth
Length	More	Less
Head	Large	Small
Angle of shaft with condyles	≥80°	<80°
Angle of neck with shaft	≥125°	<125°

6. Temporary teeth and permanent teeth (Adesh, Bathinda 2019) (North Eastern Hill University, Shillong Supple 2016)

	Temporary teeth	Permanent teeth
Color	China white	Ivory white
Size	Smaller and lighter (except temporary molars)	Heavier and stronger (except permanent premolars)
Direction of anterior teeth	Vertical	Inclined forwards
Neck	More constricted	Less constricted
Roots of molars	Smaller and divergent	Larger and less divergent

7. True hermaphroditism and pseudo-hermaphroditism (Sardar Patel University, Gujarat supple 2019)

	True hermaphroditism	Pseudo-hermaphroditism
Gonadal tissue	Both ovarian and testicular tissues	Gonadal tissue of only one sex
External genitalia	External genitalia of both sexes exist	External genitalia is of opposite sex
Karyotype	Either male or female pattern (46XX or 46XY or mosaics)	1. Male pseudo-hermaphroditism has male karyotype (nuclear sex—XY) and testes. 2. Female pseudo-hermaphroditism has female karyotype (nuclear sex—XX) and ovary.

8. Klinefelter's syndrome and Turner syndrome (Sher-i-Kashmir, Srinagar supple 2017)

	Klinefelter's syndrome	Turner syndrome
Karyotype	47 XXY	45 XO
Sex chromatin	Positive (similar to females)	Negative (similar to males)
Incidence	More common	Less common
Phenotype	Male	Female
Nuclear sex	Female	Male
Stature	Tall	Short
CVS anomalies	Rare	More common
Recognised	At puberty	At birth

CHAPTER 4

Asphyxial Deaths

LONG QUESTIONS

1. **Define asphyxia. What are the cardinal signs of asphyxia? What are the differences between antemortem and postmortem hanging?** (BFUHS, Punjab 2017)

Classify asphyxial deaths. Describe in detail the postmortem findings and causes of death in a case of a hanging. (Himachal Pradesh 2017) (Sai Tirupati University, Rajasthan, 2019)

Dead body of a middle-aged male subject was found in the state of hanging from the branch of a tree. There was evidence of a prominent ligature mark around the neck, cyanosis over finger nail beds and lips. There was presence of multiple small lacerated injuries with bleeding over both side of front of neck. How would establish: (WBUHS 2019)

a. Cause and nature of death

b. Likely internal findings during postmortem examination.

c. Time since death

(Note: Ignore the lacerated injuries over neck)

Ans:

Definition of asphyxia: It is a condition when there is reduced or no supply of oxygen to body tissues.

Cardinal signs of asphyxia

1. Congestion of organs 2. Cyanosis of ear, lips, nail beds 3. Petechial hemorrhages/Tardieu spots on face, neck, chest	**ASPHYXIAL TRIAD**

4. Right ventricular enlargement
5. Increased fluidity of blood

Classification of Asphyxial Deaths

a. *Mechanical causes*

Hanging	Strangulation	Suffocation	Drowning
1. Based on degree of suspension • Complete • Partial 2. Based on position of knot • Typical • Atypical	1. Ligature 2. Bansdola 3. Manual 4. Mugging 5. Garrotting	1. Smothering 2. Gagging 3. Choking 4. Overlaying 5. Burking 6. Traumatic asphyxia	1. Typical (wet) a. Freshwater b. Seawater 2. Atypical a. Dry drowning b. Near drowning c. Immersion syndrome d. Shallow water drowning

b. *Pathological causes:* When oxygen is not able to enter lungs due to diseases of URT/ lungs; e.g., laryngeal edema, stridor, tumor, etc.
c. *Environmental causes:* Asphyxia due to lack of oxygen. Seen in high altitude, inhalation of CO, sewer gas
d. *Positional asphyxia:* Asphyxia due to abnormal position. Seen in jack-knife position

PM FINDINGS IN CASE OF HANGING

External Findings

1. Head-inclined to side **opposite** to side of knot
2. **Face**
   - Congested and swollen
   - **Le facie sympathetique**—knot compresses the cervical sympathetic ganglion leading to opening of eyelids and dilated pupils of same side
   - Protrusion of tongue
   - **Dribbling of saliva**—From angle of mouth (opp. to side of knot) leading to salivary stain **(surest sign of AM hanging)**
   - Petechial hemorrhages over face
   - Cyanosis over lips, nail beds, ear
3. **Neck**
   a. **Ligature mark**
      - Pressure abrasion present in form of groove *(rope burns)*
      - Brown color, dry, hard, parchment like
      - Situated above the thyroid cartilage
      - Runs obliquely passing backwards, upwards on either side of the neck but leaves a gap at knot making an inverted V-shaped impression

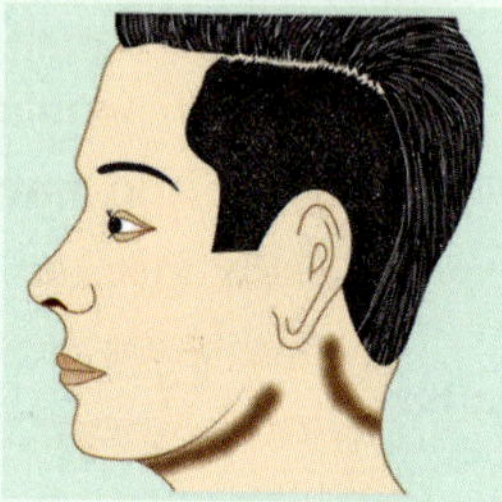

   b. Stretching of neck
   c. Bending of neck to side **opposite** to knot
4. Glove and stocking pattern of PM staining
5. Seminal discharge, involuntary discharge of feces, urine.

Internal Findings

1. Tissues underneath ligature—dry, white and glistening
2. Neck
   - Hyoid bone—anteroposterior compression fracture/abduction fracture
   - Carotid artery—Amussat's sign (transverse tear in carotid intima)
   - Larynx—congested
   - Thyroid cartilage—fracture of superior horn
3. Lungs and heart—congested and edematous with Tardieu spots
4. Abdominal viscera—congested

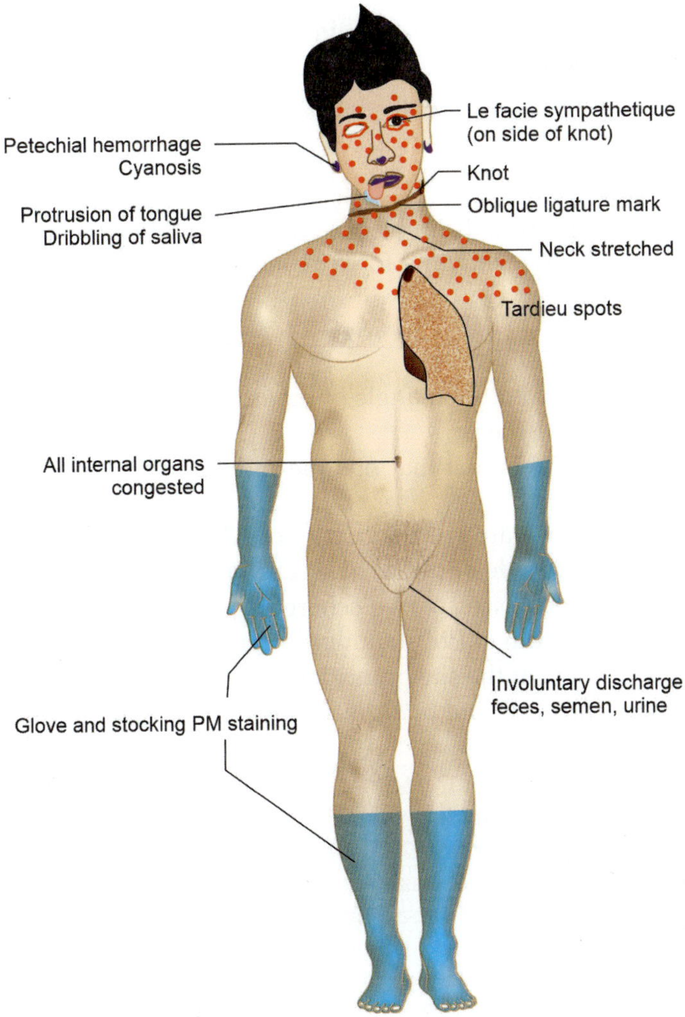

Causes of Death

Immediate causes	Delayed causes
1. Asphyxia—due to constriction force of ligature	1. Aspiration pneumonia
2. Cerebral anoxia—due to compression of carotid artery	2. Infection
3. Reflex vagal inhibition and cardiac arrest	3. Edema of lungs
4. Venous congestion—due to compression of jugular vein	4. Brain abscess
5. Fracture and dislocation of cervical vertebrae	

Refer to difference no. 2 for antemortem and postmortem hanging.
Refer to long question 3 for time since death.

2. A dead body of a female with a ligature around the neck is brought for the autopsy. Discuss in brief postmortem findings differentiating hanging from ligature strangulation. (Adesh, Bathinda 2018)

Define hanging. How are you going to come to conclusion that it is antemortem in nature? How it differs from ligature strangulation? (BFUHS, Punjab Supple 2016)

Ans:

Definition of Hanging

It is a form of violent asphyxial death produced by suspending the body with ligature tied around the neck. The constricting force is the weight of the body or part of body weight.

Signs of AM Hanging

1. Marks of dribbling of saliva from angle of mouth over clothes/skin
2. Signs of asphyxia can be seen
3. Ligature mark—dry, parchment-like, oblique and non-continuous which is present above the level of thyroid
4. Le facie sympathetique—rare but a sure sign of AM hanging
5. Protrusion of tongue on side opposite to side of knot
6. Presence of seminal, fecal or urinary discharge
7. Glove and stocking pattern of PM staining—but not a definite sign of AM hanging
8. Presence of suicide note at the site of incident

Difference between hanging and ligature strangulation: Refer to difference no. 1.

3. **A young woman of about 20 years was found hanging from ceiling of her room with a dupatta and feet dangling from the ground, in her rented accommodation by her landlord today morning 7:00 AM, she was fully clothed but her clothes were turned inside out. She was seen last alive by her landlord at about 8:00 PM the previous night when she had left for a party. Police were called and the body, with a ligature intact, was shifted to the mortuary by 8:00 AM. Paper were prepared for postmortem examination and presented at about 10:30 AM. You are the doctor conducting the postmortem examination.** (Rajasthan University 2017)
   a. **What findings on the body will help you arriving at the probable time since death in this case? Give the specific time limits of each for this particular case.**
   b. **Enumerate the specific samples that you should collect in such a case, give reasons in support of the same.**
   c. **Define hanging. Which type of hanging is present in this case?**
   d. **How will you remove the ligature material from the neck of the victim?**

Ans:

a. **The findings which may help in determining time since death are:**
   1. **Algor mortis:** Most useful in temperate countries during the first 24 h after death. The body attains environmental temperature in about 16–20 h.
   2. **Rigor mortis:** It commences in 1–2 h after death, takes about 9–12 h to develop from head to foot, persists for another 12 h, and gradually passes off in the same order as it appeared.

3. **PM staining:** Mottled patches over the dependent parts occur within 1–3 h. These patches coalesce in 4–6 h. The lividity is fully developed and fixed in about 8–12 h.
4. **Decomposition changes**
   - Greenish discoloration of the abdomen over the cecum and the flanks appears in about 12–24 h after death in summer. It spreads over the whole of the abdomen and the rest of the body within the next 24 h.
   - Marbling commences after 24 h. By 36–48 h, marbling is prominent.
   - In 12–18 h after death, gases collect in the intestines and distend the abdomen. From 18–36 or 48 h, gas formation is abundant.
   - Putrefactive odor is noticed by 24h.
5. **Food in stomach:** A light meal usually leaves the stomach within 1–2 h, a medium-sized meal in 3–4 h, and a heavy meal within 5–8 h. If the stomach is full and contains undigested food, it can be said that death occurred within 2–4 h of eating of the last meal, and if the food is digested (indistinguishable), then >4 h.
6. **Eye changes:** Segmented blood in retinal vessels seen up to 1 hr after death **(Kevorkian sign)**. Temporary opacity of cornea occurs by 2 hrs and permanent by 8–12 hrs. Tache noire is seen in 3–4 hrs. Rise in vitreous potassium is seen in up to 100 hrs after death.
7. **Insect activity:** By 18–36 h, flies lay their eggs. The eggs hatch into maggots or larvae in about 12–24 h. In the course of 4–5 days, maggots develop into pupae.

b. **Specimens to collect and preserve:**
   1. Ligature material
   2. Clothings
   3. Viscera
   4. Fingernail scrapings
   5. Blood (grouping, alcohol, drugs)
   6. Vaginal swabs
   7. Any other stains

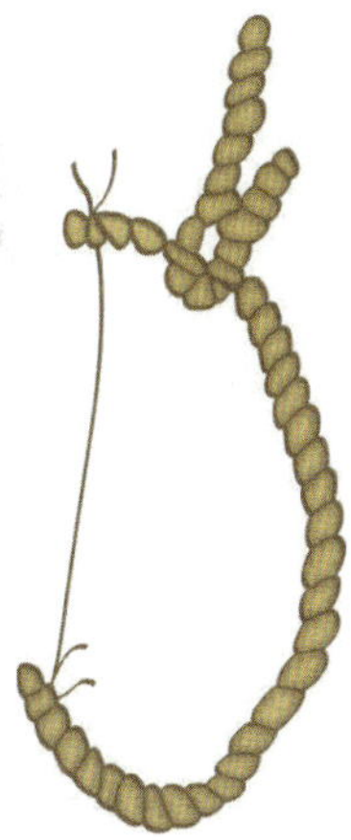

c. For definition refer to long question 2 above.

   The hanging was homicidal in nature; must be postmortem hanging as the clothes were turned inside out. Exact cause and nature of death is given depending on the findings.

d. The ligature is preserved and should be cut away from knot and reconstructed by joining cut ends with tape or another cord. This is done to verify and corroborate with the findings of autopsy subsequently.

4. Classify violent asphyxia deaths. Discuss the postmortem findings in case of freshwater drowning. (Andhra Pradesh 2015) (North Eastern Hill University, Shillong Supple 2020)

Define drowning. Enumerate types of drowning and discuss postmortem findings and laboratory investigation in a case of wet drowning. (Sher-i-Kashmir Institute, Srinagar 2020, 2015) (University of Health Sciences Rohtak 2019) (North Eastern Hill University, Shillong 2015, Supple 2016) (Sardar Patel University, Gujarat Supple 2015) (BFUHS, Punjab 2016) (VNS, Gujarat 2018)

What is atypical drowning? Discuss briefly the postmortem findings of a case of drowning. (Adesh, Bathinda Supple 2016) (Sai Tirupati University, Rajasthan, 2018)

Ans: Classification of violent asphyxia deaths: Refer to long question no. 1.

Definition of Drowning

It is a type of violent asphyxial death where entry of air into lungs is prevented due to submersion of mouth and nostrils into water or any liquid medium.

Types of Drowning

Typical drowning (wet drowning)	Atypical drowning
1. Fresh water drowning	1. Dry drowning
2. Sea water drowning	2. Immersion syndrome
	3. Near drowning
	4. Shallow water drowning

Definition of atypical drowning: It is a type of drowning in which water or fluid does not enter the lungs but death of the person occurs immediately.

1. Dry drowning: As soon as water enters the lungs, laryngeal spasm occurs leading to asphyxia
2. Immersion syndrome (hydrocution): Cold water stimulates the vagus resulting in cardiac arrest
3. Near drowning (2° drowning): Person does not dies of drowning, rather dies of complications like pneumonia, electrolyte imbalance
4. Shallow water drowning: When an unconscious person drowns even when there is little amount of water

PM Findings in Case of Wet Drowning

External findings

1. Clothes—wet and mixed with mud
2. Froth
   - Fine, white, tenacious, copious, lathery froth at mouth and nostrils
   - It reappears on pressing the chest
   - Pathognomic sign of AM drowning
3. Cadaveric spasm
   - An important sign of AM drowning
   - Grass, mud may be tightly clenched in hand
4. PM staining—present over face, neck, front of chest, upper and lower limbs (body floats with face down and buttocks up, with legs and arms hanging down)
5. Cutis anserine/goose bumps
   - Nonspecific sign (as seen in both AM and PM drowning)
   - Skin appears puckered and granular with erection of hairs due to contraction of erector pili

6. Washerman's hand and feet
   - Nonspecific sign (as seen in both AM and PM drowning)
   - Wrinkled, bleached appearance of palms, fingers due to submersion of body

Internal findings (seen in case of AM drowning)

1. Froth—present in trachea and bronchus
2. Lungs—voluminous, and show ballooning with impressions of ribs
   a. **Emphysema aquosum**—when conscious person is thrown in water
   b. **Paltauf's hemorrhage**—due to rupture of alveolar capillaries
   c. **Edema aquosum**—when unconscious person is thrown into water
3. Other changes
   - Presence of water in the middle ear
   - Presence of water in the stomach and small intestines
4. Congestion of viscera

Lab findings in Case of Wet Drowning

1. **Gettler's test**

For comparison of concentration of chloride ions in right side and left side of heart

Normally	Conc. of chloride ion same on both sides
FResh water drowning	Rt> Lt
SaLt water drowning	Lt> Rt

2. **Diatom test**
   - It is an important test of AM drowning
   - Diatoms are microscopic unicellular algae present in water
   - They have silica shell which is acid and alkali resistant
   - Best bone to analyse is bone marrow of femur
3. **Serum Mg**—increased in sea water drowning
4. **Serum strontium**—increased in sea water drowning

5. Define and classify strangulation. Describe the autopsy findings in case of ligature strangulation. (North Eastern Hill University, Shillong 2018)

Ans:

Definition of Strangulation

It is a form of violent asphyxial death caused by constriction of air passage at the neck by any means other than suspension of the body.

Classification of Strangulation

1. Ligature strangulation	Ligature is used to compress the neck
2. Manual strangulation (throttling)	Compression of neck by hands
3. Bansdola	Strangulation by bamboo or stick
4. Mugging	Strangulation by compressing neck in bend of elbow or knee
5. Garrotting	Compression of neck by a ligature which is tightened by twisting it with a lever (rod, stick)

PM findings in Case of Strangulation

External findings

1. **Face**
   - Congested and swollen
   - Subconjunctival hemorrhage
   - Bleeding from ear and nose
   - Protrusion of tongue
   - Presence of Tardieu spots all over the face (all these signs are more prominent in strangulation than hanging)
2. **Neck**
   Presence of **ligature mark** which is
   - Dry, hard, parchment-like with ecchymosed margins
   - Continuous and completely encircles the neck
   - Below the level of thyroid
   - Horizontally present around the neck
3. **Signs of struggle**
   Presence of scratches and finger nail abrasions on neck
4. **Other signs**
   Presence of cyanosis on nail beds, tip of nose
   Involuntary discharge of semen, urine, feces

Internal findings

1. Tissues beneath ligature mark
   - Show hemorrhage
   - Fracture of thyroid cartilage
2. Lungs—congested, edematous with petechial hemorrhages
3. Abdominal viscera—congested

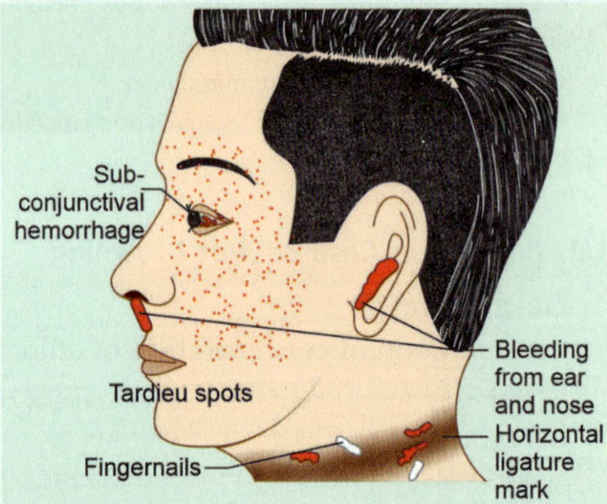

6. Describe the external and internal postmortem findings of manual strangulation. How strangulation is procured for homicidal purpose? (Rajasthan University 2015) (VNS, Gujarat supple 2018) (GMC, Chamba 2019)

Enumerate various violent asphyxia deaths. What are the postmortem findings in a case of throttling? Add a note on hyoid bone fractures. (Rajiv Gandhi University, Bengaluru 2019)

Enumerate the different types of strangulation. Write the postmortem findings in case of throttling. (North Eastern Hill University, Shillong Supple 2017)

Dead body of an adult female recovered from a bedroom. An area of pallor on otherwise suffused face along with 1.2 × 0.1 cm crescentic abrasion on the right side of face is present. (Adesh, Bathinda 2019)

a. What is your opinion regarding the cause of death?

b. Classify the violent asphyxia death.

c. What are the other postmortem findings and importance of circumstantial evidence in this specific case?

Ans:

a. The cause of death in throttling is asphyxia due to obstruction of respiration.

b. Refer to long question no. 1 for classification.

c. PM findings in case of throttling/manual strangulation.

External findings	Internal findings
1. Face • Congested with petechial hemorrhages • Subconjunctival hemorrhage 2. **Neck** a. *Abrasion—due to fingernail* Type of abrasion — Produced by 1. Crescentic abrasions — Assailant 2. Vertical abrasions — Victim So, it is important to examine the nails of the victim and fingernail scrapings of the alleged assailant when possible b. *Bruise* • May be irregular/oval shaped (six penny bruise) • More prominent of tip of thumb than tip of fingers • Presence and extent of fingertip bruising depends on relative position of victim and assailant. • In case of grip from right hand from front, there is one mark on right side (thumb impression) and four marks on left side of neck (finger impressions) 3. Involuntary discharge of feces and urine	1. Tissues beneath ligature mark • Show hemorrhage • Most significant internal sign 2. Fractures a. Thyroid cartilage — Fracture of superior horn b. Cricoid cartilage — Typical sign of homicidal throttling c. Hyoid bone — Inward compression fracture occurs Hyoid bone fracture most commonly seen in throttling 3. Lungs: Congested, edematous with petechial hemorrhages 4. Abdominal viscera: Congested

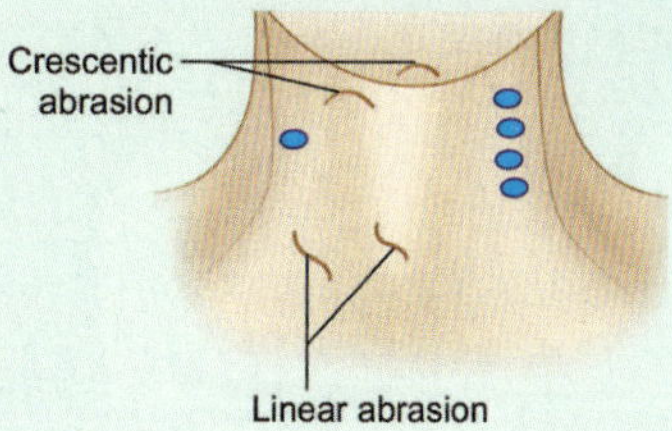

Hyoid Bone Fractures

1. Abduction fracture (anteroposterior fracture)	2. Adduction fracture (Inward compression fracture)	3. Side to side compression fracture	4. Avulsion fracture
Fractured segment is displaced outward due to anteroposterior compression, Divergence of greater cornu is increased causing fracture	Fractured segment is displayed inwards as the fingers of the grasping hand squeeze the throat, the greater cornu of hyoid causing fracture of the bone on the outer side and not on the inner.	Fractured segment displaced to inwards on one side and outwards on other side	Also called TUG fracture Occurs due to hyperextension of the neck
Seen in hanging	Commonly seen in throttling	Hanging/accidents	Convulsions

1. Abduction fracture (anteroposterior fracture)	2. Adduction fracture (inward compression fracture)	3. Side to side compression fracture	4. Avulsion fracture

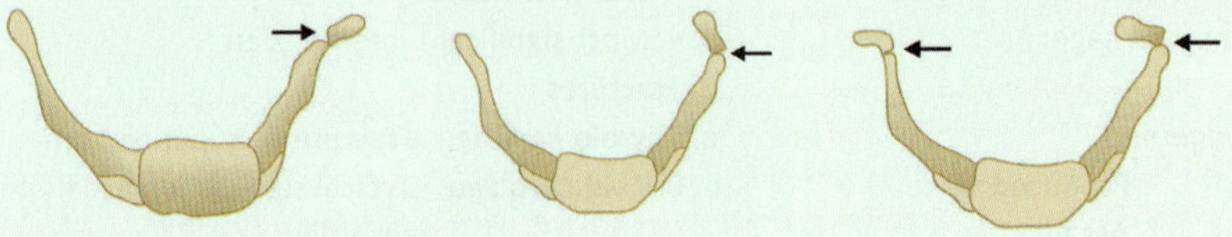

SHORT NOTES

1. Diatoms test (Adesh, Bathinda Supple 2020) (BFUHS, Punjab 2020) (VNS, Gujarat 2016)

Ans:

- Diatom test is an important laboratory test of AM drowning
- Diatoms are microscopic unicellular algae present in water
- They have silica shell which is acid and alkali resistant
- During drowning, diatoms (size up to 60 μ) can enter circulation
- Best bone to analyze is bone marrow of femur

In AM drowning	In PM drowning
Water with diatoms enter airway ↓ Reaches alveoli and finally enters circulation ↓ Reaches distant organs—sign of AM drowning like BM, spleen, kidney Bone marrow of femur (best site for analysis)	Diatoms able to enter lungs but diatoms are not found in distant organs

- MLI
  a. Diatoms resist putrefaction
  b. Can differentiate AM and PM drowning
  c. Diatom test is not useful in—dry drowning and hydrocution
  d. Gold standard test for diagnosis of typical drowning.

2. Smothering (BFUHS, Punjab 2020)

Ans:

Definition of Smothering

It is a form of violent asphyxia caused by mechanical obstruction of nose and mouth by hand, cloth, plastic bag or other materials.

Types

1. Homicidal	Most common type of smothering
2. Accidental	• Commonly seen in alcoholics or epileptics, when they fall accidentally in mud

	• In autoerotic asphyxia • In case of children, while playing with plastic bags over the head
3. Suicidal	Rare

PM Findings

- Abrasions and bruises around the mouth and nostrils. But not seen if soft materials, like cloth or pillow has been used.
- Presence of contusion/lacerations on inner side of lip

3. Café coronary (North Eastern Hill University, Shillong Supple 2020) (GMC, Chandigarh 2016) (AIIMS, Patna 2018) (BFUHS, Punjab Supple 2018) (Adesh, Bathinda 2017) (VNS, Gujarat supple 2019)

Ans:

- Café coronary is a condition of accidental choking wherein a bolus of food produces complete obstruction of the larynx.
- It's called café coronary because it mimics a heart attack and is usually seen in an intoxicated person.

Causes

1. Impairment of gag reflex	Seen in • Alcohol consumption • Overdose of CNS depressant
2. Ingestion of large bolus	Stimulates recurrent laryngeal nerve (vagus)—leading to cardiac arrest

Cause of Death

1. Asphyxia
2. Reflex cardiac arrest (vagal inhibition)

Typical history: Victim apparently healthy while eating, collapses suddenly turning blue.

Treatment

- First aid—Heimlich maneuvre
- A blow on the back or on the sternum may cause coughing and expel the foreign body.
- If the object cannot be removed—tracheotomy/cricothyrotomy.

4. Emphysema aquosum (BFUHS, Punjab 2019) (VNS, Gujarat 2017)

Ans: Emphysema aquosum is the condition of lungs seen in typical (wet) antemortem drowning.

Seen when the victim is live and conscious, so respiratory efforts are present. Therefore, water enters the lungs actively, leading to formation of froth in the air passages plus water in the lungs.

On Autopsy

- Lungs appear, voluminous, bulky, overinflated, that completely covers the heart and chest cavity resulting in impressions of rib over the lungs.
- And on dissection of lung, presence of froth and blood-stained froth comes out.

5. Shallow water drowning (North Eastern Hill University, Shillong Supple 2019)

Ans:

Shallow water drowning is a type of atypical drowning; seen when:

- An unconscious person (under influence of alcohol, drugs)
- Epileptic patient

May be drowned even in little amount of water because of direct contact of nose and mouth with water resulting in asphyxia and ultimately death of person occurs.

6. Pathophysiology of fresh water and sea water drowning (Rajiv Gandhi University, Bengaluru 2019) (Sardar Patel University, Gujarat 2018)

Ans:

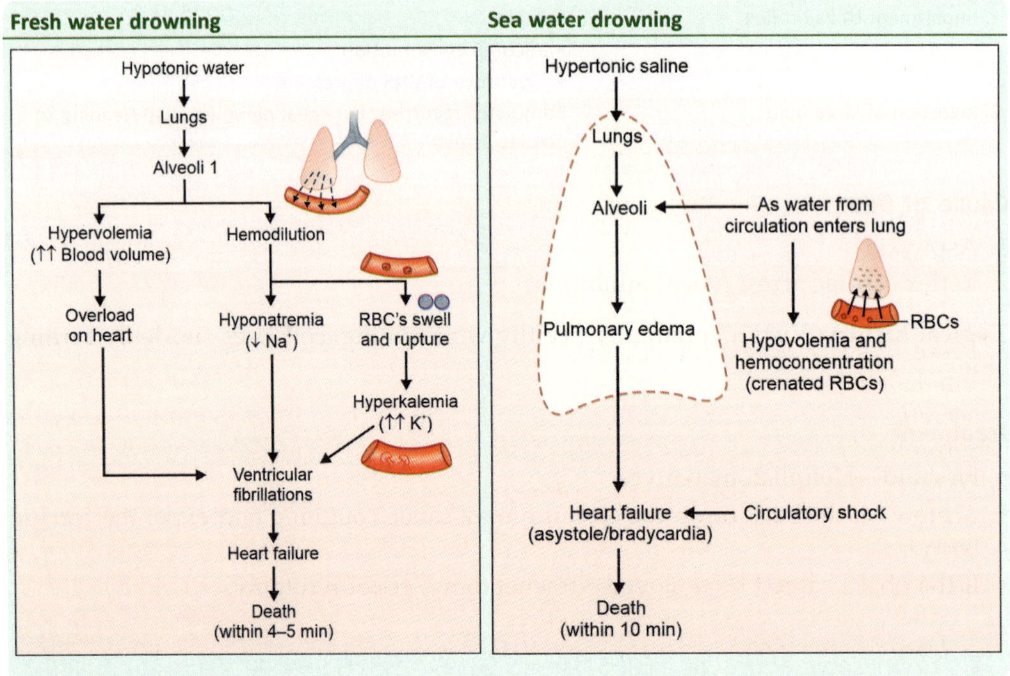

7. Short note on froth from nose and mouth in deceased (West Bengal University 2018)

Ans:

Fine and tenacious froth	Froth (not fine and tenacious)
• Fine, leathery, copious, tenacious froth is seen in case of wet drowning (typical drowning). • The mass of foam, consisting of fine bubbles, does not collapse when touched with the point of a knife. • May be absent when wiped off, but reappears again by itself or by applying pressure on chest.	Seen in death due to: 1. OPC poisoning 2. Electric shock 3. Acute pulmonary edema 4. Snakebite 5. Strangulation

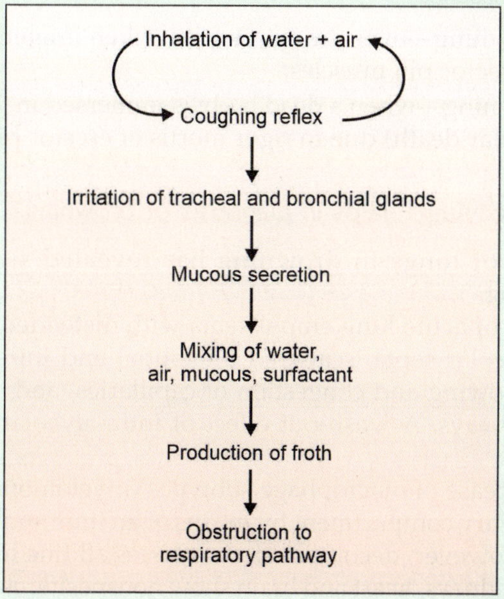

8. Absence of froth does not rule out AM drowning (West Bengal University Supple 2017)

Ans:

1. Presence of froth is characteristic of antemortem wet or typical drowning. The inhalation of water irritates the mucous membrane of air passages resulting in secretion of large quantities of mucus and edema fluid. Forceful agitation of the seromucoid secretion, surfactant, aspirated water and retained air results in froth.
2. **In atypical drowning, froth is not seen.**
3. There is very little or no inhalation of water or fluid in the air passages in many conditions.
4. Seen in:
   a. **Dry drowning:** Water does not enter the lungs due to laryngeal spasm caused by small amounts of water entering the larynx.
   b. **Immersion syndrome:** Syncope resulting from cardiac arrhythmias on sudden contact with water that is lower than body temperature.
   c. **Shallow water drowning:** Alcoholics, infants, drugged, epileptics and unconscious persons may die due to drowning in shallow water in a pit or drain.
   d. **Near drowning:** Near drowning refers to survival beyond 24 hrs after a submersion episode. Froth is not seen in such cases.

Hence, absence of froth does not rule out antemortem drowning.

9. Cutis anserine (Andhra Pradesh 2015)

Ans:
- Also called goose skin/goose flesh/goose bumps
- It is not a specific sign of pregnancy (as seen in both AM and PM drowning)
- Skin appears puckered and granular

Phenomenon of Cutis Anserina

- In case of AM drowning—over the extremities, when immersed in cold water due to contraction of erector pili muscles.
- In case of PM drowning—when a dead body is immersed in water soon after death (i.e., before molecular death) due to rigor mortis of erector pili muscles.

10. How histology of lungs helps in diagnosis of drowning? (Pondicherry 2019)

Ans: The histology of lungs in drowning has revealed significant findings in antemortem drowning.
1. Findings are—foci of acute lung emphysema with distended alveoli, thinning and rupture of the alveolar septa, scattered interstitial and intra-alveolar edema and hemorrhages, narrowing and congestion of capillaries, and sometimes exogenous particles in the airways. A wash-out effect of intra-alveolar macrophages can be seen.
2. In addition, an increase of macrophage subtypes (myelomonocyte subtypes) in the alveolar-intracapillary compartment by means of an immunohistochemical method has been found. However, decomposition removes all fine histological details.
3. Other organs like kidneys, heart and brain show nonspecific changes like generalized congestion and swelling of the capillary endothelia seen in any other form of asphyxia.

11. Lynching (Adesh, Bathinda 2018) (Andhra Pradesh 2015) (VNS, Gujarat 2018)

Ans:
- Lynching is a type of homicidal killing in which an angry mob kills an alleged offender in public often by hanging, without a legal trial.
- It was prevalent in North America, where it was practiced by whites on colored people.
- Usual methods used to kill an offender are hanging, burning, beating, etc
- Inquest in a case of lynching is done by police.
- Cause of death in lynching is asphyxia when person is hanged.

Post-mortem examination: In case of hanging, the features are of asphyxia. The body may show various injuries inflicted by the mob, e.g. contusions, abrasions, head injuries, fractures and so on.

MLI: Lynching is considered as murder/homicide. The persons belonging to a mob committing lynching are punished according to Sec. 302 IPC.

12. Traumatic asphyxia (BFUHS, Punjab 2017) (Rajiv Gandhi University, Bengaluru 2015 (KHMS, Tamil Nadu 2015) (North Eastern Hill University, Shillong Supple 2018)

Ans:

Definition of Traumatic Asphyxia

It is a form of violent asphyxia resulting from respiratory arrest due to mechanical fixation of chest preventing normal chest wall movements.

Causes

a. Person buried under the collapsed building.
b. Stampede by crowd due to fire in a movie theatre or public gathering.
c. Run over by a heavy vehicle.
d. Fall of tree or big rock over the person.

Postmortem Examination

External findings	Internal findings
1. **Above the line of demarcation** *Masque ecchymotique:* (due to congestion of blood in SVC and veins of head and neck) • Cyanosis and congestion over face and neck. • Petechial hemorrhages or ecchymoses. • Bleeding from ears and nose • Facial edema 2. **Below the line of demarcation:** Pale body	• Retinal hemorrhages • Fractures of rib and clavicle (common) • Heart: Right side of heart distended • Contusions, lacerations and congestion of lungs and liver

MLI

1. Mostly accidental
2. Homicidal in case of Burking

13. Burking (North Eastern Hill University, Shillong 2017)

Ans:

- Burking is a combination of homicidal smothering and traumatic asphyxia.
- William Burke and William Hare killed many persons in Scotland and sold their bodies to Medical College in UK.
- **Method:** Invited the victim to the house and offered him alcohol. When drunk, he was thrown on the ground and Burke would sit on the chest and close the nostrils and mouth with his hands, while Hare used to pull the body by the feet till he is dead.

14. Paltauf's hemorrhage (Rajiv Gandhi University, Bengaluru 2015)

Ans:

- Paltauf's hemorrhages are multiple, large, bluish reddish colored subpleural hemorrhages of variable size seen in case of **wet drowning**
- Rupture of alveolar walls produce hemorrhages just below pleura in the lungs
- Mostly occur in the lower lobes on anterior surface of lungs
- On cut section, copious amount of frothy bloodstained discharge comes out due to presence of water within alveoli and bronchioles.

15. Describe the postmortem findings in death due to drowning (Rajiv Gandhi University, Bengaluru 2020) (Uttarakhand University 2017, 2016)

Ans: Refer to long question no. 4.

16. Postmortem features of fresh water drowning (Sardar Patel University, Gujarat 2020) (GMC, Chandigarh 2016)

Ans: Refer to long question no. 4.

17. Fractures of the hyoid bone (BFUHS, Punjab 2019) (West Bengal University 2019)

Ans: Refer to long question no. 6.

18. Enumerate types of drowning. Describe autopsy findings of antemortem drowning. (Sardar Patel University, Gujarat Supple 2019)

Ans: Refer to long question no. 4.

19. Gettler's test (North Eastern Hill University, Shillong 2019) (Adesh, Bathinda Supple 2019)

Ans: Refer to long question no. 4.

20. Describe the ligature mark of typical hanging (Rajiv Gandhi University, Bengaluru 2019) (Sardar Patel University, Gujarat Supple 2016)

Ans: Refer to long question no. 1.

21. Neck finding in manual strangulation (Rajasthan University 2018)

Ans: Refer to long question no. 5.

22. Wet drowning (Uttarakhand University Supple 2018)

Ans: Refer to long question no. 4.

23. Drowning in the sea water (Andhra Pradesh Supple 2016)

Ans: Refer to long question no. 4.

24. Throttling (BFUHS, Punjab 2015)

Ans: Refer to long question no. 6.

25. Internal finding in a case of death due to drowning (KHMS, Tamil Nadu 2017)

Ans: Refer to long question no. 4.

DIFFERENTIATIONS

1. Hanging and strangulation (GMC, Chandigarh 2015) (Adesh, Bathinda Supple 2017) (Uttarakhand University 2018, 2017) (Sher-i-Kashmir Institute, Srinagar Supple 2018) (Rajasthan University 2016)

Ans:

	Hanging	Strangulation
Signs of asphyxia	Less marked	More marked
Protrusion of tongue	-do-	-do-
Bleeding from nose, ear	Rare	More common
Ligature mark		
• **Direction**	Oblique	Horizontal
• **Continuity**	Incomplete	Complete
• **Level in neck**	Above the level of thyroid	Below the level of thyroid
• **Base**	Hard, dry, parchment-like	Soft, reddish base
• **Abrasions and bruise around ligature**	Less common	More common
• **Tissues beneath ligature mark**	White, glistening	Shows hemorrhage and ecchymosis
Fracture of thyroid cartilage	Less common	More common
Fracture of hyoid bone	More common	Less common
Stains of saliva	Common	Rare
Discharge of urine and feces	Less common	More common
Seminal discharge	Common	Rare
Manner of death	Suicidal	Homicidal

2. Antemortem and postmortem hanging (Uttarakhand University Supple 2017)

Ans:

	Antemortem hanging	Postmortem hanging
Ligature mark		
• **Direction**	Oblique	Circular
• **Continuity**	Noncontinuous	Continuous
• **Level in neck**	Above thyroid	At/below thyroid
• **Base**	Dry, hard, parchment like	No changes seen
Le facie sympathetique	Present	Absent
Stain of saliva	-do-	-do-
Fecal/urinary/seminal discharge	-do-	-do-
Stretching of neck	-do-	-do-
Signs of asphyxia	-do-	±
PM staining	Glove and stocking pattern	Not specific
Suicide note	Present	Absent

3. Wet drowning and dry drowning (Rajasthan University 2015)

Ans:

	Wet drowning	Dry drowning
Definition	Type of drowning in which water or fluid enter lungs	Type of drowning in which water or fluid does not enter lungs
Lungs	Voluminous, bulky and show impressions of ribs	Lungs do not contain water (dry)
Froth	Fine, copious, tenacious froth	Not seen
Signs of asphyxia	Present	±
Cause of death	Heart failure	Laryngeal spasm

4. Fresh water drowning and sea water drowning (Rohtak Supple 2020) (Adesh, Bathinda Supple 2019)

Ans:

	Fresh water drowning	Sea water drowning
Features in lungs		
• **Size and weight**	Ballooned, but light	Ballooned and heavy
• **Color**	Pinkish	Purplish or bluish
• **Consistency**	Emphysematous	Soft, jelly-like
• **Shape after removal**	Retained	Not retained, flatten out
• **On cut section**	Crepitus is heard, little froth and no fluid	No crepitus, copious fluid and froth
Blood volume	Hypervolemia Hemodilution	Hypovolemia Hemoconcentration
Electrolytes	Hyponatremia Hyperkalemia	Hypernatremia
Cause of death	Ventricular fibrillations	Pulmonary edema
Death	Early	Late

CHAPTER

5

Injury

LONG QUESTIONS

1. Outline the features of suicide by firearm. What is the appearance of entry wound caused by revolver shot at a distance of 3 cm and 10 cm? (Adesh, Bathinda supple 2020) (Uttarakhand University 2017) (Sher-i-Kashmir Institute, Srinagar supple 2018)

Ans:

Features of Suicide by Firearm

1. Common in males with history of previous psychiatric illness, financial loss
2. Most of the suicidal firearms have shot distance as contact or very close range shot wound with sites of entry as:
   - Temple—the most common site
   - Center of forehead
   - Mouth
   - Midline behind the chin
   - Left side or front of chest
   - Abdomen
3. The person uses his dominant hand to press the trigger, steadying the muzzle against the head with the non-dominant hand
4. Presence of powder soot may be seen on hand pressing trigger, as well as on the non-dominant hand
5. Path of bullets—the gunshot is directed in-upward or backward direction
   For example, gunshots to right temple show a front-to-back or upward path in suicides. Therefore, a downward shot or a back to front should raise suspicion despite typical shot location. Gunshots to the left chest tend to show a right-to-left path and in the mouth, an upward trajectory in suicides.
6. Only one entry and one exit wound is present
7. Cadaveric spasm may be seen with the weapon firmly grasped in the hands
8. Presence of suicide note and weapon at the scene (mostly house)

Entry wound caused by revolver shot at a distance of 3 cm and 10 cm: Refer to long question no. 2.

2. Classify firearms. Discuss the findings of entry bones caused by rifled firearm from various ranges. (BFUHS, Punjab supple 2018) (Delhi University 2017) (North Eastern Hill University, Shillong 2018) (VNS, Gujarat 2018)

Ans:

Rifled firearms	Smooth bored firearm (shotgun)
• Military rifle/assault rifle-AK-47, AK-56	• Single barrel
• Revolver	• Double barrel
• Pistol	• Cylinder bore
• Submachine gun	• Choke bore
• Machine gun	• Bolt action
• Single shot pistol	• Pump action
• Auto-loading pistol	

Findings of entry bones caused by rifled firearm from various ranges

	Effects	Range
Flame	Singeing	8 cm
Smoke	Blackening	30 cm
Gun powder	Tattooing	60–90 cm

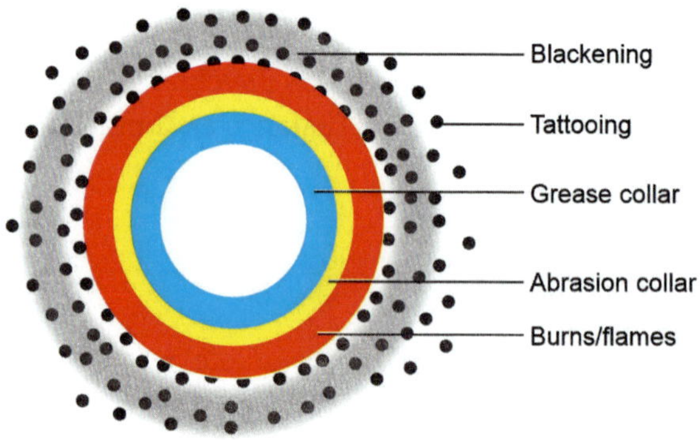

	Contact shot	Close shot	Near/intermediate shot	Distant shot
Distance	Hard contact over head	Within range of flame (<8 cm)	Outside range of flame but within range of gun powder (>8 cm–90 cm)	Outside range of gun powder (>90 cm)
Shape	Stellate/cruciate	Small, circular and inverted	Small, circular and inverted	Small, circular and inverted
Muzzle impression	+	–	–	–
Burning and singeing	– (but seen inside track of wound)	+	–	–

Contd...

	Contact shot	Close shot	Near/intermediate shot	Distant shot
Blackening	– (but seen inside track of wound)	+	–	–
Tattooing	– (but seen inside track of wound)	+	+	–
Abrasion collar	+/–	+	+	+
Grease collar	+/–	+	+	+

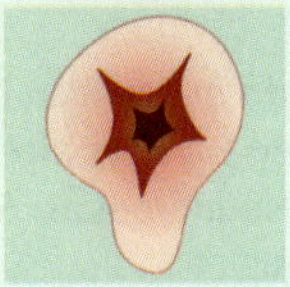
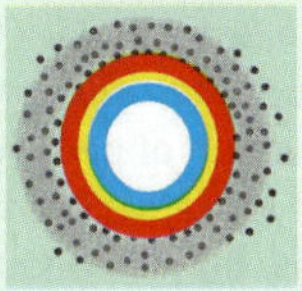
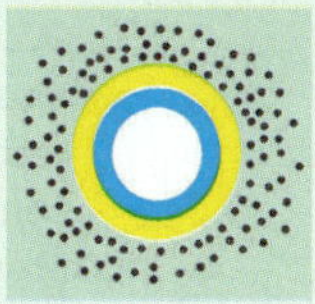

3. Define and classify burns. How will you differentiate antemortem and postmortem burns? What are the causes of death in case of burns? (Rajiv Gandhi University, Bengaluru 2019, supple 2017) (University of Health Sciences, Rohtak supple 2020)

Ans:

Definition of Burns

Burn is an injury caused by heat, or by a chemical or physical agent having an effect similar to heat.

Classification of Burns

	1st Degree	2nd degree superficial	2nd degree deep	3rd and 4th degree
Depth	Involves only epidermis	Involves epidermis and papillary dermis	Involves epidermis and whole of dermis	Till subcutaneous layer (3rd degree), muscles (4th degree)
Color	Red	Red	Red	Black and charred
Pain to stimuli	Tender	Tender	Less painful	Painless
Blisters	Present	Present	Less in number	Absent
Blanching	Present	Present	Varied blanching	Absent
Healing	Heals spontaneously in 3–5 days	Heals within 2 weeks	Heals within 3 weeks	Difficult to heal, contracture seen
Scar	Absent	Absent	Hypertropic scar	Hypertropic scar and keloid formation
Seen in	Sun burns	Scalds, flash burns	Scalds, flash burns	Contact with flame, hot surface, hot liquids
Treatment	Paraffin dressing	Silver sulfadiazine dressing	Silver sulfadiazine dressing	Early excision and skin grafting

Differences between antemortem and postmortem burns: Refer to difference no. 11.

Causes of Death in Case of Burns

Immediate causes	
1. Neurogenic shock	Due to severe pain and fear
2. Asphyxia	Due to suffocation caused by inhalation of CO and smoke
3. Laryngeal spasm and Glotticedema	Caused by smoke, fumes and gases
4. Cardiac arrest	
Delayed causes	
1. Hypovolemic shock	Due to loss of fluids and electrolytes *Causes secondary shock and death within 24–48 hrs*
2. Toxemia	Due to absorption of toxic products from burnt tissues
3. Acute renal failure	Occurs on 3rd–4th day
4. Septicemia	*Most important cause of death in survived patients* Leads to death of person after ≥ 4 days after burns Common causative agents: Pseudomonas, *Staph aureus*
5. Infective complication	Bronchitis, bronchopneumonia

4. Classify injuries. Discuss the postmortem findings in case of death due to antemortem flame burns. (North Eastern Hill University, Shillong Supple 2020) (Sai Tirupati University, Rajasthan 2018)

Ans:

Classification of Injuries

Refer to long question no. 8.

PM Findings in Case of Death due to Antemortem Burns

External findings

1. Clothes
   - Found to be burnt
   - Clothes are removed and examined for smell of kerosene, petrol
2. Face
   - Swollen and tongue protruded out with charred tip
   - Froth may be seen due to irritation of the air passages by smoke as a result of pulmonary edema
   - **Crow's feet sign:** Skin around eyes spared
3. Skin—AM burns show signs of redness
4. AM blisters
   - Contains inflammatory fluid
   - Erythemic base
   - Edges showing signs of redness
5. Singeing of scalp and body hairs
6. Degloving of skin, particularly hands and feet
7. **Pugilistic attitude:** The legs are flexed at the hips and knees, arms are flexed at the elbows and the fingers are bent like claws due to heat stiffening. Can be seen in both AM or PM burns

Internal findings (3Cs)

1. Carbon/soot particles
   - Deposition of cabon and soot particles in airway till terminal bronchioles
   - *Surest sign of antemortem burns*
2. Curling ulcers—due to mucosal ischemic acute stress ulcers are seen in gastric antrum and 1st part of duodenum
3. COHb levels in the blood raised
4. Spleen—enlarged and congested
5. Adrenals—enlarged and congested
6. Lungs—congested and edematous
7. Heart—cherry red color blood

5. Classify thermal injuries. Describe the postmortem findings in case of death due to burn injuries. (North Eastern Hill University, Shillong 2019)

Ans:

Classification of Thermal Injuries

Due to Heat	Due to Cold
1. Local effects • Burns • Scalds 2. General effects • Heat cramps • Heat exhaustion • Heat stroke • Heat syncope	1. Local effects • Frostbite • Trench foot • Chilblains 2. General effects • Hypothermia

For PM findings in case of death due to antemortem burns: Refer to long question no. 4.

6. Define grievous hurt as per Section 320 of IPC. What is dangerous weapon or means? (BFUHS, Punjab 2019)

Ans:

The grievous hurt is defined under **Sec 320 IPC** and consists of 8 clauses:

First	Emasculation
Second	Permanent privation of the sight of either eye
Third	Permanent privation of the hearing of either ear
Fourth	Privation of any member or joint
Fifth	Destruction or permanent impairing of the powers of any member or joint
Sixth	Permanent disfiguration of the head or face
Seventh	Fracture or dislocation of a bone or tooth
Eighth	Any hurt which a. Endangers life b. Causes the victim to be in severe bodily pain for 20 days c. Unable to follow his ordinary pursuits for a period of 20 days.

1. **Emasculation**
   - Means loss of masculine power
   - This clause is confined only to males
   - **Causes** of emasculation
     - i. Castration
     - ii. Cutting of penis
     - iii. Injury to penis
     - iv. Injury to lumbosacral spine leading to impotence

2. **Permanent privation of the sight of either eye**
   - The loss of sight may be partial or complete but it has to be permanent.
   - *For example:* Corneal abrasions heal by leaving a scar leading to partial loss of vision
3. **Permanent privation of the hearing of either ear**
   - Loss of hearing may be partial or complete but it has to be permanent
   - *For example:* Teacher slaps a student and tympanic membrane of student ruptures and he cannot hear from that ear. So teacher is guilty of grievous hurt.
4. **Privation of any member or joint**
   - **Member** means any organ or limb of a subject responsible for performance of distinct function. It includes eyes, ears, nostrils, mouth, hands, feet, etc
   - **Joint** may be both small or big
   - *For example:* Chopping of an ear or finger
5. **Destruction or permanent impairing of the powers of any member or joint**
   For example: Cutting of a tendon cause deformity, loss of movement and weakness.
6. **Permanent disfiguration of the head or face**
   - Opinion of disfigurement should be given after complete healing
   - Chopping of an ear or nose, laceration on face as it leaves a scar on healing
7. **Fracture or dislocation of a bone or tooth.**
   - **Fracture** includes any type of fracture, cut on bone, hairline fracture, skull fracture, etc.
   - **Dislocation:** For example, shoulder dislocation
8. **Any hurt which**
   a. **Endangers life**
   b. **Causes the victim to be in severe bodily pain for 20 days.**
   c. **Unable to follow his ordinary pursuits for a period of 20 days,** for example, not able to brush his teeth, eat food or take bath.

Dangerous Weapon or Means

Any instrument if used as a weapon of offence is likely to cause death, like weapon used for shooting, stabbing or cutting; or by means of fire or any heated substance, poison or any corrosive substance, explosive or any substance which is harmful to the human body to inhale, to swallow or to receive into blood or by means of any animal.

Sections which Deal with Dangerous Weapon

	Offence	Punishment
Sec. 324 IPC	Voluntarily causing simple hurt by dangerous weapons	Imprisonment: Up to 3 years and fine
Sec 326 IPC	Voluntarily causing grievous hurt by dangerous weapon	Imprisonment: Up to 7 years and fine

7. Enumerate various skull fractures. Add a note on subdural hemorrhage. (Sher-i-Kashmir Institute, Srinagar supple 2019)

Ans:

Skull Fractures

Skull Vault Fracture

1. **Fissure fracture**

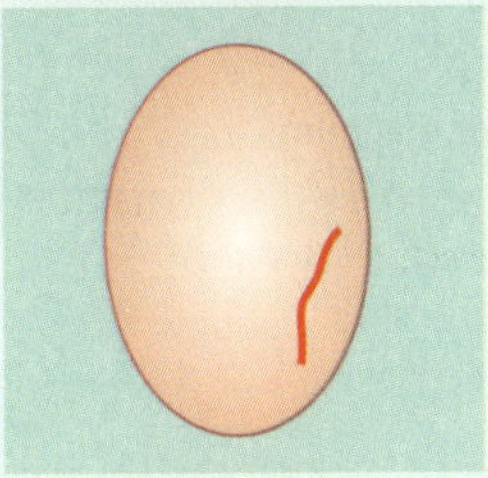

- Also called **linear fracture**
- Most common type of skull fracture
- It is produced by:
  - Blow with blunt weapon having broad striking surface
  - When head strikes a flat surface on ground

2. **Depressed fracture**

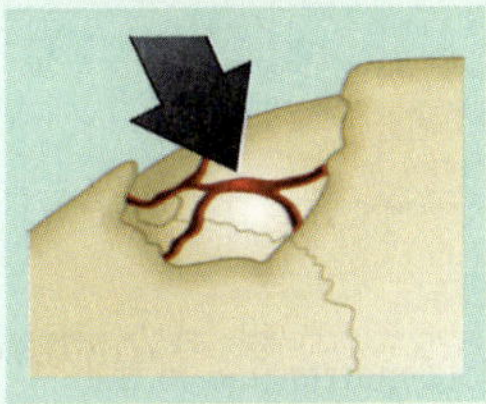

- Also called **signature fracture**
- It is produced by heavy weapon with small striking surface like hammer, axe, etc.

3. **Comminuted fracture**

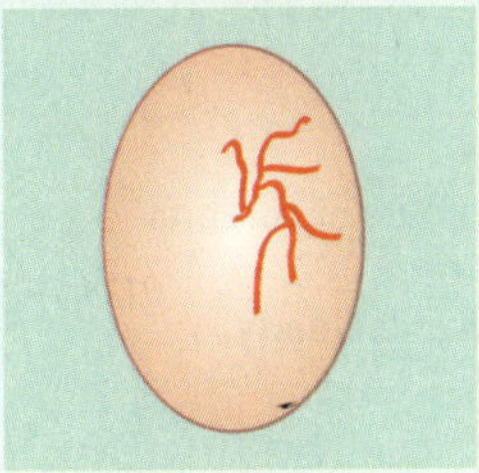

- Also called **spider web fracture/mosaic fracture**
- In this type of fracture, bone is broken into several pieces of different sizes
- It is caused by:
  - Vehicular accidents
  - Fall from height on a hard surface
  - Blow on head with heavy object

4. **Gutter fracture**

- In this outer part of the skull bone is chipped off by a tangential force so as to form a gutter
- It is produced by oblique bullet not penetrating the skull

5. **Indented fracture**

- Also called **pond's fracture**
- It is seen in case of infants (as elastic skull)
- It is caused by obstetrics forceps delivery

6. **Diastatic fracture**

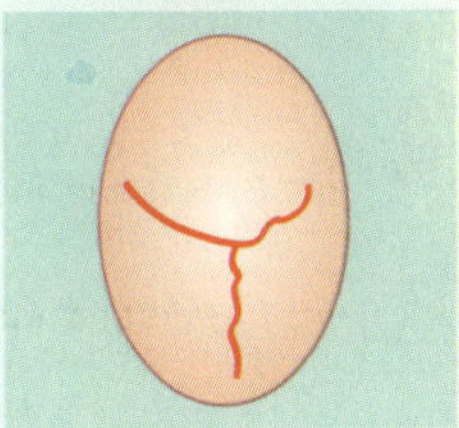

- Also called **sutural fracture**
- Fracture lines run across the suture
- Commonly seen in young individuals

Skull Base Fracture

1. **Hinge fracture** 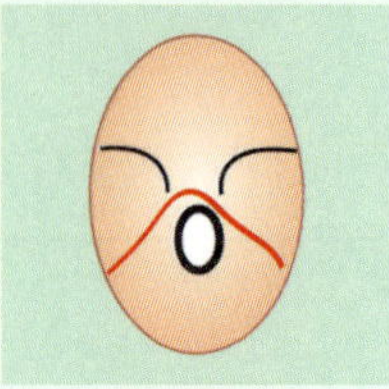	• Also called **motorcyclist fracture** • It divides the entire base of skull into two parts • It is the fracture of middle cranial fossa • Seen in motorcyclist
2. **Ring fracture** 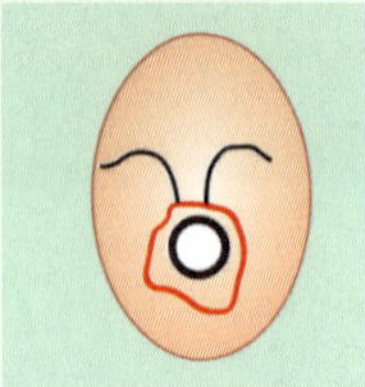	• Type of fissured fracture encircling foramen of magnum • It is the fracture of posterior cranial fossa • It is produced by fall from the height
3. **Orbital Blow out fracture**	• Fracture of medial wall and floor of orbit • On CT tear drop sign is seen

(Mnemonics—**BCDeFGHI**)

Subdural hemorrhage

Definition	Bleeding in the space between dura and arachnoid matter (i.e. in the subdural space)
Causes	1. Trauma 2. Intense shaking (in infants/child)
Vessels involved	1. Rupture of bridging or communicating veins 2. Tears in the dural venous sinuses
Site	Fronto-temporal region with preservation of contours of cerebral convolutions
Predisposing factors	1. Age—chronic SDH commonly seen in **Children** and **Elderly** 2. Alcoholics
Types of SDH	1. **Acute SDH** • Symptoms start immediately or within 3 days after trauma • Treatment: Burr holes or emergency craniotomy 2. **Sub-acute SDH:** Symptoms start within 4–21 days after trauma 3. **Chronic SDH** • Appear >3 weeks after trauma • Seen in Infants and elderly
Clinical features	1. Drowsiness 2. Headache 3. **Lucid interval:** Seen in 30% of cases 4. Confusion 5. Forgetfulness 6. Hemiparesis
Diagnosis	On CT scan—concavo convex opacity
MLI	1. In battered baby syndrome—SDH is the most consistent feature 2. Age of SDH correlates with events prior to death

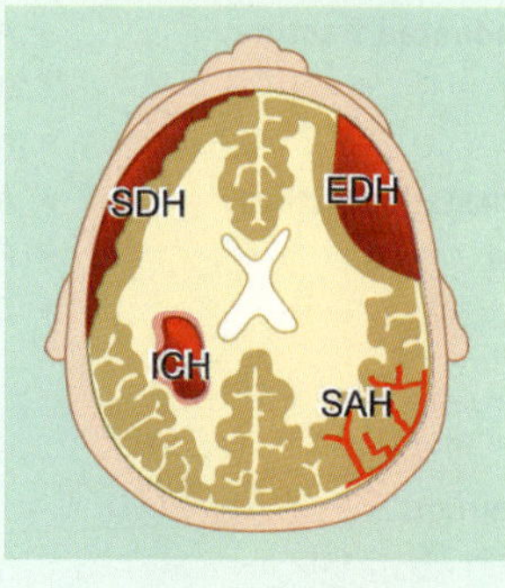

8. Define injury. Write medical, legal and medico-legal classification of injury. How will you differentiate suicidal cut throat injury from homicidal cut throat injury? (AIIMS, Patna 2018)

Ans:

Definition of Injury

As per Section **44 IPC**, injury is defined as any harm, whatever illegally, caused to any person in **M**ind, **R**eputation, **B**ody or **P**roperty. (Mnemonic: **MR BP**)

Classification of Injury

1. **Medical** (based on causative factors)	1. **Mechanical injuries**	
	Based on blunt force	*Based on sharp force*
	• Abrasion	• Incised wound
	• Bruise	• Chop wound
	• Laceration	• Stab wound
	• Fracture	
	2. **Thermal injuries**	
	Based on heat	*Based on cold*
	• Burns	• Frostbite
	• Scalds	• Trench foot
	• Heat cramps and heat stroke (systemic effects)	• Hypothermia (systemic effect)
	3. **Chemical injuries**	
	• Irritants—plant and animal irritants	
	• Corrosives—acid and alkali	
	4. **Other injuries**	
	• Electric injuries	
	• Blast injuries	
	• Radiation injuries	
2. **Legal** (based on severity of injuries)	1. Simple	
	2. Grievous	
3. **Medico-legal** (based on nature of injuries)	1. Suicidal	
	2. Homicidal	
	3. Accidental	
	4. Fabricated injuries	

Difference between suicidal and homicidal cut throat injury: Refer to difference no. 4.

9. What is the difference between injury, wound and hurt? How can you estimate age of contusion? (Rajasthan University 2018)

Ans:

Difference Between Injury, Wound and Hurt

1. **Injury:** Any harm, whatever illegally, caused to any person in *body, mind, reputation or property* **(Sec. 44 IPC).**
2. **Wound:** *Clinically*, it means any injury where there is breach of natural continuity of skin or mucous membrane. *In medico-legal practice*, the terms 'wound' and 'injury' are synonymous, but strictly wound will include any lesion, external or internal,

caused by violence, with or without breach of continuity of skin (not defined in any IPC or CrPC).

3. **Hurt:** Hurt means any bodily pain, disease or infirmity caused to any person (**Sec. 319 IPC**).

   It is of two types:
   i. Simple
   ii. Grievous.

Estimation of age of contusion: Refer to long question no. 11.

10. Define bruise. How can you determine age of bruise? How does parallel bruise occur? (West Bengal University 2017)

Ans:

Definition of Bruise

It is defined as extravasation of blood in the subcutaneous/subepithelial tissues due to rupture of blood vessels as a result of blunt force impact.

Age to determine bruise: Refer to long question no. 11.

How does parallel bruise occur?

Parallel bruise **(railway line or tram-line type)** is caused by blows with a rod, stick or a whip which produces two parallel, linear hemorrhages with the intervening normal skin.

Mechanism: When the weapon sinks into the skin, there is little or no damage to the blood vessels over ridges where it compresses the skin. However, traction causes marginal dermal vessels to rupture in the skin. The resulting accumulation of a small amount of blood, near the epidermis causes the formation of the patterned bruise.

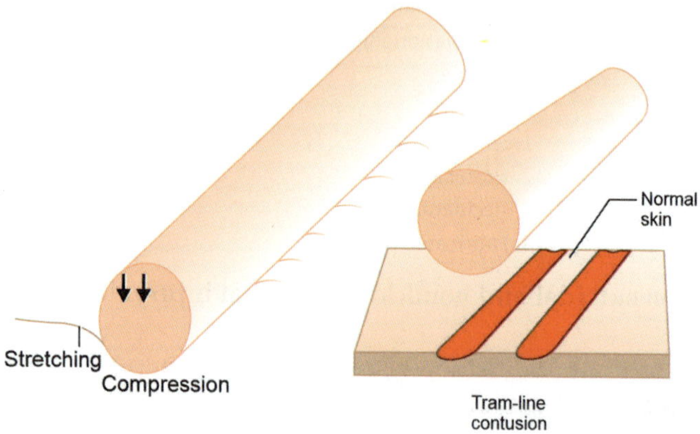

11. Define injury. Classify mechanical injuries and explain contusion in detail. (Uttarakhand University 2018) (Sai Tirupati University, Rajasthan 2019)

Ans:

Definition of Injury

Refer to long question no. 8.

Classification of mechanical injuries: Refer to long question no. 8.

Contusion/Bruise

Definition of bruise: It is defined as extravasation of blood in the subcutaneous/ subepithelial tissues due to rupture of blood vessels as a result of blunt force impact.

Classification of bruise: Bruise is classified into three types:

i. **Intradermal bruise** lies in the immediate subepidermal layer. Made by impact with a patterned object, and hemorrhage is sharply defined.
ii. **Subcutaneous bruise** is situated in subcutaneous tissue, often in the fatty layer, and the edges are blurred. Most common type of bruise.
iii. **Deep bruise:** Bleeding deeper to the subcutaneous tissues. It may take hours to 1–2 days to appear at the surface **(delayed bruising)**.

Factors Affecting Appearance of Bruise

Age	Easily produced in children and elderly
Sex	More common in females
Site	More prominent in bony prominence More prominent on loose skin (scrotum, eyelids) Less prominent on thick skin (palms and soles)
Complexion of skin	More easily visible in fair skin
Natural disease	Bruise occur easily by applying minor trauma in case of: Scurvy, hemophilia, purpura
Clothing	Difficult in case of heavy clothing

Various Types of Bruise

Ectopic bruise/migratory bruise

When extravasated blood at point of impact by a blunt weapon tracks down due to gravity along the fascial planes and may appear where the tissue layers become superficial.

Examples

Ant. cranial fossa fracture	Black eye/ Racoon's eye	Collection of blood in peri-orbital region
Mid. cranial fossa fracture	Battle sign	Collection of blood in mastoid region

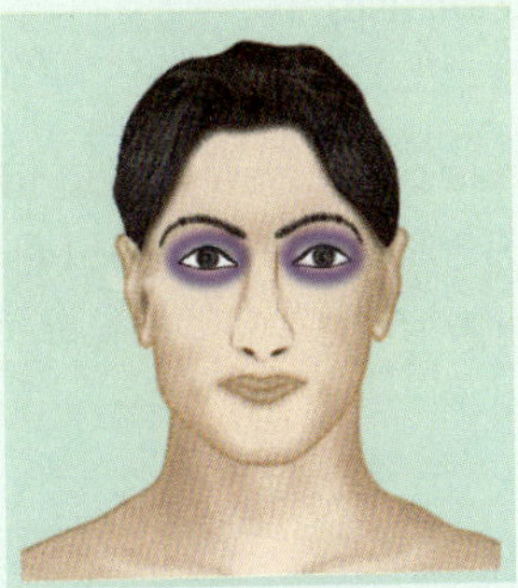

Black eye

Patterned bruise

The bruise which reflects the pattern of the object causing it

Examples

1. Railway track bruise—hit by a stick
2. Six penny bruise—in throttling
3. Steering wheel injury

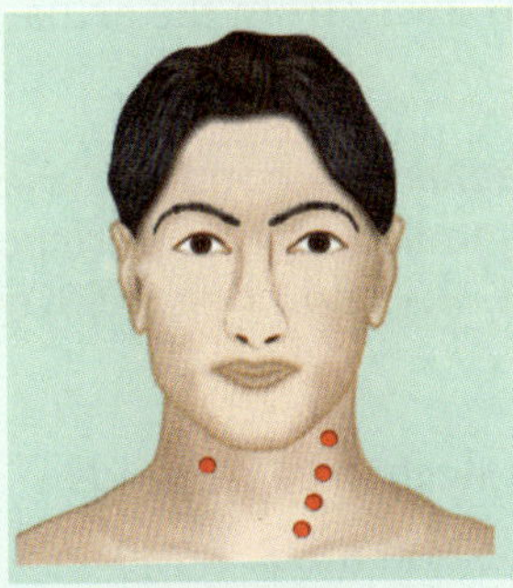

Six penny bruise

Age of Bruise

Age of bruise can be estimated by:
1. Colour changes
2. Histological changes
3. Spectrophotometry

Estimation of Age of Contusion

On basis of colour changes (Mnemonic: **VIBGYOR**)

Duration	Colour	Reason
Fresh	Red	Oxyhemoglobin
Few hr to 3 days	Violet/ Blue	Deoxyhemoglobin
4–5 days	Brown	Hemosiderin
5–6 days	Green	Biliverdin
7–12 days	Yellow	Bilirubin
≥2 weeks	Original/ Normal	Normal

- In subconjunctival hemorrhage—color changes are not seen.

MLI

1. Age of bruise helps in determining time of infliction of injury
2. Artificial bruise can be produced by applying juices of marking nut or calotropis on the skin in order to allege somebody of assault
3. Contusions/bruises near genital areas may be due to sexual assault
4. Multiple bruises in various stages of healing in case of child suggest child abuse/ battered baby syndrome
5. Character and manner of injury may be known from its distribution
   For example: Six-penny bruises are produced by forcible pressure of fingertips as in case of throttling
6. Bruises are of lesser value than abrasions as:
   a. Their size may not correspond to the size of the weapon
   b. Do not indicate the direction in which the force was applied.
   c. May take few hrs to develop
   d. May appear away from the actual site of injury (ectopic bruise)

12. Classify mechanical wounds. Describe the different types of lacerated wounds with their medico-legal importance. (North Eastern Hill University, Shillong Supple 2018) (VNS, Gujarat University 2016)

Ans:

Classification of Mechanical Wounds

Refer to long question no. 8.

Different types of lacerated wounds (Mnemonic: **CATSS**)

1. **S**plit laceration	• When blunt force is applied at the **bony prominence**, skin gets sandwiched between bone and object causing split laceration • Usually seen at: Scalp, forehead, zygomatic process, shin • As margins look regular, so these lacerated wounds are called **incised looking lacerated wounds** (look like Incised wounds) which can be differentiated from incised wound with magnified lens
2. **S**tretch laceration	• Occurs due to overstretching of skin and subcutaneous tissue • Caused by heavy forceful impact • Seen in—run over injuries, compound fractures
3. **A**vulsion laceration	• Produced by a tangential force/shearing force, seen in case of run over by vehicles in cases of RTA. • Leading to – Flaying—due to rotational force of wheel leading to detachment of skin and subcutaneous tissue over a large area – Degloving injury—entire skin comes out – Amputation injury
4. **T**ear laceration	• When objects hit the skin and skin is pulled back in opposite direction • Seen in case of car door handle
5. **C**ut laceration	• Caused by a heavy cutting weapon like axe, chopper • Fracture of underlying bone also occurs

MLI

1. Laceration is usually homicidal, accidental but not suicidal
2. Laceration over face can result in extensive scar formation on healing resulting in disfiguration of face—*grievous injury*
3. Avulsion laceration/flaying helps in determining the direction of force
4. Type of laceration can suggest shape of the blunt weapon, e.g. crescentic laceration—hammer head.

13. Classify mechanical injuries. Write down the difference between laceration and incised wound. On what parts of the body hesitation cuts are seen? (Rajiv Gandhi University, Bengaluru supple 2015)

Ans:

Classification of Mechanical Injury

Refer to question no. 8.

Differences between laceration and incised wound: Refer to difference no. 3.

Hesitation cuts are tentative cuts seen in suicides. These cuts are multiple, small and superficial often involving only the skin, and are seen at the beginning of the incised wound. They are seen over:

1. Front of wrist, chest, groin
2. Front and sides of neck
3. Back of legs
4. Frontal aspect of elbow

14. Classify mechanical injuries. Describe the characteristic features of stab and incised wound. (Sardar Patel University, Gujarat supple 2016, 2015)

Ans:

Classification of Mechanical Injuries

Refer to long question no. 8.

Characteristic Features of Stab Wound and Incised Wound

	Stab wound	Incised wound
1. **Site**	Usually over chest, abdomen or neck	Anywhere
2. **Margins**	Clean cut	Clean cut and everted margins
3. **Length**	Length of the wound is slightly less than the width of the weapon	Length is greatest dimension
4. **Width**	Width is more than the thickness of weapon	Width is greater than the width of the weapon
5. **Depth**	Depth is the greatest dimension	Length is greater than its width/depth
6. **Shape**	Spindle-shaped, but depends on weapon	Spindle-shaped
7. **Direction**	It can be vertical, horizontal or oblique in direction	Direction is given by the tailing of the wound.
8. **Surrounding abrasion and bruise**	May be seen (hilt mark)	Absent

15. Define injury. Classify mechanical injuries and describe briefly the different types of stab wounds. (Adesh, Bathinda supple 2017)

Ans:

Definition of Injury

Refer to long question no. 8.

Classification of Mechanical Injuries

Refer to long question no. 8.

Types of Stab Wound

Concealed punctured wound	Penetrating stab wound	Perforating stab wound
Puncture wounds on the concealed body parts • Caused by pins, ice picks • Usual sites—ear lobes, fontanella, genitals, axilla MLI: Needle puncture on fontanelle is a common method for infanticide	Punctured wound caused by any weapon that enters body cavity producing only entry wound	Punctured wound caused by any weapon that enters from one side of the body and exits from the other side, i.e. has entry wound and exit wound MLI—Identification of entry and exit wound • Entry wound—larger with inverted edges • Exit wound—smaller with everted edges

16. A 30-year-old male presents to causality with multiple injuries over head caused allegedly from assault by many people. In such a case: (Sardar Patel University, Gujarat 2015)

a. What features help you differentiate a lacerated wound from incised wound?

b. What features of any mechanical injury help in indication the nature of inflicting weapon?

c. What criterion is used to opine an injury as grievous?

Ans:

a. Refer to difference no. 3.
b. The margins and dimensions of the wound help in indicating the nature of inflicting weapon.
c. **Sec. 320 IPC** gives the eight clauses of grievous hurt which help in opining the injury.

17. A 20-year-old female domestic maid presents to the emergency with burns over both lower limbs. Her employer gives a history of spillage of boiling water over her body parts while she shakes her head in disagreement. The burnt areas also look suspicious and not consistent with the history given by the employer. (Sardar Patel University, Gujarat 2015)

a. How will you confirm whether the injury is due to spillage of hot liquid and not by flame or use of corrosive?

b. If the burns are confirmed to be sure to corrosive, how will you manage it?

c. What shall be your medico-legal duties in such a case?

Ans:

a. A thorough examination of the burnt area will help in identifying the causative agent. Points which may help in differentiating burns from boiling water vs corrosives are:

	Boiling water	**Corrosives**
1. **Site**	At or below the site of contact	At or below the site of contact
2. **Splashing**	Present	Present
3. **Skin**	Sodden, bleached	Corroded and devitalized
4. **Color**	Bleached	Distinctive coloration
5. **Vesicles**	Present	Absent
6. **Red line**	—do—	—do—
7. **Ulceration**	Absent	Present
8. **Clothes**	Wet, not burnt	May be burnt, with characteristic stains

Additionally, there will be pain or numbness at the site, irritation, burning, black dead skin in corrosive.

Refer to difference no. 10 for features of burns due to dry heat and moist heat.

b. **Treatment**
   1. Use of PPE—vital for the treating doctor.
   2. Airway, breathing and circulation (ABC): Stabilization of patient is vital.
   3. Remove solid debris.

4. Copious irrigation with warm water for surface burns—at least 20–30 mins.
5. Neutralization of chemicals is not indicated.
6. Complete wound evaluation—assessment of depth, debridement of blisters and non-viable tissue
7. Treatment of acid-base and electrolyte imbalance, and hypothermia.
8. Referral.

c. Since it is corrosive burns and there is suspected foul play; the doctor should inform the police and treat it as Medico-legal Case (MLC).
   - The medical officer should inform the duty constable, giving the name, age, sex of the patient and the place of occurrence of the incident and should start the treatment of the patient.
   - The treating doctor should record a proper history, examination including general condition, level of consciousness, vitals, and report of investigations and the other circumstances of the case and then analyze the injuries. He should document clearly all injuries observed by him in the MLC after taking due consent from the patient.
   - All the communication in case of MLC should be written.

SHORT NOTES

1. Hesitation cuts (Adesh, Bathinda supple 2020)

Ans:

Definition: While attempting suicide, a person undecidedly makes superficial cuts before attempting a final deeper cut. These are called hesitation cuts.

- They are also called tentative cuts, trial marks.
- It shows hesitation while gaining courage to make a final decisive cut.

Characteristics	Usual sites of hesitation cut
• Multiple	• Front of wrist
• Parallel	• Front of elbow
• Superficial cuts (involving skin)	• Front and sides of neck
• Mostly incised wounds	
• Seen on accessible parts of body	

MLI

- It suggests suicidal tendency
- These are caused by light sharp edged weapons (knife/razor)
- It indicates direction of cut (deeper at the beginning and superficial at end).

2. Section 320 IPC (Adesh, Bathinda supple 2020) (Sardar Patel University, Gujarat 2020, supple 2016) (Rajiv Gandhi University, Bengaluru 2020, 2015, supple 2015) (AIIMS Patna 2018) (Uttarakhand University 2017, supple 2016) (North Eastern Hill University, Shillong 2016) (Himachal Pradesh 2017) (BFUHS, Punjab 2015) (VNS, Gujarat 2016)

Ans: Refer to long question no. 6.

3. Self-inflicted injury/fabricated Injuries (Rajasthan University 2018) (KHMS, Tamil Nadu 2018)

Ans:

Definition: These are the wounds produced by a person deliberately on his own body or by another person with his/her consent.

Types

Self-inflicted injuries: Produced by person on his body
Self-suffered injuries: Produced by another person with his/her consent

Diagnosis

Based on the:

1. Clinical history
2. Features

1. **History**
   - History of assault incompatible with injuries
   - No defence injury despite history of assault
2. **Features**

Type	1. Incised wounds (mostly)—Multiple, superficial, parallel
	2. Abrasions
	3. Burns
Sites	1. Front of forearm
	2. Outer side of upper arm
	3. Front of chest and abdomen
	4. Top of head, forehead
	5. Outer sides of thigh
Clothes	1. Are not cut (usually)
	2. If cut—not compatible with nature of injuries
Injuries produced by	1. Knife
	2. Razor
	3. Glass piece
	4. Scissors
	5. Ice pick

MLI: These are produced with an intention:

1. To make false charge against another person with assault or attempt of murder
2. To convert simple injuries into grievous injuries
3. By women, to bring a charge of rape
4. By prisoners, to bring charge of beating by officers
5. To avoid hard duties by employees
6. By an assailant to pretend self-defence.

4. Types of skull fractures (BFUHS, Punjab 2020) (KHMS, Tamil Nadu supple 2020) (University of Health Sciences, Rohtak 2019) (JIPMER supple 2018) (Sai Tirupati University, Rajasthan 2019)

Ans: Refer to long question no. 7.

(Another Mnemonic: Love can do problem, girls please be serious)

1. **L**inear fracture
2. **C**omminuted fracture
3. **D**epressed fracture
4. **P**ond fracture
5. **G**utter fracture
6. **P**erforating fracture
7. **B**asilar fracture
8. **S**utural fracture

5. Signature fracture (KHMS, Tamil Nadu supple 2019) (Rajiv Gandhi University, Bengaluru 2015) (VNS, Gujarat 2018)

Ans:

1. Signature fracture is **depressed fracture of skull.**
2. They are so called since the shape of the depressed part of the skull corresponds and resembles the striking surface of the weapon, and it appears as if the weapon has left its signature on the skull.
3. It is produced by heavy weapon with small striking surface like hammer, axe, etc.
4. The part of the skull which is first struck shows maximum depression.
5. **MLI**
   a. Helps in identifying the causative agent/weapon
   b. Helps in determining manner of application of violence
   c. Helps in determining the relative position of assailant and victim.

6. Pond Fracture (Andhra Pradesh supple 2016)

Ans:

1. It is just a simple dent seen on the skull which looks like a depression on a ping pong ball produced by pressing thumb or a finger.
2. It is also called **indented fracture/ping-pong fracture.**
3. Fractures occur only on the outer table around the periphery of the dent but the inner table is not fractured.
4. Seen in case of:
   1. Infants—due to elastic skull
   2. Children—due to incomplete ossification of skull bones
   3. Newborns—due to forceps delivery.

7. Age of contusion (Sher-i-Kashmir Institute supple 2020) (AIIMS Patna 2018) (GMC, Chandigarh 2016)

Ans: Refer to long question no. 11.

8. Classify mechanical injuries (Pondicherry 2015)

Ans: Refer to long question no. 8.

9. MLI of incised wounds (Pondicherry supple 2017)

Ans:

1. Helps in determining the **nature of weapon.**
2. **Nature of injury** can be determined—as incised wounds usually are not fatal as they do not penetrate deep enough to damage large blood vessels. However, they are highly fatal if present over the neck, as veins of neck are present superficially.
3. Helps in determining **direction of force** (tailing present at end of incised wound).
4. **Manner of injury** can be determined (i.e. whether it is suicidal, homicidal, accidental or fabricated wounds).
5. Helps in determining **age of injury.**
6. Relative position of assailant and victim can be determined.

10. Degree of flame burns (Sardar Patel University, Gujarat 2019, supple 2020, supple 2019)

Ans: Refer to long question no. 3.

11. Heat hematoma (Sher-i-Kashmir Institute, Srinagar supple 2015)

Ans:

- Heat hematoma is an artifact and not a vital phenomena. It is seen in exposure of skull to tremendous heat which results in charring of the skull.
- It resembles extradural hematoma (EDH).

Mechanism of Formation

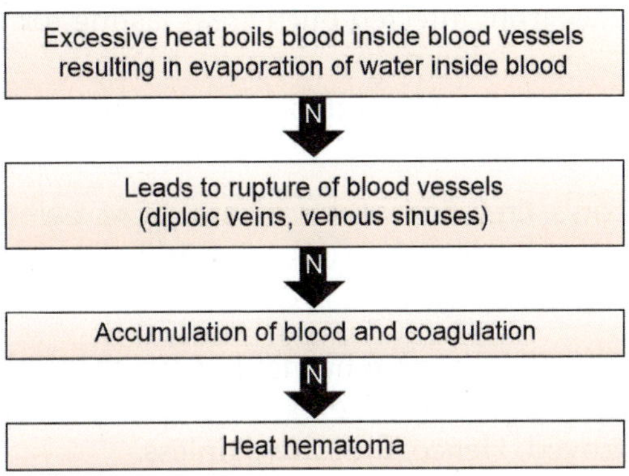

Features

1. **Distribution:** Seen diffusely around the brain (commonest site—parieto-temporal region)
2. **Position:** Usually bilateral
3. **Appearance**
   - Soft friable clot, light chocolate brown in color, sickle shaped, honeycomb appearance
   - Thickness: 1.5 mm to 1.5 cm
   - Contains up to 120 mL of blood
4. There may be **eggshell fracture** and cross suture lines (in comparison to EDH)
5. Presence of **COHb** in blood

12. Explain various causes of death in case of flame burns (Sardar Patel University, Gujarat supple 2018)

Ans: Refer to long question no. 3.

13. Complications of burns (Adesh, Bathinda supple 2017)

Ans:

Complications can occur after a few days to a few months which may lead to death of the patient.

1. **Hypovolemic shock** is quite common in burn patients. It occurs within 24–48 h due to loss of fluid and protein, causing decrease in cardiac output and multiorgan failure.
2. **Acute edema of glottis** occurs from inhalation of irritant smoke or hot gases with or without pulmonary edema.
3. **Sepsis** is seen after 4–5 days. Septicemia can be caused by burn wound infections (e.g. *Pseudomonas aeruginosa, Staphylococcus aureus*), UTI following catheterization, pneumonia, etc.
4. **Infective complications** like bronchopneumonia may be seen.
5. Suppurative discharges from infected burn areas lasting for weeks or months may occur.
6. Gangrene, tetanus, anemia, edema of dependant parts and jaundice.

14. Explain why Wilson's first degree burns are more painful than third degree burns. (West Bengal University 2018) (West Bengal University supple 2017)

Ans:

Wilson's epidermal burns (first degree burns) involve the superficial nerve endings and is extremely painful and tender. Whereas in deep burns (third degree burns), the nerve endings are destroyed. Hence, they are painless.

15. Rule of 9 (BHUHS, Punjab supple 2020) (KHMS, Tamil Nadu supple 2020) (SGRD, Amritsar 2019) (Sardar Patel University, Gujarat supple 2019) (Delhi University 2018) (West Bengal University supple 2017) (Adesh, Bathinda supple 2017) (GMC, Chandigarh 2015) (Uttarakhand University 2015, supple 2016)

Ans:
- It is a method used to estimate percentage of **total body surface area (TBSA)** that has burnt.
- It is also called **Wallace Rule of 9.**
- As per the rule, body is divided into 11 anatomical regions and each represents 9% of TBSA. Remaining 1% area is perineum.

Region	% TBSA
1. Head and neck	9
2. Upper limb: Right side	9
3. Upper limb: Left side	9
4. Chest	9 (Front) + 9 (Back)
5. Abdomen	9 (Front) + 9 (Back)
6. Lower limb: Right side	9 (Front) + 9 (Back)
7. Lower limb: Left side	9 (Front) + 9 (Back)
8. Perineum	1
Total	(9 × 11) = 99 + 1 = 100

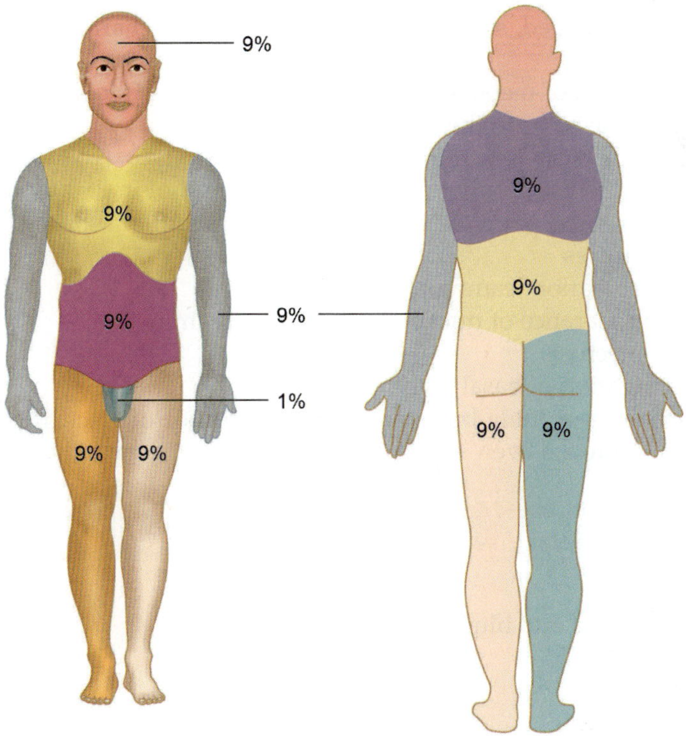

MLI

1. Gives rough estimate of TBSA involved
2. Helps to know prognosis in case of burns (as >33% TBSA burns has poor prognosis)
3. Helps in calculating amount of fluid required for resuscitation by Parkland formula.

16. Joule Burns/ Endogenous Burns (Rajiv Gandhi University, Bengaluru supple 2020) (SGRD, Amritsar 2019) (Rajasthan University 2018) (KHMS, Tamil Nadu 2017) (Uttarakhand University supple 2017) (Sher-i-Kashmir Institute, Srinagar supple 2017) (Adesh, Bathinda 2017)

Ans:

Definition: The point where electric current enters the body which is usually characterized by presence of electric mark. This electric mark (entry point) is called Joule burn.

- It is seen in cases of low voltage current with tight contact.

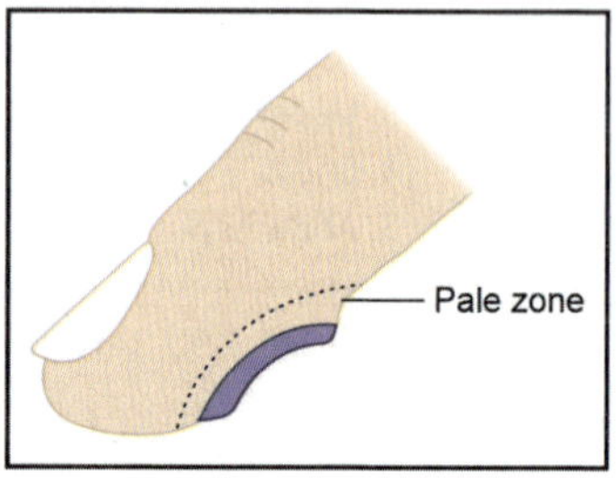

Characteristics of Joule Burns

1. **Crater**
   - Central crater with peripherally raised margins
   - Chalky white in color
   - Floor of crater is pale and lined by flattened skin
2. **Hyperemia**
   - Mild hyperemia of adjacent intact skin
   - If contact is prolonged, skin mark becomes brown or charred
3. **Metallization**
   - Due to deposition of metallic ions from the conductor into skin
   - May impart fade color to the electric mark
   - It is detected by Acro-Reaction test
   - It can be demonstrated only in Entry wounds and not in Exit wounds
4. **Sites:** Seen on exposed parts of body, especially on palmer aspect of hand.
5. **Microscopic features**
   a. Epidermal separation leading to microblisters
   b. Palisading appearance of nuclei and nuclear streaming
   c. Coagulative necrosis
   d. Nuclear elongation of basal layer
6. **MLI:** The presence of Joule burns is not itself a proof of electrocution as similar marks can be produced even after death except for the zone of hyperemia.

17. Enumerate injuries caused by hard and blunt object. Describe any one of these in detail. (Sardar Patel University, Gujarat 2020)

Ans:

Injuries caused by hard and blunt object

1. Abrasion
2. Bruise
3. Laceration
4. Fracture

For details of bruise: Refer to long question no. 11.
For details of abrasion: Refer to short question no. 18.

18. Abrasion (BFUHS, Punjab supple 2016)

Ans:
Definition: Abrasion is a type of mechanical injury caused by the removal of superficial epithelial layer of the skin, usually the epidermis by friction against rough surface.

Types of Abrasions

1. Scratch/linear abrasion	2. Graze abrasion	3. Pressure abrasion	4. Imprint abrasion
Caused by a pointed object passing across the skin, such as finger-nails, thorn or pin	Caused by horizontal or tangential friction between the skin and the hard rough surface	Caused by linear pressure of a rough object over the skin	Caused by force applied perpendicular to the skin and bears the imprint of the object causing it
Fingernail abrasions seen in throttling	Seen in road traffic accidents	Ligature mark in hanging and strangulation	Tyre-tread mark, imprint of bicycle chain

- Most common type of abrasions is graze abrasions.

Healing of Abrasion

It produces minimum bleeding, heals rapidly (in 1 week) and leaves no permanent scarring on healing.

MLI

1. Usually, it is seen in accidents and assaults.
2. Abrasions on the face or body of the victim/assailant indicates struggle.
3. Abrasions give an idea about the site of impact and direction of force.
4. **Nature of injury**: Abrasions are superficial injuries and simple in nature. Abrasions over the cornea may cause corneal opacity, which may cause grievous hurt (**Sec. 320 IPC**).
5. Patterned abrasions are helpful in connecting the wound with the causative weapon.
6. Age of injury can be determined.
7. Character and manner of injury may be known from its distribution. For example, in throttling, crescentic abrasions made by fingernails are found on the neck.

19. Filigree burns (BFUHS, Punjab supple 2018) (Rajiv Gandhi University, Bengaluru 2018) (Andhra Pradesh 2016) (VNS, Gujarat supple 2018, supple 2019)

Ans:
- **Definition:** It is defined as characteristic fern-like pattern seen on the body due to lightening strike.
- It is also called **Arborescent markings, Lichtenberg flowers.**

Characteristics

1. Superficial
2. Irregular (tortuous or dendritic)
3. Red markings over the skin
4. Resembles branch of leaf
5. **Usual sites:** Shoulder, front and back of chest, abdomen
6. Appear within 1 hr of lightening and disappear in a day or two

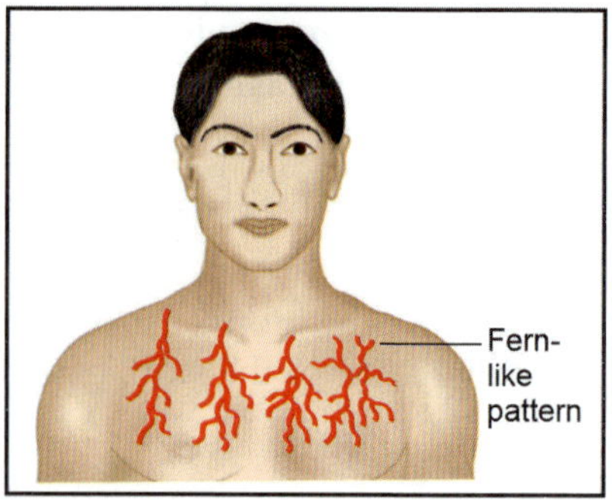

Mechanism/theories Related

1. Static electric discharge along superficial vasculature
2. Hemoglobin staining the tissues due to high current that break down RBCs in the capillaries
3. Electron showers giving rise to inflammatory reaction

MLI

a. Markings over the skin indicate path taken by discharge and usually takes long axis of body towards ground.
b. Death is accidental.
c. If anyone can recognize these features, and start immediate resuscitation, then the person can be saved.

20. Harakiri (AIIMS Patna 2019, 2017, 2015)

Ans:

- It is a method of **suicidal disembowelment** (cut open the abdomen).
- It is a type of self-inflicted injury.
- Seen in case of Japanese Samurai soldiers.
- Victim with sword produces a stab injury over the abdominal region.
- As a result of sudden evisceration of internal organs, there is decrease intra-abdominal pressure resulting into circulatory collapse and ultimately leading to death.

21. Split laceration/incised looking wounds (BFUHS, Punjab 2019, 2015) (North Eastern Hill University, Shillong Supple 2019) (Adesh, Bathinda supple 2017) (Uttarakhand University 2015, supple 2016)

Ans:

Refer to long question no. 12.

MLI

1. At the time of preparing MLC report or at time of autopsy. Incised looking lacerated wounds can be wrongly interpreted as incised wounds. The doctor may opine that the causative object as "sharp", whereas it was caused by a "blunt" object.
2. In court of law, doctor will have to explain the reason for misinterpreting it as incised wound.

22. Write MLI of Tailing of wound (West Bengal University 2019)

Ans:

1. Incised wounds show "head" and "tail" ends.
2. Tailing of wound is seen on one end due to withdrawal of the weapon. At beginning, the wound is deeper (head end) and becomes increasingly shallow till, finally, cut the skin alone.
3. **MLI:** Tailing of wound indicates the direction in which force was applied.

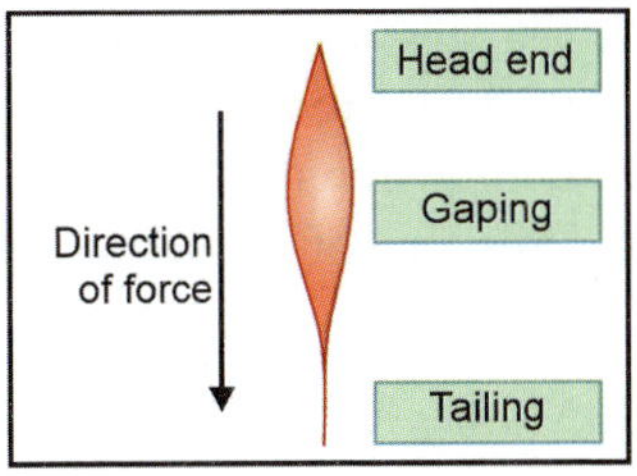

23. Delayed bruise (Rajiv Gandhi University, Bengaluru 2015)

Ans:

1. **Definition:** Bruise which takes some time to appear at the point of impact.
2. It is also called **deep bruise.**
3. In this, bleeding occurs deeper to subcutaneous tissues, i.e. either in superficial muscles or muscular fascial planes.
4. Since it is deeper, it may take hours to 2 days to appear at the surface.
5. Therefore, it is very important to reexamine the person 1–2 days after first examination.

24. Concealed puncture wounds (Uttarakhand University supple 2017)

Ans: Refer to long question no. 15.

25. Explain why stab injury over auricles is immediately fatal, whereas those over the ventricles are not (West Bengal University 2018)

Ans: Stab injury over auricles is immediately fatal, whereas those over the (left) ventricles are not.

1. This is because if ventricles are punctured, the thick muscles may restrict the bleeding, therefore allowing time for surgical emergency treatment. It may almost completely seal itself by contraction of the cardiac muscle around the defect. Death will occur due to cardiac tamponade which may take some time.
2. A stab wound through the left ventricle or through the thin-walled auricles is unlikely to re-seal itself and will bleed out into the pericardium with fatal results.

26. Chop wound (BFUHS, Punjab 2019)

Ans:

Definition: Chop wounds are large deep gaping wounds caused by a blow with heavy cutting weapons when applied with significant degree of force.

Weapons used: Axe, chopper, hatchet, butcher's knife

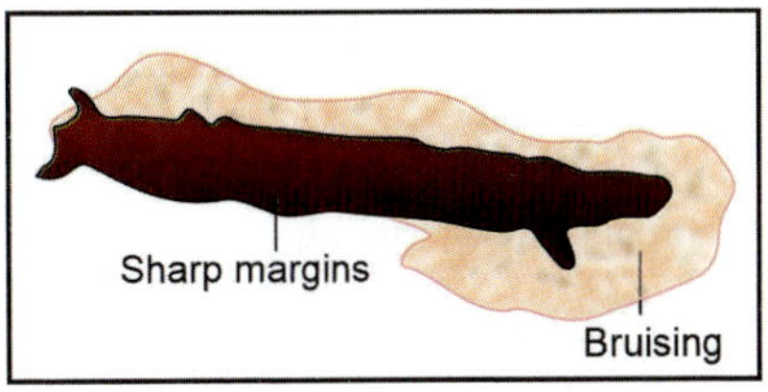

Characteristics

1. A chop wound is a combination of blunt and sharp force injury.
2. Margins—sharp and may show abrasion, bruise or laceration with severe injury to underlying tissues
3. Dimensions of the wound correspond to the cross-section of penetrating blade
4. Presence of incised wound with underlying bone fracture

MLI

1. Mostly homicidal in nature
2. Sometimes accidental or suicidal
3. Proper wound examination can give clue about the causative weapon

27. Punch Drunk syndrome (Adesh, Bathinda supple 2019)

Ans:

1. It is seen in boxers or may occur late in their career or years after retirement as a result of repeated blows to the head resulting in cumulative effect of cerebral concussions.
2. It was also called
   a. Dementia pugilistica
   b. Boxer's encephalopathy
3. Now it is called chronic traumatic encephalopathy (CTE).
4. **Clinical features**
   a. Parkinson-like symptoms
   b. Drunken appearance
   c. Dementia
   d. Others: Delusion, intentional tremors, dysarthria, etc.
   (Mnemonic: **PD**; very common example of Mohammad Ali
   P-Parkinson D-Dementia, Drunken gait, Dysarthria, Delusion)
5. **On autopsy:** Chronic SDH, DAI may be present

28. Heat stroke (BFUHS, Punjab supple 2020) (Rajiv Gandhi University, Bengaluru 2015)

Ans:

Definition: Heat stroke is a life-threatening medical emergency resulting from failure of thermoregulatory mechanisms.

2. It is also called heat hyperpyrexia or thermic fever.

Predisposing Factors

Environmental factors	Non-environmental factors
1. High humidity	1. Obesity
2. High temperature	2. Extremes of age
3. Strenuous exercise	3. Alcohol intoxication
	4. Malignant hyperthermia
	5. Thyrotoxicosis

Clinical features

1. High fever with core temperature >**41°C**
2. Absence of sweating—leading to dry skin
3. CNS symptoms—delirium, stupor, disorientation, etc.
4. Miosis
5. Tachycardia and hyperventilation
6. Low BP

Treatment

1. Lower the temperature by active cooling (cold bath and sponging) and passive cooling (removing clothes)
2. Correct dehydration—by oral or IV glucose or saline
3. To control shivering—IV diazepam and IV chlorpromazine
4. Supportive treatment.

Complications

a. Hepatic necrosis
b. DIC
c. Adrenal hemorrhage
d. Myoglobinuria

PM findings

1. PM caloricity
2. Necrosis and edema in Purkinje layers of cerebellum
3. Lungs—congested
4. Heart—subendocardial hemorrhages
5. Rigor mortis sets in early and passes off early.

29. Whiplash injury (BFUHS, Punjab supple 2018) (Pondicherry supple 2017) (North Eastern Hill University, Shillong 2017) (Delhi University 2015) (VNS, Gujarat 2016, supple 2019)

Ans:

Definition: Whiplash injury is seen commonly in occupants of front seat in motor vehicle when a moving car suddenly stops, resulting in acceleration-deceleration mechanism of transfer of energy to the neck.

Causes

1. Rear end or side impact motor vehicle collisions
2. When a car suddenly stops
3. Blow on the chin

Mechanism

1. Hyperflexion followed by hyperextension—when a car suddenly stops
2. Hyperextension followed by hyperflexion—when a car is hit from behind

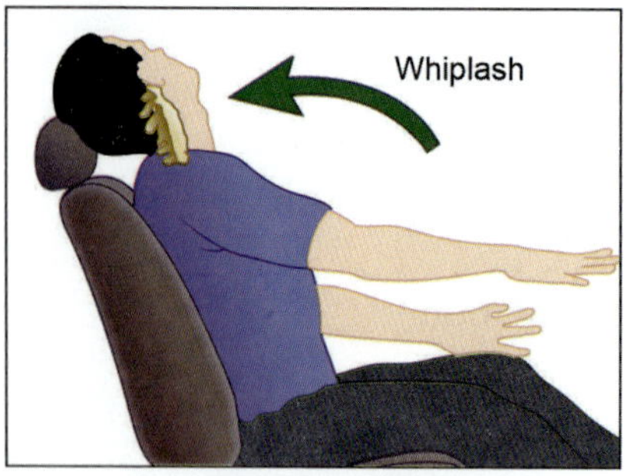

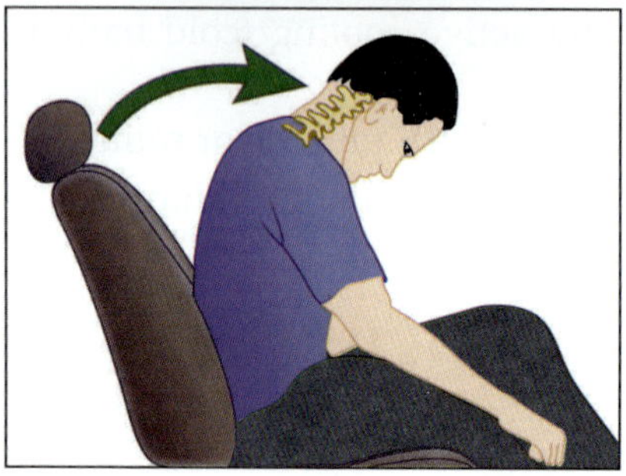

Out of hyperflexion and hyperextension injuries, hyperextension is more dangerous as it leads to tearing of anterior longitudinal ligament resulting in injury to cervical region of spinal cord (C5-C6 dislocation is more common than C1-C2 dislocation).

Signs and symptoms

1. Pain and stiffness of neck
2. Headache, dizziness
3. Numbness, tingling
4. Pain in arms, legs
5. Blurred vision

Prevention

1. Wear seat belts
2. Presence of head rests in car seats

30. Stab injury (Uttarakhand University 2017, 2016)

Ans:

- **Definition:** Stab injury is produced by penetration with long narrow instruments having pointed ends into the depth of the body.
- It is characterized by depth which is more than its length.

Weapons used

1. **Sharp:** Knife, dagger, scissors, pens, needle
2. **Blunt:** Screw driver, iron rod, cricket stump

Types of stab wound: Refer to long question no. 15.

Various Shapes of Stab Wounds

Weapon	Shape	
1. Single-edged knife	Wedge/triangular Fish tail	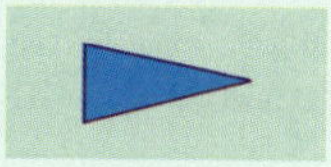
2. Double-edged knife	Spindle-shaped	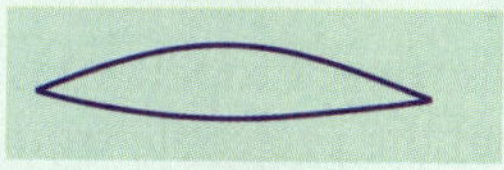
3. Arrow	Circular	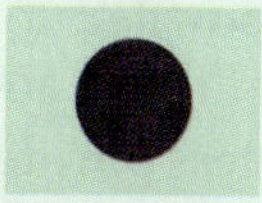
4. Fork	Circular wounds (3–4 in no.)	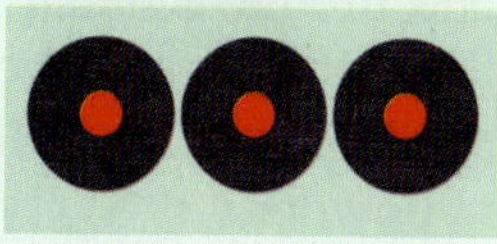

Characteristics of Stab Wound

1. **Depth** is the greatest dimension
2. **Breadth** is more than the thickness of blade due to gaping
3. **Length** is usually less than the width of stab wound because of stretching of skin
4. **Margins** are clean cut. But in case of full penetration—patterned abrasion/bruise can be seen (hilt mark)

MLI

1. Concealed punctured wounds suggest homicide
2. Depth of the wound—suggests amount of force used
3. Foreign material can be seen in the wound
4. Shape of the weapon—suggests type of weapon
5. Manner of production can be determined

31. Lacerated wound (Sardar Patel University, Gujarat 2018) (BFUHS, Punjab 2017)

Ans:

Definition: It is defined as tearing of skin, mucous membrane, muscle or internal organs caused by blunt force impact producing shearing or crushing force

Weapons used: Blunt weapons (cricket bat, hammer, iron rod, hockey, etc.)

Characteristics

1. **Margins:** Irregular
2. **Bruise and abrasion**—present around the margin
3. **Hair bulbs**—crushed
4. **Blood vessels**—crushed
5. **Hemorrhage**—less (due to crushing of blood vessels)
6. **Tissue bridges**—present and is the hallmark of lacerated injury

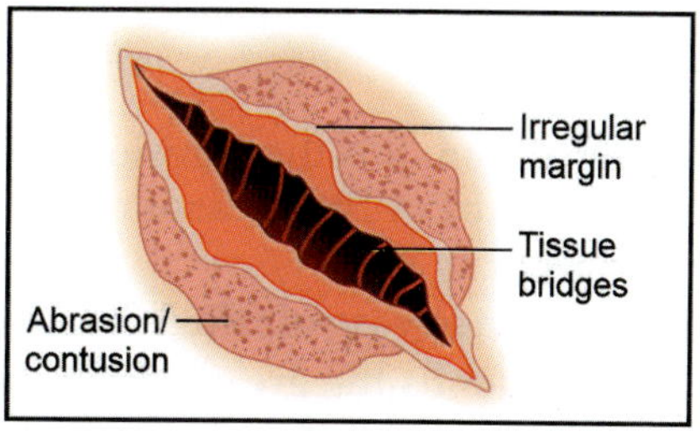

Types of laceration: Refer to long question no. 12.

MLI: Refer to long question no. 12.

32. Propellant (Sher-i-Kashmir Institute, Srinagar supple 2019)

Ans:

Definition: Propellant is an explosive substance used to propel (to move forward with force) the projectile from a gun. They are of following types:

1. **Black powder:** It produces flame, smoke and heat, and consists of sulphur (10%), charcoal (15%) and potassium nitrate (75%).
2. **Smokeless powder:** It is more effective than black powder as it burns more efficiently and produces much less smoke, resulting in less blackening and tattooing around the entry wound. It can be:
   a. **Single base powder** consists of nitrocellulose. Most common type of commercial powder.
   b. **Double base powder** consists of nitrocellulose and nitroglycerin.
   c. **Triple base powder** consists of nitrocellulose, nitroglycerin and nitroguanidine.
3. **Semi-smokeless powder:** It consists of mixture of 80% black and 20% smokeless type.

33. Tandem bullet (North Eastern HIll University, Shillong 2019) (Adesh, Bathinda supple 2017) (VNS, Gujarat 2019)

Ans:

1. "Tandem" means two things arranged one in front of the other.
2. When a rifled firearm is fired, bullet gets stuck in the barrel and fails to come out of the muzzle, so when the gun is fired again, the second bullet hits the first bullet from behind and forces the first bullet to move forward. Therefore, both the bullets are seen coming out of the muzzle as a single projectile.
3. It is also called **Piggy bank bullet**.
4. Seen in case of old unused guns where one bullet follows the other bullet.
5. This phenomena is used practically in "Duplex bullets" wherein there are two bullets by design so as to hit the target at different points.

34. Abrasion collar (KHMS, Tamil Nadu 2018) (Andhra Pradesh 2016) (GMC, Chandigarh 2016) (Rajiv Gandhi University, Bengaluru 2015) (VNS, Gujarat supple 2019)

Ans:

1. **Definition:** It is the abrasion of the skin caused by a bullet around the entry wound.
2. It is seen in case of rifled firearm.
3. It surrounds the grease collar and itself can be surrounded by blackening or tattooing.

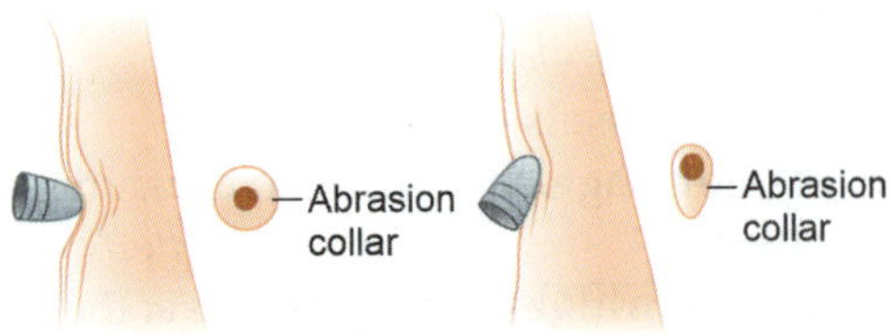

4. Sometimes, contusion is present in place of abrasion collar and is called contusion collar.
5. **Mechanism:** As the bullet strikes the skin, it first indents and then stretches the skin surface and then it penetrates the tense area of skin. So, rubbing of the bullet against the inverted skin epidermis and heat is responsible for the development of abrasion collar.
6. **MLI**
   a. It is a proof of entry wound.
   b. Abrasion collar is circular in shape—if bullet strikes perpendicular to the body surface.
   c. Abrasion collar is eccentric in shape—if bullet strikes the surface in an oblique direction to the body surface.
   d. Abrasion collar is not seen on palms and soles due to thickness and keratinization of epidermis.

35. Coup and contrecoup injuries (Andhra Pradesh 2016)

Mechanism of coup and contrecoup injuries and its MLI (Rajiv Gandhi University, Bengaluru 2018) (Pondicherry 2016)

Ans:

Coup Injury

It occurs immediately beneath the site of impact, and results directly by the impacting force.

- Caused when the **head is fixed** and there is violent impact over the skull
- There will be fracture and underlying brain damage (contusion) will be located beneath the site of impact

Contrecoup Injury

The injury is located in the brain opposite to the site of impact.

- Caused when the **moving head** is suddenly decelerated by hitting a firm surface, e.g. striking on the wall
- Common in road traffic accidents (RTAs)
- Contrecoup injury is rare in <3 years of age.

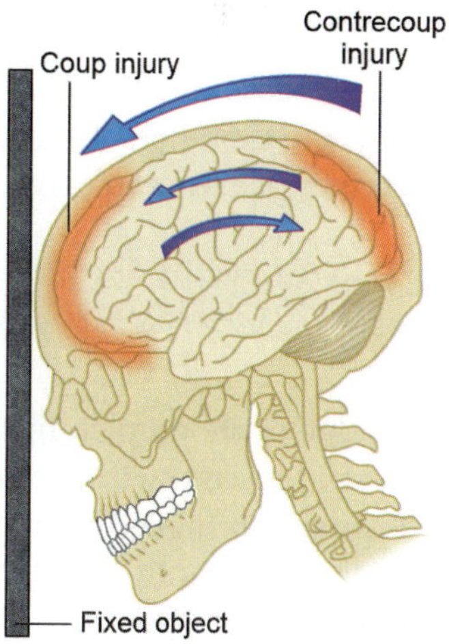

Mechanism

1. When head strikes a fixed surface, a momentary deformation of skull occurs with increase in pressure which may struck on the underlying brain causing compression—*coup injury*.
2. At the same time, opposite area of the skull will bulge outward to accommodate the deformation—*'struck-hoop'* theory. There is formation of vacuum as brain lags behind the moving skull. The vacuum exerts a suction effect that causes shear strain by pulling the brain—*contrecoup injury*.

Site: Common site for coup injury is the occipital lobe and for contrecoup injury is the frontal lobe in case of RTAs.

MLI: It is possible to determine if injury resulted from a fall or assault on the basis of location of the injuries.

1. In *assaults*, brain shows much larger contusions underlying the area of impact (coup) than on the site opposite to impact (contrecoup).
2. In head injuries caused *by falls* (RTAs), the contrecoup injuries are usually located in inaccessible portions and are larger than the coup contusions (e.g. occipital lobes).

36. Choking in a firearm (SGRD, Amritsar 2019)

Ans:

Definition: It is defined as the narrowing or constriction of the barrel at its muzzle end in a shotgun.

Types of Shotguns

1. **Cylinder bore:** When the entire barrel (from breech to muzzle) is of same diameter in a shotgun
2. **Choke bore:** When 7–10 cm of bore near muzzle end is constricted in a shotgun

Degree of choking in ascending order of choking

1. Cylinder bore
2. Improved cylinder choke
3. Modified choke
4. Full choke

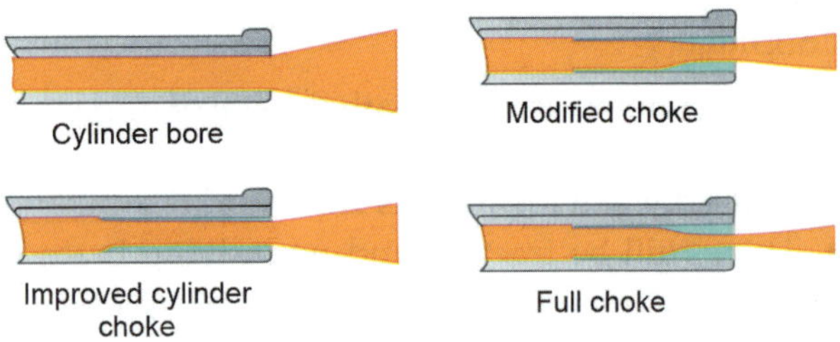

Advantages

1. To decrease dispersion of pellets
2. To increase range of the shotgun by increasing velocity
3. To increase the explosive force

37. Cartridge of shotgun (West Bengal University supple 2017) (BFUHS, Punjab 2016) (VNS, Gujarat 2017)

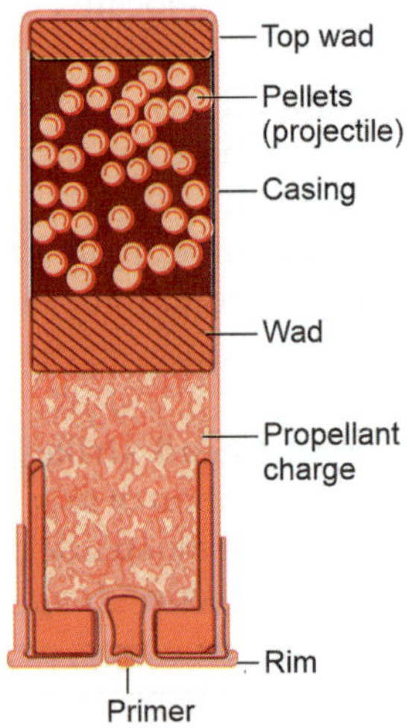

Ans:

Cartridge of shotgun comprises:

1. Cartridge case with percussion cap containing **primer.**
   Primer: It is highly inflammable that burns into flame and explodes the gun powder.
2. **Gunpowder**- it is the explosive material that is burnt by a spark generated in primer to propel shots.
3. **Wad:** It is disc-shaped cushion made up of cardboard or plastic.
   It acts as lubricant and functions like a piston by pushing the lead shots out.
4. **Lead pellets:** These are spherical lead balls used in smooth bored firearm.

38. Characteristics external features of contact shot wound by rifled firearm. (Sardar Patel University, Gujarat 2019, 2015)

Ans: Refer to long question no. 2.

39. Entry wound in firearm injury (KHMS, Tamil Nadu supple 2020) (VNS Gujarat, supple 2018)

Ans: Entry wound is one that results when a projectile enters a body.

Characteristic features are:

1. In skull, entry wound is clean cut on outer table and beveled in the inner table.
2. Smaller than the diameter of the bullet (except contact shot)
3. Edges are inverted
4. Bruising, abrasion and grease collar, burning, blackening, tattooing can be seen.
5. Bleeding is less as compared to exit wounds.
6. Singeing of hair will be there (close range)
7. Wound track is cherry-red due to COHb.
8. Fibers of clothes are turned in.

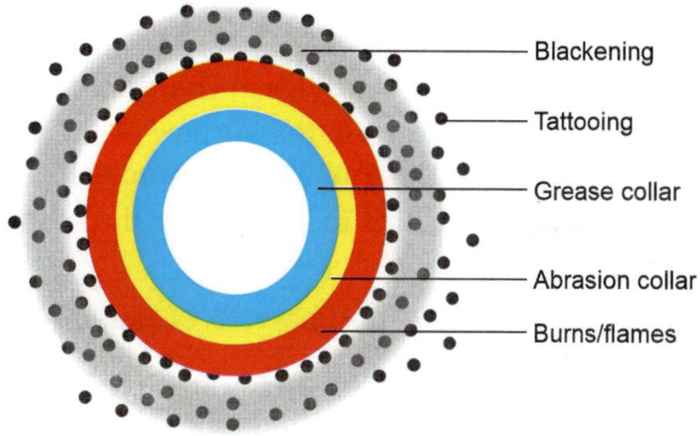

40. Caliber (Andhra Pradesh 2015)

Ans:

In case of rifled firearm	In case of smooth bore firearm
• It is defined as the diameter of the interior of the barrel measured between diagonally opposite lands. • It is expressed in mm or inches.	• It is defined as the number of spherical lead balls of size fitting the barrel of a shotgun which can be made from 1 pound of lead. • It is also called **Bore**.

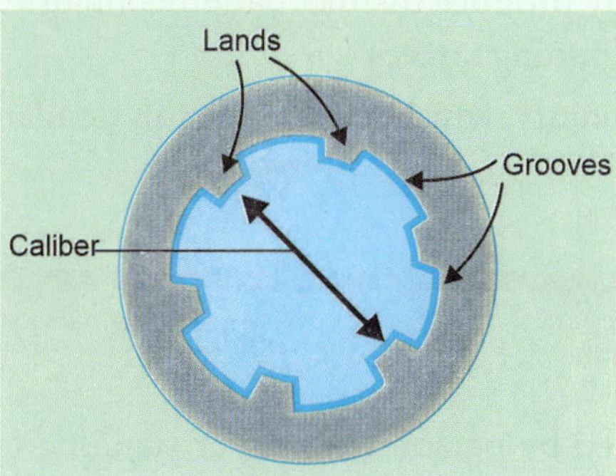

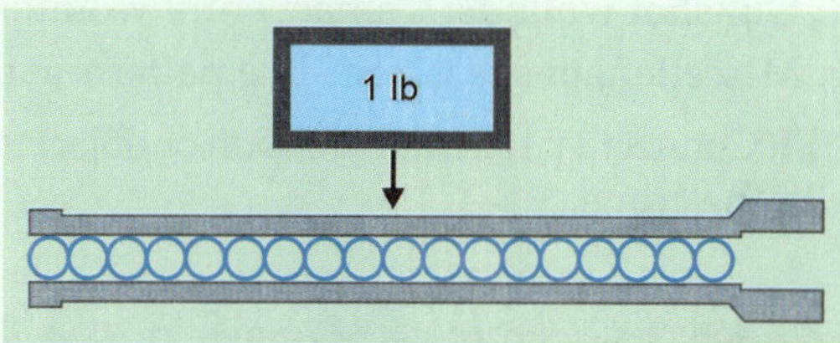

18 bore

41. Bullet fingerprinting (AIIMS Patna 2016)

Ans: Bullet fingerprinting comprises primary marking and secondary markings.

1. **Primary markings:** It occurs due to rifling, i.e. presence of lands and grooves on the interior wall of a barrel (parallel shallow spiral grooves from breech end to muzzle end).
    - It is also called "class characteristics"
    - Class characteristics in a fired bullet identification would be
        a. Number, diameter and width of lands and grooves.
        b. Depth of grooves
        c. Direction and degree of rifling twist
    - **Advantage:** Helps in identifying the make and model of a gun.
2. **Secondary markings**
    - It is also called "individual characteristics"
    - **Cause:** Produced on the surface of the bullet due to irregularities in the barrel (occur during manufacturing process)
    - **Advantage:** Helps in identifying the specific gun which was fired.

42. Patterned injuries (University of Health sciences, Rohtak supple 2020)

Ans:

Definition: Pattern injuries are one which has a distinct pattern that may reproduce the characteristics of the object causing the injury.

- Most common are patterned abrasion and patterned bruise.
- For example: "Railway track bruise"—by stick, "six penny bruise" in throttling, tyre mark pattern in RTAs, etc.

Patterned injuries can be categorised into type of force involved:

i. **Blunt force injuries:** These are the most commonly seen group. Caused by abrasions, bruising and lacerations.
ii. **Sharp force injuries:** Stab wounds may show characteristics of the blade—hilt guard mark, or stab wound with screwdrivers or scissors.
iii. **Gunshot wounds:** Contact entry wounds may produce distinct patterned injuries.
iv. **Miscellaneous,** e.g. fern-like pattern with lightning strikes.

MLI: Connect a particular weapon or object to an injury, which may connect an assailant with the crime.

43. Injuries seen in pedestrians in road traffic accidents (KHMS, Tamil Nadu supple 2020)

Ans:

Definition: These are the blunt injuries sustained by person walking or standing on the ground when hit by a vehicle.

Types

Primary impact injuries	Secondary impact injuries	Tertiary impact/secondary injuries
Definition: These are the injuries caused by the **first** impact of the vehicle on the victim	**Definition:** These are the injuries caused by **second** impact of the body with the vehicle (after the primary impact)	**Definition:** These are the injuries caused when the person falls on the ground
Cause: Bumper impact	**Cause:** 1. Bonnet impact 2. Windshield impact	**Cause:** 1. Ground impact 2. Run over injuries
Injuries seen: 1. Abrasions, contusions and lacerations on legs, thighs/ buttocks 2. **Bumper fracture:** It occurs when the victim is struck by front of vehicle, (e.g. bumper). Leads to fracture of tibia which is wedge shaped	**Injuries seen:** 1. Head injury 2. Skeletal fracture 3. Cervical injuries	**Injuries seen:** 1. Abrasions 2. Lacerations 3. Head Injury

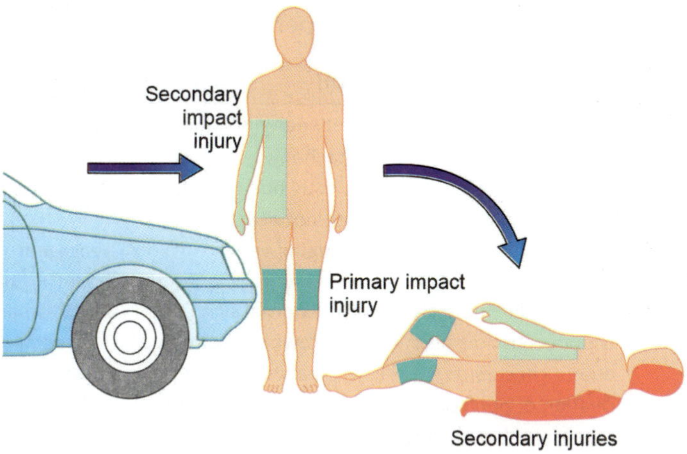

44. Primary impact injury (KHMS, Tamil Nadu 2017, supple 2019) (GMC, Chamba 2019)

Ans: Refer to short question no. 43.

45. Close firing may not be evident on examination of gunshot wound (West Bengal University 2019)

Ans:

1. In contact and close range firing, whole of the discharge containing flame, gases, powder smoke and metallic particles will be blown under pressure into the track taken by the bullet through the body, often leaving little evidence that one is dealing with a contact wound.
2. There is little or no evidence of burning, singeing, blackening and tattooing.
3. Burning, blackening and powder grains deposits will be found in the depths of the wound.
4. The characteristic features look like that of a distant shot.

46. Intra-cranial hemorrhages (BFUHS, Punjab 2019, 2015) (Uttarakhand University 2015)

Extradural hemorrhage (Delhi University 2017) (BFUHS, Punjab supple 2016) (Pondicherry 2015)

Sub-arachnoid hemorrhage (Uttarakhand University 2017) (Andhra Pradesh supple 2015)

Ans:

Definition: Intracranial hemorrhages are localized collection of blood in the skull/ brain, usually clotted or partially clotted.

Types: Classified by anatomical location:

1. Extradural
2. Subarachnoid
3. Subdural
4. Intracerebral

- Intracranial hemorrhage is a common complication of head injury, and is the most common cause of death in patients who experienced a lucid interval.

	EDH	SDH	SAH
Location	Between skull and dura	Between dura and arachnoid	Between arachnoid and pia
Cause	Always due to head injury	Mostly due to injury but not always	Both natural and traumatic
Vessel involved	Middle meningeal artery	Bridging veins	Leakage from vessels on brain surface
Externally	Swelling under the scalp	No external sign	No external sign
Clinical course	• Loss of consciousness due to concussion. • Dilation of pupil on the side of hemorrhage with conjugate deviation of eyes to opposite side • Bilateral fixation of pupils • **Lucid interval**—due to compression of accumulated blood	• Drowsy or comatose (may have *lucid interval*) from the moment of injury • Unilateral headache, hemiparesis • Enlarged pupil on the same side	• Sudden onset of severe headache ('*thunderclap headache*') • Nausea and vomiting • Neck stiffness, photo-phobia, drowsiness or agitation
Situation	Unilateral	Unilateral or bilateral	Focal, diffuse or bilateral
Space occupying	Can be space occupying	Space occupying	Space occupying, if it is arterial
Effect on brain	Brain surface ironed out by dura	Brain compressed, but less ironed out	Brain surface not distorted
Confusion with other condition	Can be confused with heat artifact	Seldom confused with other bleeding	Can be artifact from opening the skull

Refer to long question no. 7 for details on SDH.

Intracerebral Hematoma

Hemorrhage found within the cerebral parenchyma that is not in contact with the surface of the brain.

1. **Causes:** Hypertension, trauma and cerebral amyloid angiopathy
2. **Artery involved:** Spontaneous hemorrhage in the region of basal ganglia by rupture of lenticulo-striate artery
3. **Site:** Well-demarcated homogenous collection of blood seen most frequently in the white matter of the frontotemporal lobe
4. **Clinical features**
   i. Abrupt onset of focal neurologic deficit.
   ii. Diminished level of consciousness.
   iii. Signs of increased intracranial pressure, such as vomiting and headache.
   iv. Contralateral hemiparesis.

47. All murders are homicides but all homicides are not murder. (West Bengal Supple 2019)

Ans:

Murder as defined under Sec. 300 IPC is killing of a person with malice aforethought. If *the act by which death is caused*:

- With the intention of causing death.
- With the intention of causing such bodily injury which is *likely to cause death* of the person or *sufficient in ordinary course of nature to cause death.*

In murder, the mens rea (guilty mind) should be there, i.e. the mental element of a person's intention to commit a crime.

Homicide is the killing of a human being as a result of conduct of the other. It may be *lawful or unlawful.*

a. **Lawful homicide:** It can be justifiable by the circumstances that led to killing of the person (like judicial execution, self-defence, etc) or excusable and caused unintentionally (like causing death by accident/misadventure or death following lawful operation).
b. **Unlawful homicide:** Implies both, the fact of death and an accompanying state of mind known as *'malice aforethought'* on the part of the killer (murder).
   Hence, all murders are homicides but all homicides are not murder.

48. Explain why, in extremes of age EDH is rare but SDH is common. (West Bengal University 2017)

Ans:

1. EDH is rare in extremes of age [elderly and young (<2 years)] due to greater adherence of dura to the skull in both these age groups, and absence of a bony canal for the artery in the young.
2. Whereas SDH is common in infants (<6 months) and in the elderly (>60 years) because of delicate nature of blood vessels, large head-to-torso ratio with less developed neck muscles to hold the head steady and underdeveloped brain (more

room for the brain to move) in former, and cardiovascular changes, on anticoagulants and decreased brain weight leading to an increase in extracerebral volume in the latter.

DIFFERENTIATIONS

1. True bruise and artificial bruise (Adesh, Bathinda supple 2020) (KHMS, Tamil Nadu Supple 2019) (Sher-i-Kashmir, Srinagar supple 2018)

Ans:

	True bruise	Artificial bruise
1. **Caused by**	Trauma	Juice of marking nut, Calotropis
2. **Site**	Anywhere	Accessible parts of body
3. **Color changes**	Seen	Only dark brown colour
4. **Signs of inflammation**	At site	Surrounding the site
5. **Margins**	Irregular	Regular and well defined
6. **Blisters and itching**	Absent	Present
7. **Content**	Blood	Acid serum

2. Incised and incised looking wounds (BFUHS, Punjab Supple 2020) (Uttarakhand University 2017)

Ans:

	Incised wounds	Incised looking wounds
1. **Produced by**	Sharp object	Blunt object
2. **Seen**	Anywhere on the body	Bony prominence (shin, scalp, forehead)
3. **Margins**	Regular and clean cut	Regular (to naked eye) but using hand lens—Irregular margins
4. **Tissue bridging**	Absent	Present
5. **Underlying bone fracture**	Absent	Present (may be)
6. **Foreign bodies**	Absent	Present (may be)
7. **Hair bulb**	Cut	Crushed
8. **Blood vessels**	Cut	Crushed

3. Incised and lacerated wound (Jammu and Kashmir 2017) (Rajasthan University 2017) (Sher-i-Kashmir supple 2015) (North Eastern Hill University, Shillong 2015) (GMC, Chandigarh 2016)

Ans:

	Incised wounds	Lacerated wound
1. **Produced by**	Sharp object	Blunt object
2. **Site**	Anywhere	Bony prominences
3. **Shape**	Spindle shaped	Irregular
4. **Margins**	Smooth and clean cut	Irregular
5. **Dimensions**	Length greater than depth, gaping	Variable
6. **Abrasion/ bruise around the wound**	Absent	Present

7. **Tissue bridges**	Absent	Present
8. **Foreign matter**	Absent	Present
9. **Hair bulbs**	Clean cut	Crushed
10. **Blood vessels**	Clean cut	Crushed

4. Suicidal and homicidal cut throat injuries (Rajiv Gandhi University, Bengaluru 2020) (West Bengal University 2019) (KHMS, Tamil Nadu 2018) (Delhi University 2017) (Andhra Pradesh 2015) (GMC, Chandigarh 2016)

Ans:

	Suicidal cut throat	Homicidal cut throat
1. **Location**	Left side of neck	On the sides of neck
2. **Direction**	• Oblique from left to right, or • Above downwards	• Horizontal, or • Below upwards
3. **Level**	Above thyroid cartilage	Below thyroid cartilage
4. **Severity of wound**	• Superficial (multiple) • Less severe	• Deep (multiple) • More severe
5. **Carotid artery**	Not cut	Cut
6. **Hesitation cuts**	Present	Absent
7. **Defense wounds**	Present	Absent
8. **Weapon at crime scene**	Present	Absent
9. **Suicidal note**	Present	Present
10. **Signs of struggle and foreign materials**	Absent	Present

5. Contusion and postmortem staining (KHMS, Tamil Nadu 2016, supple 2020) (Adesh, Bathinda 2017) (North Eastern Hill University, Shillong supple 2017) (Delhi University Supple 2016) (Sardar Patel University, Gujarat 2016) (University of Health Sciences, Rohtak 2017) (GMC, Chamba 2019)

Ans:

	Contusion	Postmortem staining
1. **Occurs due to**	Rupture of vessels	Distension of blood vessels
2. **Site**	Anywhere	On dependant parts
3. **Margins**	Irregular	Regular
4. **Blanching**	Absent	Present
5. **Color changes**	Present	Absent
6. **Extravasations**	Present	Absent
7. **Effect of pressure**	No change	Blanch when pressure is applied
8. **On incision**	Blood present in surrounding tissues, cannot be washed by water	Blood present in blood vessels, can be washed easily by pouring water

6. Difference between antemortem and postmortem injuries (Uttarakhand 2015) (Adesh, Bathinda 2018)

Ans:

	Antemortem injuries	Postmortem injuries
1. **Bleeding**	Profuse	Slight/ Absent
2. **Source of bleeding**	Arterial	Venous
3. **Extravasation of blood**	Present	Absent
4. **Signs of spurting**	Present	Absent
5. **Coagulation**	Present	Absent
6. **Vital reaction**	Present	Absent
7. **Chances of Infection**	Present	Absent
8. **Infiltration by cells**	Present	Absent
9. **Enzyme activity**	Present	Absent

7. Suicidal and homicidal wounds (GMC, Chandigarh 2016)

Ans:

	Suicidal wounds	Homicidal wounds
1. **Wounds**	Incised/ Stab	Incised/Stab/Lacerated
2. **Seen on**	Accessible parts only	Anywhere on the body
3. **Number of wounds**	Single	Multiple
4. **Hesitation cuts**	Present	Absent
5. **Severity of wound**	Superficial, less severe	Deep, more severe
6. **Multiple deep wounds**	Absent	Present
7. **Signs of struggle**	Absent	Present
8. **Clothes**	Not cut	Cut
9. **Weapon at crime of scene**	Present	Absent
10. **Suicide note**	Present	Absent

8. Exogenous and endogenous burns (Adesh, Bathinda 2019)

Ans:

	Exogenous burns	Endogenous burns
Cause	Burns is produced by the flame which produced outside the body.	Burns produced by the steam due to heating of the tissues (for example, by the electric current)
Mechanism	Direct transfer of thermal energy to body	Electrical energy is converted to thermal injury within tissues
E.g.	Flash burns	Joule burns

9. Coup and contrecoup injuries (KHMS, Tamil Nadu 2017)

Ans:

	Coup injury	Contrecoup injury
1. **Site**	At side of Impact	Opposite to side of Impact
2. **Severity of Injury**	Mild	Severe
3. **Produced due to**	Direct impact on brain	Vacuum and suction force
4. **External injury**	Present	Absent
5. **Caused when**	Head is fixed	Moving head strikes
6. **Most common site**	Occipital lobe	Frontal lobes

10. Burns from dry heat and moist heat (Sardar Patel University, Gujarat 2017)

Ans:

	Dry heat burns	Moist heat burns
1. **Produced by**	Flames	Steam or hot liquid
2. **Site**	Below upwards	Above downwards
3. **Clothes**	Burnt	Wet
4. **Splashing**	Absent	Present
5. **Singeing**	Present	Absent
6. **Charring**	Present	Absent
7. **Color**	Black	Bleached
8. **Vesicles**	On the edges	All over the affected area
9. **Scar**	Thick	Thin

11. Antemortem burns and postmortem burns (University of Health Sciences, Rohtak 2019) (Himachal Pradesh 2017) (Delhi University supple 2016) (GMC, Chandigarh 2015)

Ans:

	Antemortem burns	Postmortem burns
1. **Line of redness**	Present	Absent
2. **Blisters**	Contains inflammatory fluid	Contains gas bubbles
3. **Base of blister**	Red, swollen	Dry, hard and pale
4. **Vital reaction**	Present	Absent
5. **Sign of healing**	Present	Absent
6. **Soot particles in airway**	Present	Absent
7. **Infection**	Present	Absent
8. **COHb in blood**	Present	Absent

12. Heat Hematoma and EDH/Heat hematoma and Traumatic Hematoma (Adesh, Bathinda 2018, Supple 2019) (West Bengal University 2018) (GMC, Chamba 2019)

Ans:

	Heat hematoma	EDH
1. **Cause**	Heat	Blunt trauma
2. **Vessels ruptured**	Venous sinuses and diploic veins	Middle meningeal artery
3. **Position**	Bilateral	Unilateral
4. **COHb in blood**	Present	Absent
5. **Appearance**	Honeycomb like, soft, friable	Disc-shaped, rubbery
6. **Suture lines**	Hematoma may cross suture lines	Do not cross suture line
7. **Fracture**	Egg shell fracture	Linear radiating fracture
8. **Injury to brain**	Absent	Present

CHAPTER 6

Sexual Jurisprudence and Infanticide

LONG QUESTIONS

1. Classify sexual offense. Define Rape under Section 375 IPC and 376 IPC. (Sher-i-Kashmir Institute, Srinagar supple 2017)

Ans:

Classification of Sexual Offenses

Natural	Unnatural	Sexual perversions
R- Rape	Bestiality	Fetishism, Frotteurism
I-Incest	Buccal coitus	Sexual Asphyxia
A-Adultery	Lesbianism	Masochism, Masturbation
	Sodomy	Others like:
		Urophilia
		Sadism
		Exhibitionism
		Transvestic fetishism
		Voyeurism
RIA	BCLS	FAMOUS EXHIBITION on TV

Definition of rape as per Section 375 IPC:

A man is said to commit rape, if there is:

a. Penetration of penis into vagina, anus, urethra or mouth
b. Insert any object or body part (not being his penis) into mouth, vagina, urethra or anus
c. Applies mouth to vagina, urethra or anus
d. Manipulates any part of victim's body for penetration into vagina, anus or urethra.

If any of the above act is done:

1. Against her will
2. Without her consent
3. With her consent, if consent is obtained by
   - Fear of death or hurt
   - Impersonation or fraud
   - Insanity or intoxication
4. With or without consent when she is <18 years of age: **Statutory rape**
5. When she is unable to communicate her consent.

Exception: Any medical intervention shall not constitute rape

Punishment of rape is as per Section 376 IPC:

376(1)	Rape committed on a girl ≥18 yrs	10 yrs to LI + Fine
376(2)	Rape under special circumstances 1. Custodial rape 2. Rape of pregnant female 3. Rape during communal violence 4. Rape by armed forces 5. Rape on same female repeatedly	10 yrs to LI + Fine
376(3)	Rape of a girl <16 yrs.	≥20 yrs to LI + Fine
376 A	Rape causes persistent vegetative state/ death of the victim	≥20 yrs to LI/death
376AB	Rape of a girl <12 yrs.	≥20 yrs to LI + fine/death
376 B	Sexual intercourse by husband with his wife during separation **B = Bride/Biwi**	2 yrs to 7 yrs
376 C	Sexual intercourse by person in authority not amounting to rape	5 yrs to 10 yrs
376 D	Gang rape	≥20 yrs to LI + Fine
DA	Gang rape of woman <16 yrs	LI + Fine
DB	Gang rape of woman <12 yrs **D= Delhi = Gang rape**	LI + Fine/death
376 E	Repeat offender **E = Eat – Repeat**	LI to death

*LI –Life imprisonment

2. Define Rape. How will you proceed for examination of a case of a 14-year-old girl survivor of sexual offence? Enumerate various evidences to be preserved in such case. (North Eastern Hill University, Shillong 2017, 2016, supple 2020) (BFUHS, Punjab 2017, supple 2016) (Sher-i-Kashmir Institute, Srinagar 2015) (Sai Tirupati University, Rajasthan, 2018, 2019)

Ans: Definition of rape: Refer to long question no. 1.

Examination of Rape Survivor

1. General particulars
   - Preliminary particulars: Name, height, weight, brought by, marital status, two identification marks.
   - Informed consent

Age of girl	Consent form is signed by
<12 yrs. of age	Guardian/parents
≥12 yrs. of age	Survivor

   - Victim is preferably examined by or under supervision of female doctor.
   - Examination is carried out with minimum delay.
2. **History**
   a. Medical and surgical history
   b. Sexual history—any history of sexual intercourse, if yes, then date of last consensual sexual intercourse
   c. Menstrual history
   d. Obstetric history
   e. Physical violence

Specific history about the incident:

- Date, time and place of commencement of act
- Any physical violence
- Details of events—bathing, cleaning, changing clothes, etc.

Examination of victim of rape–under Section 164-A CrPC

Physical examination

1. General

- Stature
- Weight
- Nutritional status
- Gait
- Behavior of survivor

2. Clothes of victim

- Should stand over a clean sheet of paper and then remove all her clothes herself, in front of doctor
- Look for the tears/loss of portion of clothes, torn buttons, foreign hair
- Examined for stains, soiled areas
- After drying in shade, clothes are packed in paper bag and sent for chemical examination

3. Extra-genital injuries

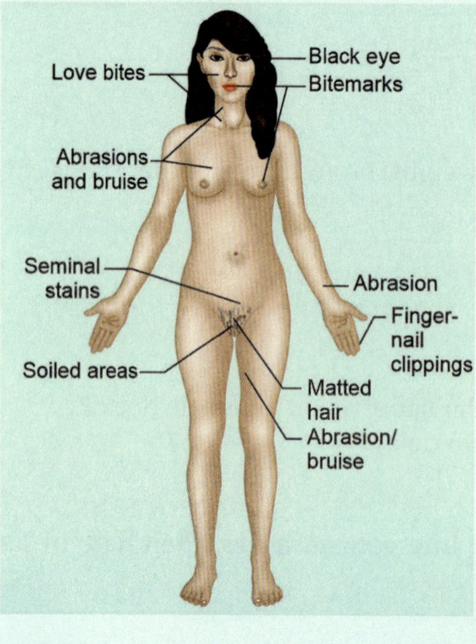

Local examination

Done in lithotomy position

- High vaginal swab
- Low vaginal swab
- Cervical swab
- Swabs from introitus and perineum
- Matted pubic hair

Genital Examination

1. Vulva—assessed for tears, swelling, abrasions, or discharge
2. Hymen
   - Tears at postero-lateral position (most common), edema
   - An intact hymen does not rule out sexual violence
3. Vagina
   - Bruises seen on anterior vaginal wall (lower 1/3) and posterior wall (upper 1/3)
   - Look for vaginal discharge
4. Cervix—presence of abrasions (away from external os)

Local injuries

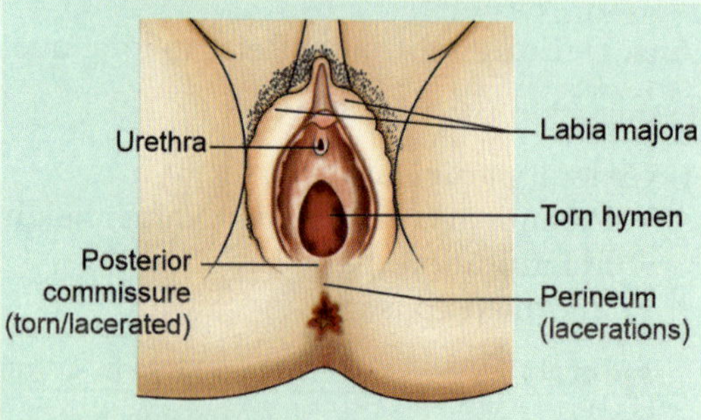

Evidences to be preserved

Samples preserved	Remarks
Clothes	Worn at time of alleged incident to detect blood/ semen
Swabs	1. Soiled areas 2. Anal swab 3. Buccal swab
Hair	1. Loose hairs on the body 2. For comparison—pubic hair 3. Matted pubic hair
Fingernail clippings	Tissue sample, blood of the accused
Blood	1. ABO blood grouping 2. Alcohol/drugs 3. HIV/Hepatitis B
Scrapping	1. Dried blood stain 2. Dried seminal stain
Saliva	Secretor grouping

3. Define Rape as per S.375 IPC. What is the role of informed consent in examination of such cases? (BFUHS, Punjab 2019)

Ans: Definition of rape: Refer to long question no. 1.

Informed consent should be obtained before the examination, collection of specimens, release of information to authorities and taking of photographs.

1. In emergency conditions, the doctor may start the treatment without consent **(Sec. 92 IPC).**
2. **Informed consent:** The survivor is informed about the nature and purpose of examination:

a. Examination may involve an examination of the mouth, breasts, vagina, anus and rectum.
b. Evidence may be collected like clothing, hair, foreign substances from the body, saliva, samples from the vagina, anus, rectum, mouth and blood sample.
c. She may refuse examination or collection of evidence or both, but that refusal will not be used to deny treatment. The refusal should be documented.
d. She has a right for partial examination—whether she wants a physical examination and/or genital examination, and allow collection of bodily evidence.
e. The doctor is bound to inform the police. However, if she does not wish to, she has the right to refuse to file FIR and it would not result in denial of medical examination and treatment. At the time of intimation being sent, a note stating 'informed refusal for police intimation' should be made.
f. Any evidence obtained may be used in court, and that she will then be exposed to publicity and cross-examination.

3. The consent form should be signed by:

Age of girl	Consent form is signed by
<12 yrs of age	Guardian/parents
≥12 yrs of age	Survivor

4. The form should be signed by the survivor, a witness and the examining doctor.

4. Define Rape. What are the precautions to be taken while examining a victim of rape? (Adesh, Bathinda 2018)

Ans: Definition of rape: Refer to long question no. 1.

Precautions to be taken while Examining A Victim of Rape

1. The doctor should not refuse to examine a rape survivor on the ground that she was not brought by the police or she came on her own.
2. Even if the rape occurred outside the jurisdiction of the hospital, the survivor must first be examined and treated, before referring her to the hospital in the appropriate area.
3. The examination should be conducted without delay (priority case) by a government doctor or any other doctor with the consent of the patient or guardian, and she should be sent to a doctor by the police within 24 hrs from the time of receiving the information relating to the commission of such offence.
4. Senior medical faculty instead of junior doctors should examine the patient.
5. If possible, the survivor is examined by or under the supervision of a female doctor. If a board of doctors is examining her, at least one doctor must be a female. Otherwise, a female nurse/attendant should be there, if she is examined by a male doctor. If the survivor requests, her relative may be present while the examination is done.
6. Privacy and confidentiality should be maintained.
7. The patient should be informed about the nature and purpose of examination. The doctor should prepare a detailed report and describe the material taken from the person of the woman for DNA profiling.
8. Even if there is informed refusal for medico-legal examination, medical treatment should not be denied.
9. In case of refusal for police intimation, the doctor is duty bound to inform the police.
10. Per-vagina examination, commonly referred to as 'two-finger test', must not be conducted for establishing rape/sexual violence.
11. A small child survivor must never be held down during examination of the genital area, this is equivalent to sexually assaulting the child.

5. Define infanticide. Write in detail about battered baby syndrome. (Sher-i-Kashmir Institute, Srinagar supple 2019)

Ans: Definition: It is killing of an infant at any time from birth up to the age of 12 months.

- It is punishable under Sec. 302 IPC.

Battered Baby Syndrome

- It is also known as Caffey-Kempe syndrome,
- A battered child is one who has received repetitive physical injuries as a result of non-accidental violence produced by a parent or a guardian.

Features related to:

Child	Parent/Guardian
1. Age <3 yrs.	1. Unmarried couple
2. Males > females	2. Young age
3. Illegitimate/unwanted child	3. Low education status
	4. Themselves were victims of battering during childhood

Clinical Features

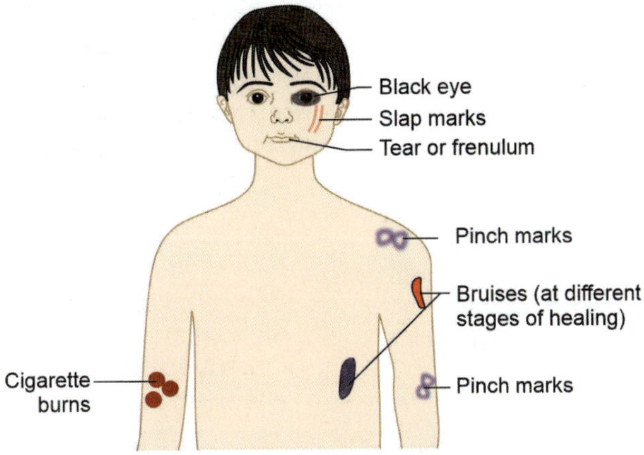

Soft tissue injuries	CNS injuries	Skeletal injuries (on X-ray)	Others
a. Abrasions	*Triad of injuries*		
b. Bruise	1. SDH (most common)	1. Long bones	1. Burns-small pitted burns indicate deliberate stubbing of cigarette ends on skin
c. Slap marks	2. Encephalopathy	• Corner's fracture	2. Scalds
d. Skin pinch marks	3. Retinal hemorrhage	• Bucket handle fracture	3. Visceral injuries
e. Black eye	Violent shaking of child leads to intracranial hemorrhage called **shaken baby syndrome** (SBS)	• Fractures at different stages of healing	
f. Laceration-Torn upper lip frenulum		2. Skull	
		• Egg shell fracture	
		• Fissure fracture	
		3. Ribs	
		• Knob fractures	
		Fractured ribs heal by callus formation leading to a knob and on X-ray give **'string of beads'** appearance in paravertebral gutter.	
		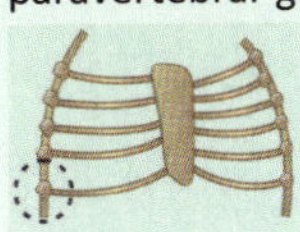	

Conclusive diagnosis

1. Injuries in different stages of healing
2. Discrepancy between history and findings
3. Delay in seeking advice

MLI: Any suspected child abuse case should be reported to the police.

6. Define infanticide. Describe in brief various acts of omission and commission in relation to infanticide. (North Eastern hill university, Supple, 2019)

Ans: Definition of infanticide: Refer to long question no. 5.

Acts of commission	Acts of omission
These are the acts done positively to cause death of an infant.	Intentional failure on part of the mother in providing the essential care to the newborn that results in death of the infant.
1. **B**urning—newborn is burnt alive 2. **S**mothering to death with use of hand or clothes 3. Strangulation—by ligature /umbilical cord 4. **C**oncealed punctured wound—caused by nail/needle through fontanelle 5. **P**oisoning—insecticides are commonly used as poison 6. **H**ead injury—banging the head of the child against the wall leading to SDH/EDH 7. **D**rowning—throwing baby in water (Mnemonic–**BSC PHD**)	1. Not providing proper assistance during labor 2. Not tying the cord, after it is being cut 3. Not providing food to the child 4. Not providing adequate clothes resulting in fetal hypothermia

7. Define infanticide. Discuss signs of live birth. (Sher-i- Kashmir Institute, Srinagar 2015)

Define infanticide. Discuss in detail the postmortem findings of a liveborn infant. (Delhi University, 2018)

What is infanticide? Write in brief about the signs of live birth. (North Eastern Hill University Supple 2016) (VNS, Gujarat 2016)

Ans: Definition of infanticide: Refer to long question no. 5.

External changes

1. **Changes in skin**
   - Absence of vernix caseosa
   - Skin color changes from bright red to brick-red to yellow and finally normal by 1st week
2. **Changes in umbilical cord**

Changes	Time since birth
Shrunken cord	Day-1
Inflammatory line at base of stump	Day-2
Mummified changes	Day-3
Cord **f**alls	Day-5
Scar	Day-10

(Mnemonic—**SIMF**all**S**)

3. Presence of caput succedaneum and cephalohematoma

Internal findings (from head to toe)

1. Closure of posterior fontanelle at birth
2. Changes in middle ear **(Wredin's test)**

- Before birth—presence of gelatin in middle ear
- When baby respires—presence of air in middle ear

3. Closure of fetal channels (umbilical vessels, ductus arteriosus and ductus venosus)
4. **Changes in chest**
   - Color—red/pink, mottled appearance
   - Consistency—soft, spongy, elastic
   - Level of diaphragm—6–7th rib
   - **Fodre's test**
     – Weight of lungs increases due to increase in vascularity
     – Weight of respired lungs (both)—60 g
   - **Ploucquet's test**

     $$\text{Ploucquet test} = \frac{\text{Weight of lungs}}{\text{Weight of body}}$$

     Respired lungs = 1:35 (as weight of lungs increases with vascularity)
   - **Positive hydrostatic test**
     – Based on the principle of specific gravity
     – Specific gravity of respired lungs–0.94
     – So lungs float on water
5. **Changes in stomach**
   - Presence of milk in the stomach
   - **Breslau's second life test:** Stomach and intestines are cut together and placed in a bowl of water
     – If floats—baby respired (as when baby respires, air is also swallowed into stomach)
     – If sinks—baby not respired
6. Absence of meconium in large intestine

8. What are the positive signs of pregnancy? Discuss the signs of recent delivery.

(North Eastern Hill University, Shillong 2019) (Adesh, Bathinda supple 2017)

Ans: Positive (conclusive) signs of pregnancy are:

1. Fetal heart sounds	1. Most definitive signs of pregnancy 2. Can be heard between 18 and 20th week with a stethoscope 3. FHR—160 beats/min at 5th month and 120–160 beats/min at 9th month 4. Not audible in—fetus <18 weeks, dead fetus, obese females
2. Fetal movements and parts	Can be felt by 20–22nd week on abdominal palpation.
3. Fetal RBCs in maternal blood (KB test)	Can be detected by 5th week of pregnancy
4. USG	1. 5th week: TVS can detect cardiac activity 2. 6th week: Gestational sac can be seen 3. 11th–13th week: Sex of baby can be determined
5. X-ray	1. Vertebrae: Series of small dots in a linear arrangement 2. Skull: Crescentic or annular shadows

Signs of recent delivery in living are:

General changes	1. Exhausted 2. Mild fever with tachycardia
Breast	1. Full and prominent 2. Colostrum expressed

	3. Montgomery tubercles
	4. Dark, pigmented areola and nipples enlarged
Abdomen	1. Flabby with wrinkled skin
	2. Stria gravidarum
	3. Linea nigra
External genitalia	1. Fourchette ruptured
	2. Labia majora and minora—tender, bruised, swollen
Vagina	Roomy, loss of rugosity, episiotomy wound
Cervix	Soft, dilated
Uterus	Involution of uterus
Lochia	1. Lochia rubra (1–4th day)
	2. Lochia serosa (5–9th day)
	3. Lochia alba (11–15th day)

9. Enumerate and explain findings in a victim of alleged sexual offence of sodomy (Adesh, Bathinda 2017) (JIPMER supple 2018) (VNS, Gujarat 2016, 2018)

Ans: Sodomy is the anal intercourse between two males (homosexual sodomy) or between a male and a female (heterosexual sodomy).

Findings seen in victim of sodomy are

Non-habitual passive victim	Habitual passive agent
Examination is done in left lateral decubitus position	Examination done in knee chest position
1. Pain and tenderness during digital rectal examination (DRE)	1. No pain and tenderness during DRE
2. Substances found in/around anus—fecal matter, lubricants, semen, loose foreign hair	2. No inflammation around anus
3. Inflammation around anus	3. Shaving of anal hair may be present
4. Bleeding due to laceration	4. **Lateral traction test**—external anal sphincter relaxes reflexly during bimanual traction of buttocks
5. Loss of normal anal tone	5. Loose foreign hair and lubricants
6. Injuries • Perianal abrasions—due to frictional shearing force by penetrating penis • Bruises—may be mistaken for hemorrhoids • Laceration • Anal fissures—wedge shaped, present in posterior quadrant and radially towards the anal canal	6. Perianal skin—thickened, keratinized due to constant regular friction 7. Anal sphincter—lax and patulous and dilated anal canal with old, healed fissures 8. Anal opening—deeply situated giving **funnel-shaped depression** of buttocks 9. Evidence of venereal disease
7. Swabs taken from inside and outside anus for microscopic examination	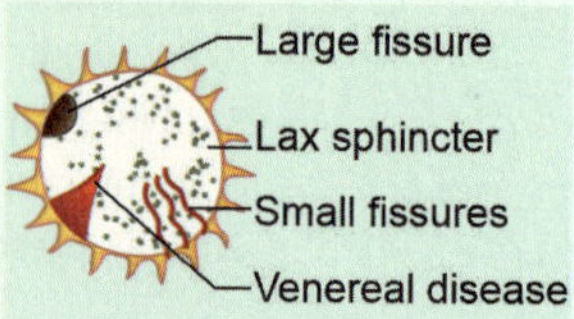

10. Define artificial insemination. What are the types? What are the medico-legal problems of AID and precautions must be followed by a doctor. (North Eastern Hill University, Shillong 2017) (Sardar Patel University, Gujarat 2019) (JIPMER supple 2018)

Definition of artificial insemination: It is the artificial introduction of semen of husband or donor into the reproductive tract of female so as to bring about pregnancy which is not attained by sexual intercourse.

Types of artificial insemination (AI)

1. AIH (artificial insemination homologous)
2. AID (artificial insemination donor)

Refer to difference no. 4 for AIH and AID.

Precautions to be followed by doctor

1. Donor should be of age less than 40 years and should have completed his family.
2. Donor should be healthy and not suffering from any hereditary disease.
3. Donor's identity should not be revealed.
4. Consent of wife, husband, donor and donor's wife should be taken.
5. Donor must not be related to woman or husband.
6. Donor should not know the recipient and the outcome of the technique.
7. Delivery should not be done by the physician who has performed artificial insemination.
8. Donor should have same blood group and there should be no Rh incompatibility.

Medico-legal Problems

1. **Legitimacy:** A child born through AID shall be presumed to be legitimate, born within wedlock, with consent of both the spouses.
2. **Adultery:** AID used for married woman with the consent of the husband does not amount to adultery on part of the wife or the donor.
3. **Litigation:** The doctor may be sued following the birth of a defective child.
4. **Nullity of marriage and divorce:** It is not a ground for divorce, if AI is done for sterility. If AI is due to impotency, it is a ground for nullity in favor of the wife due to non-consummation of marriage.
5. **Psychosocial aspect:** Problems may arise if it is known that the husband consented to AID and the husband was not capable of consummating the marriage.
6. **Incest:** There may be chance of incest among offspring born by AI and children of donor.

11. Define abortion. Write medical and legal classification of abortion. Write in brief about MTP Act, 1971. (University of Health Sciences, Rohtak 2019, Supple 2020) (AIIMS Patna 2018, 2016) (North Eastern Hill University, Shillong supple 2018) (Sardar Patel University, Gujarat 2017)

Ans:

- **Legal definition:** Expulsion of products of conception any time before full term is called abortion.
- **Medical definition:** Expulsion of products of conception before the period of viability.

Medical and Legal Classification of Abortion

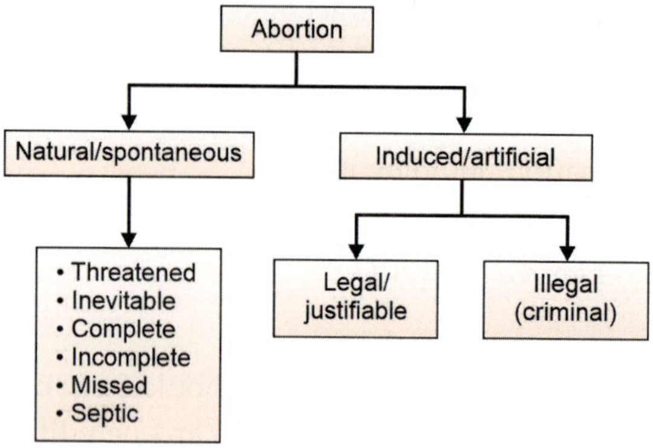

MTP ACT, 1971

Clauses of MTP

1. Indications of termination of pregnancy

Therapeutic	When continuation of pregnancy is a risk to the life of a pregnant female (risk can be in terms of physical/mental risk to health of female), e.g. toxemia, epilepsy, cervical or breast cancer, etc.
Eugenic	When it is known that child born would be suffering from severe physical or mental abnormalities, e.g. anencephaly, Down's syndrome, TORCH infections, chickenpox
Humanitarian	Pregnancy occurred due to rape
Social	Pregnancy occurred due to failure of contraceptive methods

2. Where can it be done?

Hospitals established/maintained by the Government

Place approved by government/district level committee with CMO/DHO

3. Who can perform it?

Conducting MTP up to <12 weeks	Conducting MTP up to 20 weeks
Doctor who has assisted in 25 MTP cases, out of which at least 5 MTPs should be performed independently	Any doctor with • Diploma/degree in Obs-Gynae • 6 months of house job in Obs-Gynae • 1 year of experience in Obs-Gynae department

In case of emergency, to save life of a female, even an MBBS doctor can also perform MTP.

Duration of pregnancy

a. **Up to 12 weeks of pregnancy:** Opinion of one doctor is required
b. **Between 12 and 20 weeks:** Opinion of two doctors is required
c. **More than 20 weeks of pregnancy:** Pregnancy cannot be terminated as per MTP Act, except in case of emergency when continuation of pregnancy is a risk to life of the mother.

Consent for termination of pregnancy

- Informed consent is taken from females ≥18 yrs. of age.
- In case female <18 yrs. or mentally ill—consent given by parents/guardian
- Consent of husband is not necessary

12. Define liveborn, stillborn and deadborn. How will you differentiate stillborn and liveborn infant? (AIIMS, Patna 2015)

Ans: Definition

1. **Liveborn:** The child which is born after period of viability (i.e. after 28 weeks) and shows signs of life after birth.
2. **Stillborn:** The child which is born after period of viability (i.e. after 28 weeks) but does not show any signs of life after birth.
3. **Deadborn:** The child which is found to be already dead in the uterus before beginning of the birth process and shows signs of intrauterine death.

   Difference: Refer to difference no. 1.

13. Define infanticide and methods usually adopted for carrying out infanticide. Add a note on macerated fetus. (Rajiv Gandhi University, Bengaluru 2017)

Definition of infanticide: Refer to long question no. 5.

Methods for carrying out infanticide: Refer to long question no. 6.

Macerated fetus: Refer to short question no. 40.

SHORT NOTES

1. Causes of impotency in males (Adesh, Bathinda supple 2020) (KHMS, Tamil Nadu 2017)

Ans: Causes of impotency in males are:

Medications	• SSRIs • Antipsychotic
Injuries	• Fractures—spinal cord, pelvis, penis
Psychological	• Fear, anxiety, absence of desire • Dislike of partner and disgust of act • **Quoad hoc**—a person is impotent with a particular woman (wife) but not with others
Age	• Boy is sterile before puberty but not impotent • ED is usually observed in old age
Poisoning	• Chronic lead poisoning • Arsenic poisoning
Anomalies (congenital and developmental)	• Penis—absent penis, hypospadias, epispadias • Testis—absent, cryptorchidism
Operation	• Vasectomy • Removal of testis • Amputation of penis
Nutritional deficiencies	• Vit C • Zinc • Malnutrition
Systemic diseases	• Neurological disorders—tabes dorsalis, multiple sclerosis· Endocrine causes—diabetes, hypothyroidism
Addiction	• Alcohol

	• Barbiturates
	• Opium
Local diseases	• **Penis—Phimosis, paraphimosis, peyronie disease**
	• Testis-orchitis, elephantiasis
Exposure to X-rays	• Leads to azoospermia

(Mnemonic—**MI PAPA ON SALE**)

2. Medico-legal Aspects of Impotency (GMC, Chandigarh 2015)

Ans: a. Impotence and sterility cases arises in:

Civil cases	1. Nullity of marriage 2. Disputed paternity and legitimacy 3. Claims for damages resulting in impotency 4. Adoption
Criminal cases	1. Rape 2. Adultery 3. Sodomy 4. Bestiality

b. Marriage versus impotence and sterility:

Marriage is not considered null and void nor divorce can be obtained	1. If impotence develops after marriage 2. If sterility is present at the time of marriage 3. If sterility develops after marriage
Marriage will be considered null and void	1. Impotence at time of marriage. 2. Permanent impotency is a ground for nullity of marriage but sterility is not.

3. Examination of a person alleging Impotence (Adesh, Bathinda 2019)

Ans: Examination of a person alleging impotence is done as per the protocol:

Prerequisite	1. Obtain the order of Court/Police. 2. Identification and obtain consent: Informed consent of accused should be obtained.
History	1. History of present illness (including sexual history, Surgical history, Psychological history, e.g. anxiety, depression) 2. Medical history, e.g., smoking, obesity, diabetes, nocturnal tumescence, peripheral neuropathy and medication 3. History of previous illness
Examination	1. General physical examination: Pulse, BP, secondary sexual characteristics. 2. Systemic examination: CNS, CVS, respiratory and abdominal. 3. Local examination of penis and testis: Look for deformity in penis such as phimosis, fibrous plaques, etc. or size of testis, hydrocoele, absence of testis **Bulbocavernosus reflex test:** Done to detect nerve sensation in the penis. The doctor squeezes the glans of the penis which immediately causes the anus to contract if nerve function is intact.
Lab investigations	1. Blood levels of HbA1c, lipids, thyroid, FSH and testosterone. 2. Examination of semen 3. **Nocturnal penile tumescence test:** Useful in differentiating psychogenic causes from organic causes.

4. **Duplex USG:** To check the atherosclerosis or calcification inside the penile vasculature.
5. Other tests: Penile biothesiometry, cavernosography.

4. Surrogate motherhood and medico-legal aspects (Rajiv Gandhi University, Bengaluru 2019) (Adesh, Bathinda 2017)

Ans: Definition of surrogate mother: A woman, supported by a legal agreement, carries a child for a couple or single person with the intention of giving that child up, once it is born.

Methods

1. Artificial insemination—here AI of husband's sperm to the surrogate. So, husband will be the biological father and surrogate will be biological mother.
2. Implantation of Embryo by IVF—here both husband and wife become biological parents as embryo is produced by IVF of father's sperm and wife's ovum, the surrogate will act as nonbiological mother.

Medico-legal Aspects

a. Surrogate may be emotionally disturbed on separating from the child
b. In India, surrogate is not considered as legal mother. So, after birth of the child, the child is returned to its biological father and his wife
c. Paternity of child is proved by the biological father who engaged the surrogate
d. Couple can refuse to adopt the child as the surrogate is biological mother
e. Expenses for diet, medicines are given to surrogate during the entire period of pregnancy.

5. Virginity (Rajiv Gandhi University, Bengaluru 2020) (Uttarakhand University 2017, supple 2018) (KHMS, Tamil Nadu 2016) (VNS, Gujarat 2016)

Ans: Definition

1. **Virgin:** The female who has never experienced sexual intercourse.
2. **Virginity:** The state of being virgin is called virginity.

Signs of True Virginity

Extra-genital signs

1. Breasts—small, hemispherical, firm
2. Areola—pink
3. Nipples—small, pink

Genital signs

1. Hymen—intact, rigid, inelastic, admits only tip of little finger through the orifice painfully
2. Vagina—narrow, slit like opening, marked rugosity of walls
3. Fourchette—intact
4. Clitoris—small
5. Labia majora—thick, fleshy, completely close the vaginal orifice
6. Labia minora—small, pinkish and covered by labia majora

Types of Hymen

Annular	Opening is centrally located
Semilunar or crescentic	Opening is placed anteriorly. Most common type
Vertical	Opening is vertical
Infantile	Small linear opening in the middle.
Septate	Two openings occur side by side, separated by thin strip of tissue.
Cribriform	Multiple openings
Imperforate	No opening

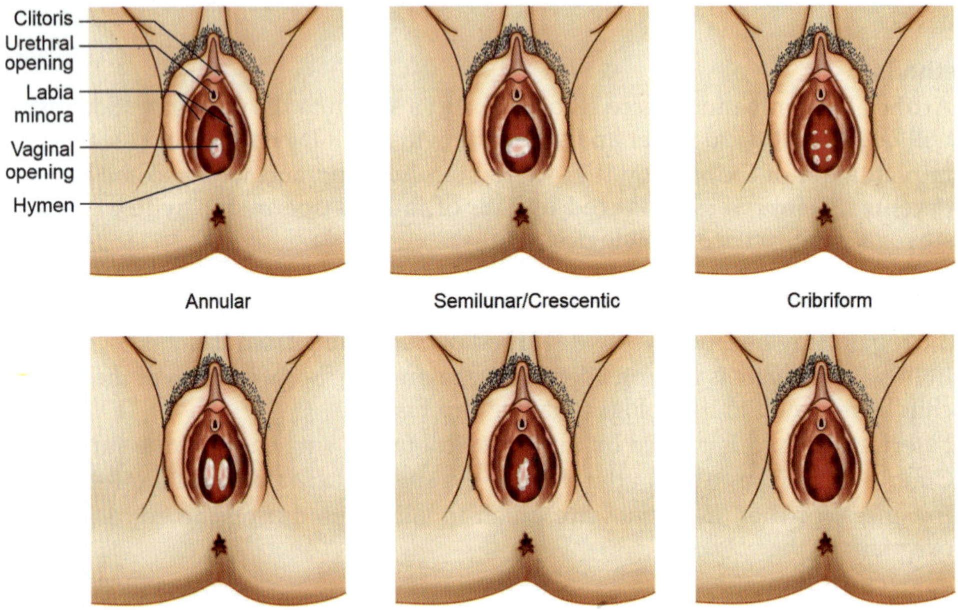

Annular | Semilunar/Crescentic | Cribriform

Septate | Infantile | Imperforate

MLI

1. The features of a deflorate woman and a false virgin are same except for the presence of hymen in the latter.
2. Hymen is completely lost after the birth of the child.
3. State of hymen is not a conclusive state of virginity.

6. False virgin (Rajiv Gandhi University, Bengaluru 2015) (KHMS, Tamil Nadu 2019) (VNS, Gujarat 2019)

Ans: Definition of false virgin: When even after sexual intercourse, if the hymen remains intact, the female is called as false virgin.

Hymen may not be ruptured due to:

1. Thick hymen
2. Loose hymen
3. Elastic hymen

The features of a deflorate woman and a false virgin are same except for the presence of hymen in the latter. For rest, refer to difference no. 3.

7. Hymen and its medico-legal significance (Rajiv Gandhi University, Shillong 2019) (University of Health Sciences, Rohtak 2017) (Uttarakhand University 2015)

Types of Hymen (AIIMS Patna 2016) (VNS, Gujarat supple 2019)

Ans: Refer to short question no. 5.

8. Precipitate labor (Rajiv Gandhi University, Bengaluru 2015) (Adesh, Bathinda supple 2018) (North Eastern Hill University, Shillong 2018, Supple 2018) (Rajiv Gandhi University, Bengaluru 2015) (VNS, Gujarat University 2019, supple 2019)

Ans: Definition of precipitate labor: It is the sudden and rapid expulsion of the fetus due to hyperactive uterine contractions.

1. A labor is called precipitate, when first and second stage of labor has < 2 hours of duration.
2. It is common in multipara.
3. **Typical history:** Mother goes to the washroom for defecation and sits on lavatory pan in an attempt to defecate and due to precipitate labor leads to the birth of the child.
4. **PM findings**
   a. Placenta is attached to the fetus
   b. Premature fetus
   c. Death of the fetus due to head injury (when baby hits the floor at time of delivery)
   d. Torn/lacerated umbilical cord (more commonly on fetal side) leading to death of fetus due to bleeding.
5. **MLI**
   a. Death of the newborn due to precipitate labor may be taken as a case of deliberate infanticide.
   b. The mother may claim infanticide (negligence on part of the doctor), but death of the newborn is due to precipitate labor.

9. Medico-legal Importance of Sterilization (West Bengal University 2018)

Ans: Medico-legal importance of sterilization

1. Doctor may be charged, if he performs sterilization without proper consent and proper indication.
2. It is desirable to sterilize only individuals above 30 years of age and having two children, one of whom is male.
3. Healthy unmarried or married persons without any issue should not be permanently sterilized, even if they volunteer for the same.
4. Failure of contraceptive measure adopted by males may lead to suspicion of wife having sexual relationship with another man who may initiate litigation—divorce, illegitimacy or disputed paternity.
5. There is no absolute guarantee to sterility after the operation, and the procedure may prove irreversible.
6. There may be failure in tubal sterilization—failure due to fistula formation or due to spontaneous reanastomosis.

10. Lochia. (Adesh, Bathinda 2017) (Rajiv Gandhi University, Bengaluru 2015) (Delhi University 2018) (VNS Gujarat, 2018)

Ans: Features of lochia are:

1. It is an alkaline discharge from female genital tract for 2–3 weeks after delivery, with peculiar, disagreeable fishy odor.
2. It is a sign of recent delivery.
3. **Types**

Lochia Rubra	Lochia Serosa	Lochia Alba
(1–4) days **Bright red in** color	(5-9 days) **Watery, pale** in color	(10–15) days **Grey-yellowish** followed by **whitish** color
Consists of • RBCs • Shreds of fetal membranes and decidua • Vernix caseosa • Lanugo hair	Consists of • WBCs >RBCs • Cervical mucus • Microorganisms	Consists of • WBCs • Mucus • Cholesterol crystals • Fatty epithelial cells • Microorganisms

11. Complications of Criminal Abortion. (Rajiv Gandhi University, Bengaluru 2020, 2015) (Sher-i-Kashmir, Srinagar supple 2018) (Pondicherry 2017) (Delhi University 2017)

Ans: Complications of criminal abortion are:

Immediate complications	1. Vagal inhibition 2. Hemorrhagic shock 3. Fat embolism 4. Air embolism 5. Amniotic fluid embolism
Delayed complications	1. Peritonitis 2. Septicemia 3. Toxemia 4. Salpingitis 5. Tetanus
Late complications	1. Pulmonary embolism 2. Endocarditis 3. Jaundice 4. Renal failure 5. Hepatic failure

12. Presumptive signs of pregnancy. (KHMS, Tamil Nadu 2016) (BFUHS, Punjab Supple 2016) (GMC, Chandigarh 2015)

Ans: Presumptive signs of pregnancy are:

Amenorrhea	• Earliest and most important symptom of pregnancy
Morning sickness	• Presence of nausea and vomiting • Starts by 1st month and ends by 3rd month of pregnancy
Breast changes	• Mainly seen in primigravidae

Hyperpigmentation	• Increase in size, tenderness of breast • Dark areola, presence of montgomery tubercles • Cholasma (pigmentation over head and cheeks) • Linea nigra • Striae gravidarum (pregnancy stretch marks on abdomen)
Fatigue	• Easy fatiguibility
Quickening	• Pregnant women feel fetal movements in her abdomen
Sympathetic disturbances	• Increased salivation, irritability and increased appetite
Urinary disturbances	• Increased frequency and micturition
Changes in vagina (Chadwick's sign)	• Bluish discolouration of vaginal mucous membrane • Seen after 4th week of pregnancy

13. Positive/Confirmatory signs of pregnancy. (Rajiv Gandhi University, Bengaluru 2020, 2015) (University of Health Sciences, Rohtak 2019, Supple 2020) (SGRD, Amritsar 2019) (KHMS, Tamil Nadu 2015, Supple 2019) (Sardar Patel University, Gujarat Supple 2018, Supple 2016) (BFUHS, Punjab 2017) (Rajasthan University 2015)

Ans: Refer to long question no. 8.

14. Artificial Insemination. (Adesh, Bathinda 2019) (BFUHS, Punjab supple 2018) (North Eastern Hill University, Shillong Supple 2018)

Ethical and legal issues in relation to Artificial Insemination (Uttarakhand University supple 2018, supple 2017) (Pondicherry 2016)

Ans: Refer to long question no. 10.

15. MTP ACT (KHMS, Tamil Nadu 2017) (BFUHS, Punjab 2016) (Adesh, Bathinda supple 2017) (Rajasthan University 2018, 2017) (North Eastern Hill University 2018) (Uttarakhand University 2017, 2015) (VNS Gujarat, supple 2018)

Indications for termination of pregnancy as per MTP ACT, 1971 (Sardar Patel University, Gujarat 2020, 2019, 2018, supple 2018)

Ans: Refer to long question no. 11.

16. Section 377 IPC. (West Bengal University Supple 2019)

1. **Sec. 377 IPC** defines punishment for unnatural sexual offence.
2. It includes offences like sodomy, lesbianism, bestiality, buccal coitus.
3. It states that 'if an individual voluntarily has sexual intercourse against the order of nature with any man, woman or animal, he is punishable with imprisonment for life or with imprisonment up to 10 years and fine.'
4. Penetration is sufficient to constitute offence under this section.
5. Consensual anal sex between two consenting adults is not punishable under this section.

17. Sodomy/Buggery. (KHMS, Tamil Nadu supple 2020) (North Eastern Hill University, Shillong 2018, Supple 2017) (AIIMS Patna 2016) (Uttarakhand University 2016) (Pondicherry 2015) (Rajiv Gandhi University, Shillong 2015) (VNS Gujarat, 2016)

Ans: Refer to long question no. 9.

18. Local findings expected during examination of habitual active and passive agents involved in sodomy. (Sardar Patel University, Gujarat Supple 2016) (VNS Gujarat, 2018)

Ans: Refer to long question no. 9.

19. Sadism. (Delhi University 2015) (VNS Gujarat, supple 2019)

Ans:

1. **Definition of sadism:** Person gets sexual gratification by infliction of pain or physical cruelty on the partner in form of beating, biting, cigarette burns or humiliation.
2. It is also called Algolagnia.
3. More common in males.
4. It is usually found in association with Masochism, and the combination of Sadism and Masochism is called as **Bondage/ sadomasochism.**
5. **MLI**
   a. Sadomasochism can lead to **Autoerotic Asphyxia.**
   b. In extreme case, it can give rise to **Lust murder.**

20. Voyeurism. (North Eastern Hill University, Shillong Supple 2019) (Rajiv Gandhi University, Bengaluru 2015)

Ans.

1. **Definition of voyeurism:** It is a sexual perversion in which person gets sexual gratification by watching other person undressing, bathing or doing sexual intercourse.
2. It is also called Peeping Tom/Scotophilia.
3. It is commonly seen in males.
4. Some voyeurs even prefer to observe their own wives being seduced by other men.
5. **MLI:** It is punishable under Section **354-C IPC.**

For 1st time offence	Imprisonment from 1–3 years and fine
For 2nd offence/ more	Imprisonment is for 3–7 years and fine

21. Fetishism. (Uttarakhand University 2017)

Ans:

Features of fetishism are:

1. It is a type of sexual perversion in person achieves sexual gratification by using inanimate objects.
2. There is recurrent intense sexual urges and sexually arousing fantasies involving specific objects.
3. **Fetish objects:** Handkerchief, dress, particularly the undergarments—panties, bras, slips, stockings.
4. The object of interest is called Fetish and the person is called Fetishist.

22. Transvestism. (Adesh, Bathinda 2018, supple 2017)

Ans. Features of transvestism are:
1. It is also called Eonism.
2. The person achieves sexual gratification by wearing the dress of opposite sex (cross dress)
3. It is usually seen in males. So, he collects items like nightgowns, slips, bras, lingerie, stockings.
4. Types:

Fetishist transvestism	Dual role transvestism
Person achieves sexual gratification with inanimate objects	There is no role of sexual arousal Rather person wants to experience opposite sex temporarily

23. Munchausen syndrome by proxy (Rajiv Gandhi University, Bengaluru 2015)

Ans: Features of Munchausen Syndrome by Proxy are:
1. It is a type of child abuse involving parent or guardian (usually mothers).
2. Children are brought to doctors by parents with fictitious history.
3. **Ways of producing symptoms**
   i. Mother may prick her finger, and add her blood to the urine sample of child and take the sample to the doctor.
   ii. She may give insulin injection to child. And take him to doctor with hypoglycemia.
   iii. Use of laxatives and emetics to produce diarrhoea or vomiting.
4. **Diagnosis**
   a. Parent's denial of knowledge of cause of symptoms.
   b. The child becomes ill or worsens when the parent or guardian is present, while recovery when separated.
   c. Signs and symptoms are not proved by laboratory/radiological investigations.

24. Superfecundation (Adesh, Bathinda 2018) (Rajiv Gandhi University, Bengaluru 2015)

Ans: Features of Superfecundation are:
1. **Definition:** It is the fertilisation of two ova in the same menstrual cycle by 2 separate acts of coitus committed at short intervals.
2. **Types**

Homoparental superfecundation	Heteroparental superfecundation
When both the ova are fertilised by the SAME person	When result of fertilisation of ova is by DIFFERENT persons

3. **MLI:** Babies may born with different complexion and features giving rise to adultery.

25. Adultery (Rajiv Gandhi University, Bengaluru 2018)

Ans: Adultery
1. **Definition:** It is a sexual intercourse by a man with another married woman without the consent of her husband.

2. It does not amount to rape.
3. **MLI**
   a. Earlier, Sec. 497 IPC dealt with adultery.
   b. But now, it is not punishable in India.
   c. It can be a ground for divorce.

26. Section 354 IPC. (Rajiv Gandhi University, Bengaluru 2015)

Ans: Section 354 IPC
1. **Section 354 IPC** deals with indecent assault.
2. **Definition of indecent assault:** Any unwanted sexual behaviour towards a person without her will/consent, with an intention to outrage her modesty.
3. **Punishment**

354	Deals with **Ind**ecent assault (1–5 years ± Fine)	**I**ndia had
354 **A**	Punishment for **Sexual harassment** (Frotteurism) (up to 3 years ± Fine)	**S**achin
354 **B**	Punishment for **Disrobe** (3–7 years ± Fine)	**D**ravid
354 **C**	Punishment for **Voyeurism** (1–3 years ± Fine –1st offence; 3–7 years ± Fine—2nd offence)	**V**VS Lakshman
354 **D**	Punishment for **Stalking** (up to **3 years** ± Fine –1st offence; up to 5 years ± Fine—2nd offence)	**S**ehwag

27. Section 375 IPC (Sher-i-Kashmir, Srinagar 2020, Supple 2019, Supple 2018) (AIIMS Patna 2019, 2017, 2015) (Jammu and Kashmir 2017) (Rajasthan University 2017, 2016)

What constitutes rape? (Sardar Patel University 2020, Supple 2016)

Ans: Refer to long question no. 1.

28. Section 376 IPC (Sher-i-Kashmir, Srinagar 2020) (Sher-i-Kashmir, Srinagar Supple 2017)

Ans: Refer to long question no. 1.

29. Signs of recent delivery in living. (Adesh, Bathinda 2018) (Rajasthan University 2018) (Andhra Pradesh supple 2015) (BFUHS, Punjab 2016)

Ans: Refer to long question no. 8.

30. Various samples collected in victim of rape (Pondicherry 2019) (BFUHS, Punjab 2015)

Ans: Refer to long question no. 2.

31. Semen Analysis (BFUHS, Punjab 2016) (University of Health Sciences, Rohtak 2017) (JIPMER 2016)

Ans: Semen examination is done as per the given protocol.

1. Screening tests

1. Physical examination	• White/yellow-white in color • Peculiar smell • Slightly viscous
2. Examination under **UV light**	Shows bluish white fluorescence
3. Chemical examination	• Florence test: Dark brown Rhombic crystals • Barberio test: Yellow Needle shaped crystals • Acid phosphatase test: Intense purple colour

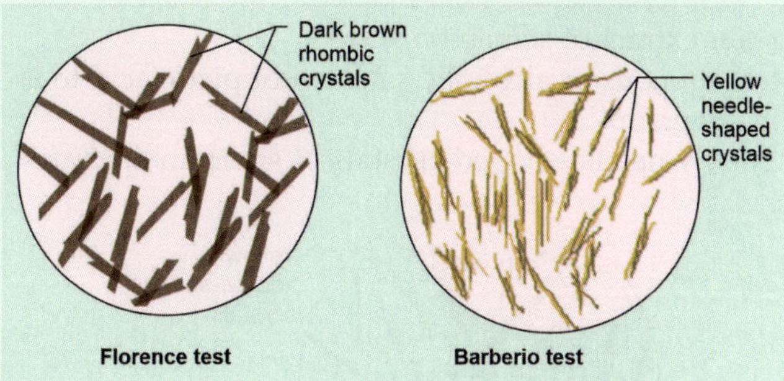

2. Confirmatory tests

1. Microscopy	• Gold standard test • Shows presence of sperms under microscope

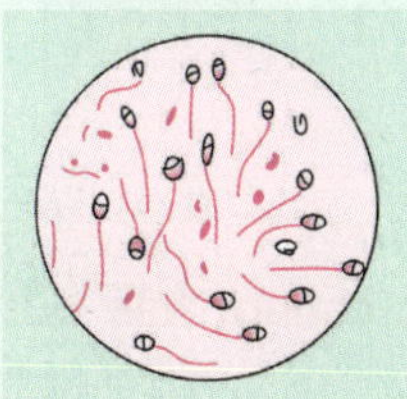

2. Prostate-specific antigen	Presence of **p-30** which is derived from prostate and found in seminal plasma
3. Acid phosphatase test	

MLI

Civil cases	Criminal cases
1. Disputed paternity	1. Proof of sexual assault
2. Legitimacy	2. Rape
	3. Murder with sexual violence

32. Benzidine test. (Adesh, Bathinda 2019) (KHMS, Tamil Nadu 2017) (VNS Gujarat, 2017)

Ans: Features of Benzidine Test

1. It is a screening test for blood stains
2. **Principle:** Presence of peroxidase in RBCs converts hydrogen peroxide to liberate nascent oxygen which acts on the reagent to change its color
   Hb (Heme with peroxidase) + **Hydrogen peroxide + Reagent → Color**
3. **Procedure**
   a. A drop of saturated benzidine solution
   b. Then add a drop of hydrogen peroxide

4. **Observation**
   Change of color to **b**lue color
5. Benzidine is a known carcinogen, hence seldom used nowadays.

33. Barberio test (Adesh, Bathinda 2019)

Ans: Features of Barberio's Test
1. It is a presumptive test for semen which must be followed by confirmatory test.
2. **Procedure**
   a. Take dried stain extract of semen on slide
   b. Add saturated aqueous or alcoholic solution of picric acid to it
   c. Cover it with coverslip
3. **Observation:** Yellow needle-shaped crystals of spermine picrate

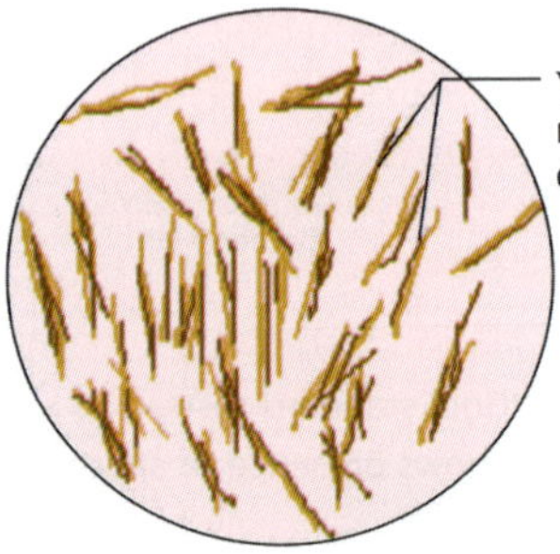

4. **Advantage:** This test is positive without presence of spermatozoa.

34. Negative findings in medical examination of an alleged victim cannot rule out rape charges. (West Bengal University supple 2018)

Ans: Although positive findings during examination of an alleged rape victim help in prosecuting the accused, but there may be situations when there may be negative findings, i.e. normal examination findings. The report should contain negative, as well as positive findings.

It should be always kept in mind that normal examination findings neither refute nor confirm the forceful sexual intercourse. Hence circumstantial/other evidence may be taken into consideration.

- For example: Complete penetration can occur in deflorate women and leaves no evidence, except for semen. The absence of injury under certain circumstances, therefore, does not exclude even complete penetration.
- In a young child, there are few or no signs of general violence, for the child usually has no idea of what is happening and also incapable of resisting. Moreover, the penis is placed either within the vulva or between the thighs. As such, the hymen is usually intact, and there may be little redness and tenderness of the vulva.

35. Autoerotic asphyxia/sexual asphyxia. (Rajasthan University 2016) (KHMS, Tamil Nadu 2018) (Pondicherry 2017)

Ans: Definition of autoerotic asphyxia: It is a paraphilia, wherein a person develops partial asphyxia in his own body by means to enhance sexual arousal.

- Degree of asphyxia is produced by mechanical means is controlled (as after experiencing orgasm, constricting force around the neck is released but death may occur in some cases).
- It is seen in association with Masochism.
- Partial asphyxia caused by pressure on carotid vessels or obstruction of air passages cause cerebral ischemia.
- Victims are usually young males, in his own house, bedroom, bathroom and the door is locked from inside.

Methods of Producing Sexual Asphyxia

1. Hanging: Most frequent method
2. Suffocation by plastic
3. Manual pressure on carotid vessels

36. Battered Baby syndrome/Caffey syndrome. (Rajiv Gandhi University, Bengaluru 2020) (KHMS, Tamil Nadu 2018, supple 2019) (Sardar Patel University, Gujarat 2019) (Andhra Pradesh 2016)

Ans: Refer to long question no. 5.

37. Sudden Infant Death Syndrome. (Adesh, Bathinda 2019) (North Eastern Hill University, Bengaluru Supple 2017)

Ans: Definition: It is defined as sudden and unexpected death of a healthy infant whose death remain unexplained even after complete autopsy.

- It is also known as **Crib death.**

General features

- Age—2 weeks to 2 years
- Sex—Males >Females
- Time of death—nighttime and early morning
- Twins—common in twins
- Addiction—smoking by pregnant mother increases risk

Causes

a. Prolonged sleep apnea (most imp.)
b. Laryngeal spasm
c. Hypersensitivity of respiratory tract

PM findings

- Negative autopsy findings
- Multiple petechial hemorrhages on heart, lungs
- Milk or blood stained froth at mouth and nostrils

38. Signs of live birth. (Sardar Patel University, Gujarat 2019)

PM findings in case of liveborn infant. (Uttarakhand University 2018)

Tests to determine live birth of infant. (Adesh, Bathinda supple 2017)

Ans: Refer to long question no. 7.

39. Dead born fetus (BFUHS, Punjab supple 2016) (Pondicherry 2017) (VNS Gujarat, supple 2019)

Ans: Definition: It is death of fetus in the uterus.

Signs of IUD (intrauterine death)

1. **M**aceration	It is aseptic autolysis (refer to short question no. 40)
2. **M**ummification	Occurs due to deficient blood supply
3. **R**igor mortis	Not seen in child <7 months of IUL
(Mnemonic—**MMR**)	

Radiological Signs of IUD

1. **Spaulding sign**	Overlapping of fetal skull bones due to shrinkage of cerebellum Seen on **5th day** after death **Most important** sign of IUD
2. **Robert's sign**	**Earliest** radiological sign (within 12 hours) It is presence of gas shadow in chambers of heart and aorta
3. **Hyperflexion of spine**	Fetus curves like a ball
4. **Deuel halo sign**	Separation of subcutaneous fat in scalp from cranial bones
5. **Crowding of ribs**	

(Mnemonic—**SRH** v/s **DC**; SRH = Sun Risers Hyderabad v/s DC= Delhi Capitals)

40. Maceration (KHMS, Tamil Nadu 2016) (BFUHS, Punjab 2017) (VNS Gujarat, 2017)

Ans: Features of maceration are:

1. It is a process of **aseptic autolysis**
2. It develops when dead fetus remains in uterus for >3 days surrounded with amniotic fluid
3. **Mechanism of maceration:** After IUD, cell membranes leak out enzymes into the extracellular space leading to autolysis of the baby
4. **Signs of maceration**
   a. Skin slippage: **Earliest sign** of maceration (seen within 12 hours of IUD)
   b. Skin blebs
   c. Bloating of abdomen
   d. Increased mobility of joints.

41. Spaulding sign (AIIMS Patna 2019, 2018, 2017) (Rajiv Gandhi University, Bengaluru 2015) (VNS Gujarat, 2018)

Ans: Refer to short question no. 39.

42. Write medico-legal importance of umbilical cord. (West Bengal University 2019, 2017, supple 2017)

Ans: Assessing the changes in umbilical cord helps in assessing liveborn or still/dead born and number of days passed after being born alive.

Day-1	**S**hrunken cord
Day-2	**I**nflammatory line at base of stump
Day-3	**M**ummification changes in cord
Day-5	**Fall**ing off umbilical cord
Day-10–12	**S**car formation (healing)

43. Hydrostatic Test (BFUHS, Punjab 2018, Supple 2019) (West Bengal University 2019) (Uttarakhand University 2017) (Himachal Pradesh 2017) (AIIMS Patna 2015) (Sai Tirupati University, Rajasthan, 2018) (JIPMER 2018) (VNS Gujarat, supple 2019)

Ans: Features of hydrostatic test

1. Also called **Lung Flotation Test/ Raygat's Test**
2. **Principle:** It is based on the fact that specific gravity of lung before respiration is more, and becomes less after respiration (less than that of water). This makes the respired lung to float.
3. **Method:** Take 3 containers having water:

Container 1	Container 2	Container 3
Place few pieces of the lungs in this container If floats—move to next step (container 2)	Lungs are taken out and squeezed and placed in this container. (to check for **Residual Air)** • If **Floats**—then **test is +ve** (means baby has respired) • If **Sinks**—the test is –ve.	Liver is placed in this container If **Sinks**—act as **control** If **Floats**—then no value of Hydrostatic test (as it suggests **Putrefaction**)

4. **MLI**
   a. Conditions in which baby respired, yet lungs **Sink** (false negative)
      - Atelectasis
      - Pulmonary edema
      - Pneumonia

   b. Conditions in which baby has *not* respired, yet lungs **Float** (false positive)
      - Putrefaction (therefore we do Control test with liver)
      - Artificial respiration

44. Rule of Hassae (Rajiv Gandhi University, Bengaluru 2015) (Sai Tirupati University, Rajasthan, 2018)

Ans: Rule of Hassae

- It is a method used to determine the age of the fetus by measuring the length of the fetus in cm (crown-heel length).

For first 5 months of pregnancy	For the last 5 months of pregnancy
Age of fetus in months is equal to the square root of length (CHL)	Age of fetus in months is equal to length divided by 5

- For example, if length is 36 cm and has crossed 5 months, then √36 = 6 months.

45. Infanticide (GMC, Chandigarh 2016)

Acts of omission and commission in relation to Infanticide (Sardar Patel University, Gujarat 2016)

Ans: Refer to long question no. 6.

DIFFERENTIATIONS

1. Respired lungs and Unrespired lungs. (BFUHS, Punjab 2019, 2015) (University of Health Sciences, Rohtak 2019, Supple 2020) (West Bengal University 2019, Supple 2017)

Liveborn and stillborn. (Adesh, Bathinda Supple 2018) (JIPMER supple 2018)

Ans:

	Respired lungs/liveborn	Unrespired lungs/stillborn
Volume of lungs	Large	Small
Colour	Mottled, salmon pink	Uniformly bluish red
Consistency	Soft, spongy	Dense, firm
Margins	Rounded	Sharp
Level of diaphragm	6–7th rib	4–5th rib
Hydrostatic test	Positive (lungs float in water)	Negative (sinks in water)
Fodere's test	Weight of lung 60–70 g	Around 30–40 g
Ploucquet's test (wt. of lung: wt. of baby)	1:35	1:70
Breslau's second life test (air in stomach)	Stomach floats in water	Stomach sinks in water
MLI	Indicates live birth	Indicates stillbirth/deadborn infant

2. Multiparous uterus and Nulliparous Uterus (Adesh, Bathinda Supple 2020)

Ans:

	Multiparous uterus	Nulliparous uterus
Size	Large	Small
Weight	80–100 g	40–50 g
Body: cervix	2:1	1:1
External os	Transverse patulous slit	Circular, dimple like
Upper surface of fundus	Higher level than the line of broad ligament	Same level as broad ligament
Uterine cavity	Rounded and spacious	Triangular and smaller
Cervix	Cylindrical shape	Conical shape
Scar for placental attachment	Present	Absent

3. True virgin and false virgin. (University of Health Sciences, Rohtak 2019 , Supple 2020) (Jammu and Kashmir 2017) (North Eastern Hill University 2015) (GMC, Chandigarh 2015) (BFUHS, Punjab 2015) (Delhi University Supple 2016)

Ans:

	True virgin	False virgin/defloration
Definition	Woman has never experienced sexual intercourse with intact hymen	Woman has experienced sexual intercourse but her hymen is intact (ruptured in defloration)
Hymen	Admits only tip of little finger through orifice	Easily admits two fingers through orifice
Clitoris	Small	Enlarged
Labia minora	Small, pinkish and covered with labia majora	Enlarged, pigmented, separated from majora
Labia majora	Fleshy and completely close the vaginal orifice	Less fleshy, separated
Vagina	Narrow with marked rugosity	Roomy with less rugosity
Fourchette	Intact	Ruptured
Posterior commissure	-do-	-do-
Nipples and areola	Small and pink	Enlarged and pigmented

Note: In defloration, the hymen is ruptured, rest of the features are same as false virgin

4. Artificial insemination homologous (AIH) and Artificial insemination donor (AID). (Delhi University Supple, 2016)

Ans:

	AIH	AID
Indications	Erectile dysfunction, hypospadias, cervical stenosis	Sterile husband, hereditary disease, Rh incompatibility
Donor	Husband	Other person
Donor's age	Not specific	Should be <40 years
Disclosure of identity	Not an issue	Donor and recipient must not know each other
Doctor who conducted AI	May deliver the child	Should avoid delivery of child
Outcome of AI	Known to husband	Donor must not know
Consent	From both husband and wife	From husband, wife, donor and donor's wife
Confidentiality maintained	No	Yes
MLI	No legal issues, except for divorce	Litigation against doctor, illegitimacy, inheritance claims, divorce, incest and mental trauma

(Mnemonic—**DOC**)

5. Natural abortion and criminal abortion. (Adesh supple 2019, supple 2018) (University of Health Sciences, Rohtak 2017)

Ans:

	Natural abortion	Criminal abortion
Cause	Predisposing disease	In unmarried woman/widow
Marks of violence on abdomen	Absent	Present
Fetal injuries	-do-	-do-
Injuries on genital organs	-do-	-do-
Toxic effects on drugs	-do-	-do-
Sepsis	-do-	-do-
Foreign body in genital tract	-do-	-do-

CHAPTER

7 Forensic Psychiatry

LONG QUESTIONS

1. Explain the term "Feigned Insanity". Mention four salient features to differentiate true insanity from feigned insanity. Add a note on civil and criminal responsibility of an insane. (Rajiv Gandhi University, Bengaluru 2018)

Ans:

Feigned Insanity

Definition: It means that the person is pretending to be mentally ill/ insane in order to deceive and for gain.

The person has some motive behind this act, e.g.,

a. to avoid inquiry
b. to avoid trial
c. to avoid conviction
d. to avoid punishment
e. to avoid going to prison

Hence, it is the duty of the doctor/psychiatrist to distinguish between two.

It is also necessary that no sane person is confined to a psychiatric hospital.

Difference between True and Feigned Insanity: Refer to difference no.1.

Civil responsibility of Insane

Management of self and property	The court may appoint a guardian to take care of the mentally ill, and may appoint a manager to manage the property.
Contracts	A contract made by mentally ill person, who does not understand the nature and quality of the contract will be considered invalid. However, he is liable for contracts if made during lucid interval.
Marriage and divorce	Marriage is invalid, if one of the parties, at the time of ceremony, was suffering from mental illness.
Adoption	Taking/giving adoption of a child is not allowed, if either of the parents is mentally ill.
Witness	A mentally ill person cannot be considered as competent to give evidence in the court of law. He can be regarded as competent during lucid interval.
Consent	The consent given by a mentally ill person is not valid because he is unable to understand the nature and consequence of that to which he gives the consent.

Testamentary capacity	Will made by mentally ill person is considered invalid because mentally ill person does not have the capacity to make a valid will. Will is valid made during lucid interval.
Guardianship	A mentally ill person is not considered as a legal guardian of a minor.

Criminal Responsibility of Insane/McNaughton's Rule

- McNaughton's rule deals with criminal responsibility of an insane person.
- **History:** In 1843, Mr. Edward Drummond, the private secretary of the then Prime Minister of England, Sir Robert Peel, was shot dead by Daniel McNaughton who was suffering from delusion of persecution and believed that his life was in danger due to the acts of persecution by the Tory Party on him. He shot dead Mr. Drummond on the belief that he killed Mr. Peel. Later, it was established that McNaughton suffered from paranoid delusions and was acquitted on the ground of insanity. The new rules that were framed for criminal responsibility of the insane were named after McNaughton.
- According to these rules, it must be proven by the defence that at the time of committing the act, the accused was laboring under such a defect of reason from disease of mind (known and nameable disease) as not to know the nature and quality of the act, or if he did know this, that he did not know what he was doing was wrong or contrary to law.
- The legal test of insanity is laid down in **Sec. 84 of IPC** "Nothing is an offence which is done by a person who, at the time of doing it, by reason of unsoundness of mind, is incapable of knowing the nature of the act or what he is doing is either wrong or contrary to the law."

2. Define McNaughton rule. How is it incorporated in Indian law? Discuss criminal responsibility of an insane. (Sher-i-Kashmir Institute, Srinagar 2020)

Ans:

McNaughton rule: *Refer to long question no. 1.*

McNaughton rule is incorporated **under Sec. 84 of IPC in Indian law**. It states that "Nothing is an offence which is done by a person who, at the time of doing it, by reason of unsoundness of mind, is incapable of knowing the nature of the act or what he is doing is either wrong or contrary to the law."

Criminal responsibility of an insane: Refer to long question no. 1.

3. Define and classify insanity. What is delusion? Describe various types of delusions. (Rajiv Gandhi University, Bengaluru Supple 2015) (Sher-i-Kashmir Institute, Srinagar Supple 2018)

Ans:

Definition of insanity: It is the disease of the mind, which affects the personality, mental status, critical faculties, emotional processes and interaction with the social environment.

Mentally-ill person: Any person who is in need of treatment by reason of any mental disorder other than mental retardation.

ICD-10 Classification of Mental Illness

Classification	Types
Organic mental disorders	Delirium, dementia
Psychoactive substance use disorders	Acute intoxication, withdrawal state
Schizophrenia and delusional disorders	Schizophrenia, psychotic disorder
Mood disorders	Manic, depressive, bipolar, mood disorders
Neurotic and somatoform disorders	Anxiety, phobic disorder, OCD
Behavioral syndromes	Eating disorders, sexual dysfunctions
Adult personality and behavior disorders	Personality or impulse disorders
Mental retardation	Mild, moderate, severe mental retardation
Disorders of psychological development	Speech, language, scholastic skills disorders
Behavioral and emotional disorders in children	Hyperkinetic, conduct and tic disorders

Definition of Delusion

False but firm belief in something which is not a fact despite proof to the contrary. It is a disorder of content of thought.

Types of Delusion

Hypochondriacal delusion	Patient believes of having some serious disease (like cancer) based on his own interpretations of physical signs and symptoms.
Delusion of infidelity (**O**thello syndrome)	• Patient believes that his partner is unfaithful to him or her. • Seen in patients with alcohol dependence
Delusion of **R**eference	Person believes that everyone is looking at him or talking about him. For example, if patient sees anyone smiling, then says he was laughing at me.
Nihilistic delusion	• Patient denies the existence of their body, their mind or even world in general. • Seen in patients of depression.
Delusion of **In**fluence	Patient complains that his thoughts, feelings and actions are being influenced and controlled by some outside agency, e.g., radio.
Delusion of **L**ove/Erotomania	• Patient believes that a person of higher socioeconomic status is in love with her/him. • Usually common in females.
Delusion of **P**ersecution	• Most common delusion. • The person thinks that people around him are trying to kill him/harm him/making conspiracy against him. • Commonly seen in schizophrenia.
Delusion of **G**randiosity	• Person imagines himself to be very rich/powerful, although in reality he may be poor. • Seen in patients with mania and schizophrenia.
(Mnemonic—**HORN In LPG**)	

4. Write in detail about Mental Health Act, 2017. (Sher-i-Kashmir Institute, Srinagar Supple 2019)

Ans:

- The Mental Healthcare Act 2017 provides for mental healthcare and services for persons with mental illness. It is presumed that all persons have the capacity to make mental healthcare and treatment decisions.

- Under this Act, the person can make an advance directive in writing the way he wishes to be cared for or not to be cared for and treated for a mental illness and appoint a nominated representative to take decisions on his behalf when he is incapable to decide.
- This Act has also decriminalized attempt to commit suicide.

Rights of Persons with Mental Illness

1. Right to access mental healthcare and treatment from mental health services
2. Right to information about proposed treatment and its side effects
3. Right to live in, be part of and not be segregated from society
4. Right to live with dignity
5. A child <3 years of a woman receiving treatment should not be separated from her during her stay in such hospital.
6. Right to confidentiality in respect of his mental health, care and treatment, and no release of even a photograph in media.

Admission and Discharge (Restraint of Mentally Ill Patient)

A mentally ill person needs to be restrained for his own safety or for the safety of others. If the lawful guardian of the patient is unable to keep him under control, or if there's no guardian, then the state is legally justified to take charge of the patient and put him under restraint.

a. **Supported admission:** Seen in case of minor (age <18 yrs)
   - Patient is admitted on the decision of Nominated Representative. Any such admission shall be informed by medical officer (MO) in-charge to the concerned board within 72 h.
   - Nominated person shall stay with the minor for the entire duration of admission. When a minor attains the age of 18 yrs, the MO in-charge shall classify him as an 'independent patient'.
   - If nominated representative requests discharge of the minor, the minor shall be discharged by mental health establishment. Also, any admission of a minor which continues for a period of 30 days shall be immediately informed to the concerned board.

b. **Independent admission:** Any person of ≥18 yrs of age, who considers having a mental illness and desires to be admitted may request the MO in-charge of the psychiatric hospital to be admitted as an independent patient for treatment, only after informed consent. On request, MO in-charge shall discharge the patient immediately.

   Mentally ill person who requires treatment beyond 30 days should be reviewed by two psychiatrists.

c. **Involuntary admission:** This is done if the patient:
   - Recently threatened/attempted or is threatening/attempting to cause bodily harm to himself;
   - Recently behaved/is behaving violently towards another person or caused bodily harm to another person

This involuntary admission can be for a period of 30 days. It is only when this period is to be extended beyond 30 days that the Board must confirm the admission.

Emergency

Any doctor may provide treatment for mental illness of a person with informed consent of the nominated representative where it is immediately necessary to prevent:

a. Death of the person; or
b. Serious harm to himself/others; or
c. Serious damage to property, which is directly related to his mental illness.

Treatments Prohibited

- Direct ECT without use of muscle relaxants and anaesthesia
- ECT for minors (performed only after taking permission from caretaker and prior permission from board)
- Psychosurgery (performed only after taking permission from caretaker and prior permission from board)
- Sterilization as a treatment for medical illness.

Restraints and Seclusion

It is needed only when:

1. It is the only means available to prevent immediate harm to the person or to others, and
2. It is authorised by the psychiatrist in charge

- The Nominated Representative should be informed of restraint within 24 h, and concerned Board monthly.
- He shall be kept in a place where he can cause no harm to himself or others.

Offences and Penalties

Any doctor knowingly serves in mental health establishment not registered under this Act will be fined ₹25,000.

Anyone contravening any of the provisions/rule/regulation is to be punished:

- First contravention— imprisonment up to 6 months with/without fine up to ₹10,000.
- For any subsequent contravention—imprisonment up to 2 years with/without fine ₹50,000 to ₹5 lakhs.

SHORT NOTES

1. Hallucination. (Sardar Patel University, Gujarat supple 2018) (North Eastern Hill University, Shillong supple 2018) (Uttarakhand University 2016, 2015) (Rajasthan University 2015) (Rajiv Gandhi University, Bengaluru 2015) (Sher-i-Kashmir, Srinagar supple 2015) (VNS, Gujarat 2017)

Ans:

a. Hallucination is false perception by senses without any external object or stimulus.
b. Seen in insanity, high fever, drug intoxication and during withdrawal from drug addiction.

c. **Types**

Auditory hallucination	• False perception of sound (noises, music) without any source, e.g., hearing sound when there is none. • Seen in schizophrenia • Most common hallucinations
Visual hallucination	• Patient observes something without anything being present. • Seen in delirium tremens
Olfactory hallucination	• False sense of smell (pleasant/unpleasant) without any source. • Seen in medical disorders (temporal lobe), schizophrenia
Gustatory hallucination	• Patient experiences different tastes (sweet/bitter/sour) without any food or drink. • Seen in temporal lobe epilepsy
Tactile hallucination (touch)	• Patient experiences crawling of insects/rats over his body. • Seen in cocainism, schizophrenia

d. **MLI:** Hallucinations are not under voluntary control and a person will not be responsible if he is incited to commit homicide.

2. Illusion (North Eastern Hill University, Shillong Supple 2019) (Rajiv Gandhi University, Bengaluru 2018, 2015) (BFUHS, Punjab Supple 2018)

Ans:

a. Illusion is a false interpretation by the senses of an external object or stimulus which has a real existence.

b. **Types**

Universal illusions	• Found in all individuals and same for all individuals • For example, the rail tracks appear to be converging to all of us.
Personal illusions	• Differ from individual to individual • For example, a person sees a dog and mistakes it for lion, or imagines a string hanging in his room to be snake.

c. A sane person may experience illusion, but can correct the false impressions. An insane person continues to believe in the illusions, even though the real facts are clearly pointed out.

3. Doctrine of Diminished Responsibility. (Adesh, Bathinda supple 2020)

Ans: The Doctrine of Diminished Responsibility was introduced in UK as a defence to murder. If this defence is established, it will entitle the offender to be found guilty of manslaughter (culpable homicide) instead of murder and will be given a lesser punishment. It states that:

a. Where a person kills someone or is a party to killing, he will not be guilty of murder if he was suffering from some abnormality of mind and is mentally incapable of taking responsibility for his acts.

b. A person who would be liable under this section, whether as a principal or as an accessory, will be convicted of manslaughter instead of being convicted of murder.

In order to prove he was suffering from diminished responsibility a defendant must show:

1. He was suffering from an abnormality of mental functioning;
2. From a recognised medical condition;
3. Which substantially impaired his ability to understand his conduct, form a rational judgment or exercise self-control;
4. Which provides an explanation for being party to the killing.

4. Lucid interval (West Bengal University 2017) (Andhra Pradesh Supple 2015) (VNS, Gujarat 2019) (GMC, Chamba 2019)

Ans:

Lucid interval is seen in two conditions:

1. Insanity
2. Head injury

	Lucid interval in insanity	Lucid interval in head injury
Definition	It's a period between two episodes of mental illness in which all the signs and symptoms of mental illness completely disappears (i.e., the person behaves normally)	Period of consciousness between two phases of unconsciousness
History	Of insanity	Of trauma
Seen in	Bipolar disorders	Head injury (EDH)
MLI	Person is responsible for all his civil and criminal acts performed during this period of lucid interval	If a patient in lucid interval approaches a doctor and the doctor without examining him properly discharges him, the doctor may be sued for negligence if the patient dies due to complications

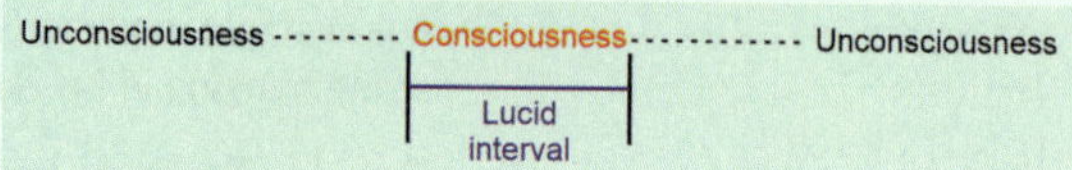

5. Marriage contract with an insane person is not valid. (West Bengal University 2019)

Ans:

a. As per Hindu Marriage Act, if one of the parties at the time of ceremony was suffering from mental illness, then the marriage is not valid and is considered null and void.
b. But insanity occurring after marriage is not the ground for divorce, but at times when any of the partners become insane after marriage, then the other sane person can demand a divorce provided that the insanity is seen to be incurable, even after his continuous treatment for a period of more than 3 yrs.
c. As per Muslim Marriages Act, a woman can obtain divorce on ground of husband's insanity within 2 years of marriage.

6. Impulse. (BFUHS, Punjab supple 2020) (AIIMS Patna 2018) (Adesh, Bathinda Supple 2018) (Andhra Pradesh supple 2016) (VNS, Gujarat 2017)

Ans:

Definition

Impulse is an uncontrolled, sudden and irresistible urge which compels the person to conscious performance of an act. A sane person is capable of controlling an impulse, but an insane person cannot.

Diagnosis of Impulsive Control Disorder

- Failure to resist the impulse, which is harmful to self or others
- Before the act—feeling of increased tension
- After performing it—person has sense of relief and finally feels guilty

Types

Kleptomania	An irresistible desire to steal articles of low value
Pyromania	Impulse to set the things on fire
Oniomania	Impulse of shopping
Dipsomania	An excessive desire to drink alcohol
Mutilomania	A desire to maim animals

7. Legal test of insanity (Rajasthan University 2018)

Ans:

The legal test of insanity is also known as the **'Right or Wrong' test**.

Under this test, a person is not criminally responsible, if at the time of the crime, he did not know the nature of the act or that it was wrong. It has the following requirements:

i. There should be evidence of mental disease.
ii. This mental disease or defect must exist at the time of commission of crime.
iii. It should be of such degree that the person is unable to understand that the act is wrong and/or contrary to the law.

It means if a person accused of a crime is found to be a normal, sound person, he will be punished. But if a person is found to be mentally ill, then the person is not punished.

8. Phobia (AIIMS Patna 2016)

Ans:

Definition

Phobia is morbid and irrational fear in the presence of stimulus and person tries to avoid the situation.

Types

Agoraphobia	Social phobia	Specific (simple) phobia
Morbid fear of places from which escape is difficult	• Fear of socially demanding situations • Fear of embarrassment	• Strong, persistent and irrational fear of an object or situation • Most common type of phobia
E.g., Crowd, market, stores	E.g., Stage fear, public speaking	E.g., Claustrophobia, hydrophobia, zoophobia

9. Testamentary capacity (SGRD, Amritsar 2019) (North Eastern Hill University, Shillong 2019, Supple 2017) (University of Health Sciences, Rohtak 2017) (Pondicherry 2017) (Delhi University Supple 2016) (KHMS, Tamil Nadu 2015) (West Bengal University 2017) (Rajiv Gandhi University, Bengaluru 2015)

Ans:

Testamentary capacity is the capacity of a person to make a valid will. The law defines it as the possession of a sound disposing mind (compos mentis) which must be certified by a doctor.

a. **Will made by mentally ill person:** Considered invalid because mentally ill person does not have the capacity to make a valid will.
b. **Will made in lucid interval:** Considered valid because in lucid interval the person is normal (i.e., of sound mind) and is able to judge and foresee the consequences of his acts.
c. **Will made by drunk person, or under insane delusions:** Invalid as the testator is incapable of understanding the nature and consequences of his own judgements.

Salient features of a valid will

1. Should be executed by a testator
2. Should be sound mind
3. Should be major (age ≥18 years)
4. Should be signed by testator in the presence of at least two witnesses

10. Responsibility of Mentally Ill person (Rajiv Gandhi University, Bengaluru 2020) (Sardar Patel University, Gujarat 2020) (KHMS, Tamil Nadu 2018) (BFUHS, Punjab 2017, 2016) (Himachal Pradesh 2017) (Pondicherry 2019, 2016, 2015) (Andhra Pradesh 2015) (GMC, Chandigarh 2015) (JIPMER supple 2018)

Ans: Refer to long question no. 1.

11. Delusions (Adesh, Bathinda Supple 2019) (West Bengal University Supple 2019) (University of Health Sciences, Rohtak 2019, Supple 2020) (AIIMS Patna 2019, 2017, 2015) (Uttarakhand University Supple 2017) (KHMS, Tamil Nadu 2016, supple 2019) (Rajasthan University 2017) (Sardar Patel University, Gujarat 2018, 2016) (Rajiv Gandhi University, Bengaluru 2015) (Delhi University 2016) (North Eastern Hill University, Shillong 2017, 2015) (Rajiv Gandhi University, Bengaluru 2015) (VNS, Gujarat supple 2019)

Ans: Refer to long question no. 3.

12. McNaughton's rule/ Section 84 IPC (KHMS, Tamil Nadu Supple 2020) (Adesh, Bathinda 2019) (BFUHS, Punjab Supple 2019) (Sher-i-Kashmir, Srinagar Supple 2017) (Delhi University Supple 2016) (Sardar Patel University Supple 2015) (Uttarakhand University 2016) (VNS, Gujarat 2017)

Ans: Refer to long question no. 1.

13. Feigned insanity (KHMS, Tamil Nadu Supple 2020) (Adesh, Bathinda 2018)

Ans: Refer to long question no. 1.

14. Restraint of insane (Pondicherry Supple 2017) (JIPMER 2016)

Ans: Refer to long question no. 4.

15. Types of Mental Disorders (Rajiv Gandhi University, Bengaluru 2015)

Ans: Refer to long question no. 3.

DIFFERENTIATIONS

1. True insanity and False insanity (West Bengal University 2019) (Delhi University 2018) (Rajasthan University 2017) (Adesh University, Bathinda Supple 2017) (University of Health Sciences, Rohtak 2017) (Uttarakhand University 2016)

Ans:

	True Insanity	False Insanity
Onset of disease	Gradual/slow	Sudden
Predisposing factor	Usually present, h/o insanity	Absent
Motive	Absent	Present (h/o crime)
Facial expression	Peculiar vacant/agitated look	Normal/exaggerated
Fatigue on exertion	Does not get fatigue	Easily fatigued
Insomnia	Present	Absent
Dressing up	Poorly dressed/ careless	Reasonably dressed up
Habits	Dirty and filthy	No ill habits
Whether examining or not	Features always present	Features exaggerate on examination
Repeated examination	Not worried	Resists

2. Psychosis and Neurosis (Adesh University, Bathinda 2019) (West Bengal University 2018)

Ans:

	Psychosis	Neurosis
Insight	Absent	Present
Empathy	-do-	-do-
Delusions/hallucinations	Present	Absent
Dealing with reality	Impaired	Preserved
Behavior	Not within socially acceptable norms	Within acceptable norms
Examples	Schizophrenia	Anxiety, phobia

3. Delusion and hallucination. (Uttarakhand Supple 2018)

Ans:

	Delusion	Hallucination
Definition	False but firm belief in something which is not a fact despite proof to the contrary	False sense of perception without any external stimulus
Disorder	Content of thought	Perception
Seen in	Schizophrenia Depression Mania Alcohol dependence	Schizophrenia Organic mental disorder Cocaine, cannabis, LSD intoxication

4. Illusion and delusion. (BFUHS, Punjab Supple 2019)

Ans:

	Illusion	Delusion
Definition	False interpretation of external object which has real existence	False but firm belief in something which is not a fact despite proof to the contrary
Stimulus	External, explicit and distinct	Internal, not clear and within the person
Nature	Universally experienced by all	Personal experience
Situation	Can happen in normal state of mind	Happens in abnormal condition (schizophrenia, mania)

CHAPTER

8 Toxicology

LONG QUESTIONS

1. What are the legal responsibilities of a doctor in a suspected case of poisoning? (Adesh, Bathinda Supple 2020) (Pondicherry supple 2018) (North Eastern Hill University, Shillong supple 2020) (VNS, Gujarat 2018)

Ans:

Legal Duties of a Doctor in Suspected Case of Poisoning

1. It is the duty of the doctor to inform the police in all cases **(in case of government medical officer)**.
2. In case of **private medical practitioner:** He should inform police/magistrate only in case of **homicidal poisoning**:
    - But he is not bound to inform police in case of suicidal/accidental poisoning (but should inform all cases for his safety).
3. If doctor does not inform the police, he will be punished under **Sec. 176 IPC.**
4. Note the preliminary particulars of the patient (name, identification marks, age, sex, occupation, etc.)
5. History—he should take proper history of poisoning, if it is suicidal, homicidal or accidental and how much quantity taken.
6. He should inform his senior doctor about the case.
7. Collection of evidence—the doctor should collect gastric lavage, food, vomitus, blood, urine, feces and preserve and then seal it properly and then send it for chemical analysis in FSL.
    - Failure to do so is punishable under **Sec. 201 IPC** (destruction of evidence).
8. He should prepare MLC report with consent.
9. If condition of patient is serious and about to die, he should make arrangements for Dying Declaration.
10. In case the patient dies, he should not issue Death Certificate but instead send the body for PM examination.
11. Any opinion regarding the nature of poison should be given only after getting the report from FSL.

2. Classify poisons and write briefly about barbiturate poisoning. (Rajiv Gandhi University, Bengaluru 2020)

Ans:

Classification of Poisons

1. Corrosives	a. Strong acids	i. Mineral acids—HCl, HNO_3, H_2SO_4 ii. Organic acid—oxalic acid, carbolic acid
	b. Strong alkalis	NaOH, KOH, NH_4OH
	c. Metallic salts	Zinc chloride, Ferric chloride
2. Irritants	a. Inorganic	i. Metallic—As, Pb, Hg, Cu ii. Nonmetallic—phosphorus, iodine
	b. Organic	i. Plants—*Abrus precatorius*, castor ii. Animals—snakes, scorpions
	c. Mechanical	Powdered glass, diamond dust
3. Neurotics	a. Cerebral	**S**: Somniferous—opium **I** : Inebriants—alcohol **D**: Deliriants—dhatura, cocaine, cannabis
	b. Spinal	Strychnine
	c. Peripheral	Curare
4. Cardiac	Digitalis, Oleander, Aconite, Hydrocyanic acid	
5. Asphyxiants	CO, H_2S, CO_2	
6. Miscellaneous	a. Agrochemicals	

Pesticides	Fumigants	Herbicides	Rodenticides
• OPC • Carbamates	• Alphos	• Paraquat	• Thallium sulfate • Zinc phosphide

b. Drugs of dependence—antidepressants, hallucinogens
c. Petroleum products—kerosene, petrol
d. Food poisoning—bacterial, chemical

(Mnemonic—**CINCAM**)

BARBITURATE POISONING

Clinical Features

1. CNS depression	• Drowsiness, delirium, excitement, hallucinations, ataxia, • Coma with positive Babinski sign, loss of superficial and deep reflexes
2. Respiratory system	• **Respiratory centres are depressed** leading to rapid and shallow, or slow and laboured breathing
3. CVS	• **Cardiac output decreased** leading to hypotensive shock, cyanosis, bradycardia
4. GIT system	• In comatose patient – **Absence of Bowel sounds** (bad prognosis)
5. Renal system	• Urine is scanty and suppressed • Contains albumin and sugar
6. Skin	• **Barbiturate blisters**
7. Body temperature	• Decreased (hypothermia) • Fever—in case of bronchopneumonia

(**Mnemonic**—when a person goes to BAR, he enjoys and feels relaxed. So all his functions are reduced like CNS depressed, CO reduced, GIT activity reduced, Resp. reduced, urine decreased and body temperature decreased)

Management

1. Maintain airway, breathing and circulation (ABC)
2. Gastric lavage is done with 1:1000 $KMnO_4$ solution and activated charcoal
3. **Elimination by Forced Alkaline Diuresis**—by use of sodium bicarbonate in 5% dextrose IV slowly
4. Antibiotics to prevent bronchopneumonia
5. **Scandinavian method** (combination of 1+2+3+4 steps)
6. Hemodialysis
7. Exchange transfusion
8. Supportive care.

PM Findings

External findings	Internal findings
1. Signs of asphyxia	• Lungs—congested and edematous
2. Cyanosis	• Stomach—hemorrhagic, congestion and erosion of mucosa
3. Barbiturate blisters	• Kidneys—degeneration of convulated tubules
4. Froth at nose and mouth	

3. Define and classify poisons. Discuss the various methods for removal of absorbed poison from a patient. (BFUHS, Punjab 2020)

Ans:

Definition of Poison

Any substance in any form (solid, liquid, gas) which if introduced into the body through any route (ingestion, injection, inhalation, contact) will produce ill health or death by its local or constitutional effects or both.

Classification of Poison

Refer to long question no. 2.

Methods for Removal of Absorbed Poison from Patient

1. Forced diuresis by urine alkalinisation	• Urine is made alkaline by use of sodium bicarbonate • Helps in promoting excretion of acidic drugs through urine • Done in salicylate, barbiturate poisoning
2. Forced diuresis by urine acidification	• Urine is made acidic by use of ammonium chloride • Helps in promoting excretion of alkaline drugs through urine • Done in poisoning/overdose of amphetamines, quinine, TCA
3. Whole bowel irrigation	Refer to short note no. 4.
4. Hemodialysis	• Hemodialysis is done in: (Mnemonic—**LABS**) **L:** Lithium **A:** Alcohol **B:** Barbiturates **S:** Salicylates
5. Hemoperfusion	• Blood is circulated extracorporeally from an arterial source through a filter filled with activated charcoal and then back to patient's venous blood • Done in case of poisoning due to caffeine, barbiturates, mushroom
6. Diaphoretics	• Increases excretion of drugs by increasing perspiration • Leading to increased excretion of toxic agents
7. Exchange transfusion	• This involves slowly removing the poisoned patient's blood and replacing it with fresh donor blood or plasma, useful if antidote is not available.

4. Describe the scientific name, active principle, signs and symptoms, medicolegal significance/aspects, postmortem findings and treatment in a case of Dhatura poisoning. (Sher-i- Kashmir Institute, Srinagar, 2020) (Himachal Pradesh,2017) (North Eastern Hill University, Shillong 2019) (Sai Tirupati University, Rajasthan, 2018) (VNS, Gujarat supple 2019)

Give the active principles and fatal dose of Dhatura. Enumerate the 10 Ds of Dhatura poisoning. (BFUHS, Punjab Supple 2019)

A person, whose belongings were stolen, found in semiconscious state in train with high fever, flushed face and dry mouth. On examination pupil was dilated. How will you diagnose and manage the case? (AIIMS Patna 2019, 2018, 2017)

Ans:

Scientific name: *Datura stramonium*

Common name: Thorn apple, Jimson weed, Devil's trumpet

Active principles

1. Hyoscine
2. Hyoscynamide
3. Atropine

Fatal dose

- 80–120 seeds
- Stupefying dose: 40–60 seeds

Signs and Symptoms (10 Ds)

1. Dryness of mouth
2. Dysphagia—difficulty in swallowing
3. Dysarthria—difficulty in talking
4. Dilatation of cutaneous blood vessels (redness, flushing of face)
5. Dry hot skin (increase in temperature—fever)
6. Drunken gait
7. Diplopia—due to dilated pupil (mydriasis)
8. Drowsiness
9. Delirium, may show **pill-rolling movements** or pulls imaginary threads from clothes
10. Dysuria due to retention of urine

Diagnosis

1. **Mydriatic test:** A drop of the suspected specimen is instilled in the eyes of the rabbit resulting in dilation of pupils
2. **Pilocarpine test**
   - Instil 2–3 drops of 1% pilocarpine in patient's eye
   - If no constriction of pupil, suggests Dhatura poisoning
3. Atropine can be detected by Radioimmunoassay.

Treatment

1. Maintain airway, breathing and circulation (ABC)
2. Give emetics
3. Perform gastric lavage with tannic acid, $KMnO_4$ or activated charcoal
4. Physiological antidote

   Physostigmine is the antidote of choice as it can cross BBB

   Dose: 0.5–1 mg slow IV over 5 min with ECG monitoring
5. Purgatives and colonic lavage is done
6. Cold sponging—to control high temperature
7. IV Diazepam—for sedation and seizures
8. Short acting barbiturates—to control delirium
9. Catheterization in case of urinary retention/dysuria.

PM Findings

External	Internal
Show signs of asphyxia	• GIT—inflamed mucosa containing seeds and its fragments • Lungs—edematous and congested • Brain—edematous and congested • Other organs—edematous and congested

MLI:

1. **Rail-road poison:** It is mostly used by criminals as stupefying agent for the purpose of robbery, rape, etc. Therefore also called rail-road poison.
2. Used as abortifacient
3. Accidental poisoning in case of children
4. Resists putrefaction
5. Used as an adulterant in country liquor to enhance kick effect
6. Used in Chinese herbal medicines to treat asthma.

5. Define stupefying agents. Describe clinical features and management of acute Dhatura poisoning. (Delhi University, 2017)

Ans:

Definition of Stupefying Agents

- Substances which are used to daze a victim or putting the victim in state of drowsiness or unconsciousness.
- It is used by criminals for the purpose of robbery, kidnapping or rape during travel in bus, train and railway station. It is usually mixed with food or drink.

Clinical Features and Management of Dhatura Poisoning

Refer to long question no. 4.

6. Classify the organophosphorous compounds. Describe the signs and symptoms, management and medico-legal duties in case of organophosphorous poisoning. (North Eastern Hill University, Shillong 2018, Supple, 2019) (Sardar Patel University, Gujarat 2020-19) (North Eastern Hill University, Shillong 2015) (Sher-i-Kashmir Institute, Srinagar 2015, Supple 2017) (Rajiv Gandhi University, Bengaluru 2017, Supple 2015) (West Bengal University 2017) (VNS, Gujarat 2018)

A patient came in the emergency with the complaints of diarrhoea, vomiting, dyspnea, incontinence of urine after working in agriculture field. On examination, there is constricted pupil and crepitation in chest. How will you diagnose and manage the case? (AIIMS Patna 2018, 2015)

A 35 years old farmer brought to your hospital with alleged history of ingestion of an unknown poisonous substance. Patient has excessive salivation, lacrimation, urination, defecation and gastric emesis. On examination, constricted pupils were found contracted. (Sardar Patel University, Gujarat Supple 2016)

a. What is the most likely diagnosis with reason?
b. Which investigations will support your diagnosis?
c. Describe treatment of this poisoning in detail.

Ans:

Classification of OPC Poisoning

On the basis of chemical composition	On the basis of toxicity
1. Alkyl phosphates • **H**ETP • **O**MPA • **T**EPP • **Mala**thion (Mnemonic—**HOT MALA**) 2. Aryl Phosphates • **D**iazinon (Tik-20) • **C**hlorthion • **P**arathion (Mnemonic—**DCP**)	1. Agricultural insecticides • TEPP • Parathion 2. Animal insecticides • Trichloroform • Ronnel 3. Household insecticides • Malathion • Tik-20

Signs and Symptoms in Case of OPC Poisoning

Muscarinic symptoms	Nicotinic symptoms	CNS symptoms
1. **S**alivation	1. Muscle fasciculation	1. **M**uscle weakness
2. **L**acrimation- Red Tears (rare)	2. Weakness of muscles	2. **A**nxiety
3. **U**rinary incontinence	3. Mydriasis	3. **D**epression
4. **D**iarrhea	4. Tachycardia	4. **R**estlessness
5. **G**IT distress	5. Hypertension	5. **A**taxia
6. **E**mesis		6. **T**remors
7. **S**pasm of bronchial muscles		(Mnemonic—**MAD-RAT**)
8. **O**thers: **P**inpoint pupil/**C**onstricted pupil (Mnemonic—**SLUDGES** in **OPC**)		

Lab Diagnosis

1. **Acetylcholinesterase** level in RBCs and plasma is decreased
   In acute poisoning, signs and symptoms generally occur when >50% of cholinesterase is inhibited
2. Liquid gas chromatography—to detect OPC in blood
3. P-nitrophenol test—in case of parathion poisoning

Treatment

1. Maintain airway, breathing and circulation (ABC)
2. Patient is removed from the source of contamination and
3. Remove clothes and wash body with soap and water—for decontamination
4. Perform gastric lavage with 1:5000 $KMnO_4$
5. Start **Atropine**

Atropine acts as an antidote for OPC and carbamate poisoning
MOA: Atropine acts by blocking Muscarinic receptors, and no action on Nicotinic receptors, therefore reversing Muscarinic manifestations but no effect on Nicotinic manifestations
Dose: 2–4 mg IV repeated after every 5 minutes till signs of Atropinization develops and then dose is adjusted to maintain it for at least 24 hrs.

6. Acetylcholinesterase reactivators—**oximes** are used to counter Nicotinic effects
   a. Pralidoxime (PAM)
   b. Diacetyl monoxime (DAM)
      - Effective only in case of OPC poisoning
      - But contraindicated in carbamate poisoning

MOA:
1. Oximes bind to anionic site of AChE and forms a bond with OPC which is already present/bound to esteric site of AChE
2. A strong bond is formed between OPC and oximes
3. Ultimately, OPC is removed from esteric site and reactivation of AChE

7. IV diazepam—to control seizures and muscle fasciculations
8. Supportive measurement

Medico-legal Duties in Case of OPC Poisoning

Refer to long question no. 1.

MLI:
1. Hospitalizing all symptomatic patients for at least 4–6 days following resolution of symptoms is needed, because of the risk of development of respiratory depression or intermediate syndrome after resolution of acute symptoms.
2. Symptoms of OPC poisoning can imitate other toxidromes and diseases. The clinician must keep in mind that misdiagnosis may occur.

3. Accidental and occupational poisoning occurs in manufacturers, packers, sprayers and in children.
4. Suicidal poisoning is common in India, both in rural and urban areas.

7. Write clinical features and management in case of accidental ingestion of parathion. What are the precautions to be taken to minimize occupational exposure? (West Bengal University 2017)

Ans:

Clinical Features and Management

Refer to long question no. 6.

Precautions to be Taken to Minimize Occupational Hazard

Occupational exposure occurs in workers involved in the manufacture of pesticides, users (e.g., exterminators of house pests), farmers and professional applicators of pesticides. Pesticide application in confined areas (e.g., green houses) also contributes to high potential for exposure through inhalation.

1. Farmers' exposure to pesticides can be reduced through less use of pesticides through alternative cropping systems (like use of natural processes) that are less dependent on pesticides.
2. Use of personal protective equipment (PPE) can be used to decrease dermal exposure. Gloves, boots, hats, long sleeve shirts, and chemical-resistant coveralls are among the most common types of PPE.
   a. The use of gloves and boots are the minimum PPE for most pesticide products.
   b. Wearing gloves has been found to be the most effective protection method.
   c. Protection is better by waterproof polypropylene fabrics compared with cotton garments.
3. Proper protection of the eyes should also be used when there is a chance of exposure to spray or dusts. Protective goggles should be used.
4. Respirators and gas masks provide protection from respiratory exposure.
5. One should not re-enter areas of application until after proper interval of time.

Doctor and nurses should be protected with water-impermeable gowns, masks with eyeshields, and use double gloves while handling the patient.

8. Classify poisons. Discuss clinical features, management and postmortem findings in acute organophosphate poisoning. What viscera shall you preserve in such cases? (Delhi University 2019)

Ans:

Classification of poisons: Refer to long question no 2.

Clinical features and management: Refer to long question no 6.

PM Findings in Case of OPC Poisoning

External	Internal
1. Smell of kerosene from nostrils and mouth	1. GIT— congested
2. Signs of asphyxia—congestion of face, cyanosis of lips, nails and mucous membrane	2. Lungs—congested and edematous
3. Blood tinged froth coming out of mouth and nostrils	3. Brain—congested and edematous
	4. Other viscera—congested and edematous

Viscera preservation in OPC poisoning: Refer to short note no 18.

9. Name the major type of poisonous snakes in India. Describe the signs, symptoms and treatment of snakebite case. (North Eastern Hill University, Shillong 2016, Supple 2020) (VNS, Gujarat 2017)

Ans:

In India, the major types of poisonous snakes are—common cobra, common krait, Russell's viper and saw-scaled viper.

Signs and Symptoms

Cobra venom produces both convulsions and paralysis, while krait causes only paralysis. Whereas hemorrhage from external orifices is seen in viperine bite.

- Puncture marks at the site bite
- Severe pain and tenderness at the site
- Nausea, vomiting, or diarrhea
- Labored breathing
- Rapid heart rate, weak pulse

Neurotoxic (cobra/krait)	Vasculotoxic
• Local necrosis causes 'wet gangrene' with a characteristic putrid smell.	• Redness, swelling, bruising, bleeding, or blistering around the bite
• Drooping of head, lower lip and eyelids with blurring of vision.	• Local necrosis is extensive which lead to dry gangrene,
• Increased salivation and sweating.	• More local reaction is seen along with pain and oozing
• Numbness or tingling around face, speech is affected, tongue paralyzed.	• Serous and serosanguineous blisters seen.
• Muscles of the extremities become weak. Paralysis of limbs, and respiratory muscles.	• Bilateral parotid swelling ('viper head').
	• Petechial hemorrhages, epistaxis, hemoptysis, hematuria,
	• Acute renal failure, hypotension

[Mnemonic (elapid bites)
5Ds—Dyspnea, Dysphonia, Dysarthria, Diplopia, Dysphagia
2Ps—Ptosis, Paralysis]

Treatment

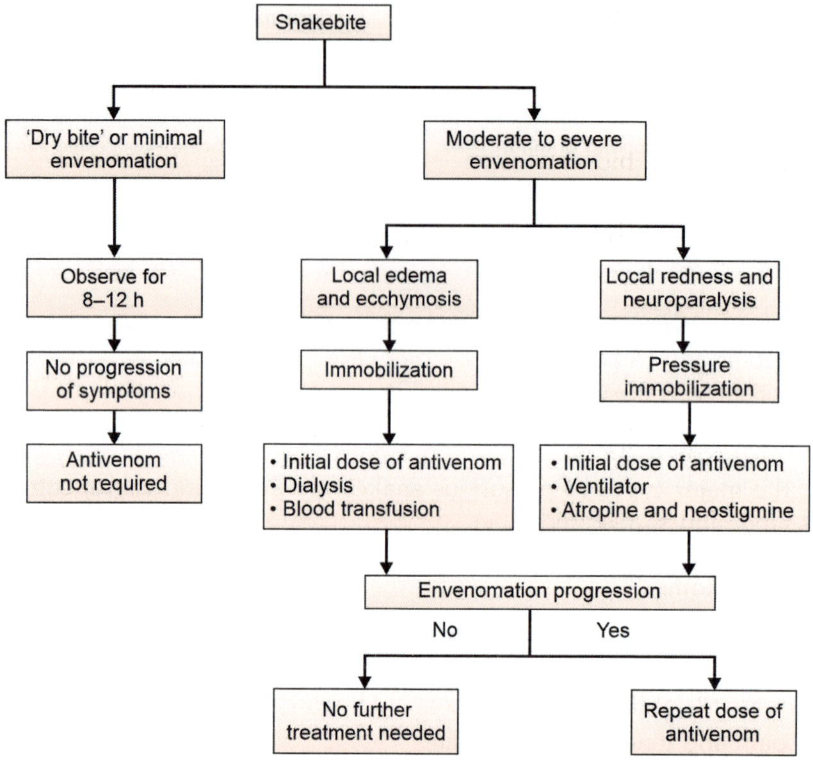

Prevention of Spread of Venom (First aid)

Dos	Don'ts
• Lay or sit down with the bite in a neutral position of comfort. • Remove rings and watches in anticipation of swelling. • Wash the bite with soap and water. • Cover the bite with a clean, dry dressing. • Pressure immobilization technique can be used for elapid bites.	• Do not apply a tourniquet. • Do not manipulate the wound. • Do not suck out the venom. • Do not apply ice or immerse the wound in water. • Do not drink alcohol as a painkiller. • Do not take pain relievers (aspirin, ibuprofen, etc.). • Do not apply electric shock.

Antisnake Venom (ASV)

1. Antivenom is indicated for patients with clinical manifestations with moderate to severe envenomation.
2. The freeze dried **polyvalent antisnake venom (ASV)** serum available in India is effective against common venomous snakes (cobra, common krait, saw-scaled viper and Russell's viper).
3. It is less potent, less immunogenic and less effective than monovalent, and has more adverse effects.

4. **Dose:** Freeze-dried antivenom serum is dissolved in water. About 80–100 mL serum should be diluted in 200–500 mL of isotonic saline and given slow IV.
5. The recommended initial dose of ASV is 8–10 vials administered slowly via IV route over a period of 1 h.

Supportive Treatment

a. Broad spectrum antibiotics.
b. Tetanus toxoid.
c. **Surgical excision:** Early surgical intervention is done to prevent extension of infection and development of gangrene.
d.

Neurotoxic bite	Vasculotoxic bite
• Patient is nursed in lateral position, and salivation cleaned to prevent aspiration. • Endotracheal intubation, O_2 supplementation and tracheostomy. • Atropine followed by neostigamine is given IV.	• Fluid resuscitation (for hypotension) with NS, Ringer's lactate, 5% albumin, fresh whole blood or FFP. Dopamine can be given. • Rehydration, diuretics or dopamine in oliguria. • Hemodialysis in acute renal failure. • Fresh blood, FFP or platelet concentrates for coagulopathy.

10. A male patient is brought to emergency with history of snakebite. Examination revealed two pinpoint puncture wounds over dorsum of right foot with oozing of blood and edema around. How will you confirm your diagnosis that it was vasculotoxic snakebite? Write in short management of vasculotoxic and neurotoxic snakebite. (West Bengal University 2018)

Ans:

Confirmation of Vasculotoxic Bite (Viperine)

20 min whole blood clotting test (20 WBCT)

1. Place a few ml of venous blood in a clean, dry, glass tube/bottle.
2. Leave it undisturbed for 20 min at room temperature.
3. Tip the tube once.
4. If the blood is still unclotted and runs out, the patient has hypofibrinogenemia ('incoagulable blood') due to venom-induced consumption coagulopathy.
   A normal 20 WBCT and clot lysis would exclude viperidae species.

Management of of Vasculotoxic and Neurotoxic Snakebite

Refer to long question no. 9.

11. Which poison is commonly known as 'road side poison'? Describe clinical feature of that poison. (West Bengal University 2018)

Ans: Refer to long question no. 4.

12. Discuss in detail mechanism, signs and symptoms, fatal dose, fatal period, treatment and postmortem findings in case of cyanide poisoning or hydrocyanic acid poisoning. (Adesh, Bathinda 2019, 2018) (Rajiv Gandhi University, Bengaluru 2018) (Pondicherry Supple 2017)

Ans:

MOA (in sequence)

1. Cyanide inhibits enzyme cytochrome oxidase/complex IV
2. Cyanide reacts with cytochrome oxidase to form cytochrome-oxidase-cyanide complex
3. Blocking the final step of oxidative phosphorylation and preventing ATP formation
4. So arrest in aerobic resp. results in histotoxic hypoxia
5. Blood is saturated with O_2 and there is O_2 supply at tissue level but tissues are not able to utilize O_2
6. Hence, conversion of pyruvate into lactate resulting in lactic acidosis

Fatal dose

- HCN: 50–60 mg
- NaCN/KCN: 200–300 mg

Fatal period

- HCN: 2–10 min
- NaCN/KCN: 30 min

Signs and Symptoms

GIT	Burning taste, throat constriction and numbness, salivation, froth at mouth and nostrils
CNS	Headache, vertigo, dizziness, coma, anxiety
CVS	Initially, hypertension with reflex bradycardia. Later, hypotension with reflex tachycardia
RS	Initially, tachypnea and dyspnea. Later, respiratory depression. Smell of bitter almond in breadth
Eyes	Prominent eyes. Pupils dilated.

Treatment

1. **Stabilization of patient:** Maintain airway, breathing and circulation (ABC) by using assisted ventilation, 100% oxygen and cardiac monitoring.
2. **Decontamination:** Remove the person from the source of poisoning. Remove clothing, brush off any powder from the skin and flush the skin with water.
3. **In case of ingestion:** Gastric lavage is done with 5–10% solution of sodium thiosulfate, followed by potassium carbonate to form Prussian blue which is inert. Activated charcoal is ineffective (because of low binding of cyanide)
4. **Antidotal therapy:** An antidote kit comprises:
   i. Amyl nitrite
   ii. Sodium nitrite

iii. Sodium thiosulfate

1st step: 0.3 ml ampoule of amyl nitrite pearl is broken in a gauze and the victim is made to inhale for 30 secs, every minute, and use a new pearl every 3 min.
2nd step: 10 ml of 3% solution (300 mg) of sodium nitrite is injected IV slowly
3rd step: 50 ml of 25% solution (12.5 g) of sodium thiosulfate over 10–20 min, by the same needle.

Cytochrome oxidase + Cyanide ion → Cytochrome oxidase - Cyanide
↓
Sodium nitrite + Hb → MetHb ⟶ Cyano-Meth-Hb
Amyl nitrite

Sodium thiosulfate + Cyano-Meth-Hb ⟶ Sodium thiocyanate
(Nontoxic) (water soluble)

5. Hydroxycobalamine/Vitamin B_{12}—introduced by IV route.
   As it binds with cyanide to form cyanocobalamine
6. Dicobalt EDTA.

Postmortem Findings

External	Internal
1. PM staining—Bright red in color	1. Smell of bitter almonds on opening the body cavity
2. Froth coming out of mouth and nostrils	2. Oral/perioral erosions
3. Smell of bitter almonds from the body	3. Stomach—smell of bitter almonds
	4. Lungs—congested and edematous
	5. Other viscera—congested and edematous

13. Rohini, a 17-year-old girl was brought to the emergency in an unconscious state and convulsions with history of consumption of bitter almonds. What is your probable diagnosis? How does the almond become toxic in the body? How will you manage the condition of the patient? (West Bengal University supple 2019)

Ans:

- The probable diagnosis is cyanide poisoning.
- Bitter almonds contain cyanogenic glycoside amygdalin (harmless). Hydrogen cyanide is released when amygdalin undergoes enzymatic hydrolysis in GIT leading to poisoning. The toxicity of amygdalin is directly related to the release of HCN. The enzymes which catalyze the hydrolysis of amygdalin are supplied by the GI flora.

Management of the Condition (Cyanide Poisoning)

Refer to long question no. 12.

14. Classify irritant poisons. Discuss in detail signs and symptoms, fatal dose, fatal period, treatment and postmortem findings in case of ALPHOS poisoning. (Adesh, Bathinda Supple 2019) (Rajasthan University 2018)

Ans:

Classification of Irritants

Inorganic	1. Metallic—As, Pb, Hg, Cu 2. Nonmetallic—phosphorus, chlorine, iodine
Organic	1. Plants—*Abrus precatorius*, castor, croton, calotropis 2. Animals—snakes, scorpions, spiders
Mechanical	Powdered glass, diamond dust

ALPHOS POISONING

Signs and Symptoms

Due to inhalation	Due to ingestion
1. **Mild:** Mucous membrane irritation, headache, dizziness, resp. distress 2. **Moderate:** Ataxia, numbness, weakness, paralysis, tremors 3. **Severe:** ARDS, arrhythmias, CHF, Coma, convulsions	1. **GIT:** Epigastric pain, retrosternal pain, vomiting 2. **CVS:** Tachycardia and arrhythmias, shock 3. **RS:** Tachypnea, dyspnea, crepitations 4. **CNS:** Restlessness, altered sensorium, convulsions 5. **Hepatobiliary system:** Jaundice, hepatitis, fever

Fatal dose

- Ingestion: 1 tablet
- Inhalation: 400–600 ppm

Fatal period: 1 to 4 days

Treatment

1. In case of inhalation poisoning—remove the patient from source of contamination into an open area
2. Maintain airway, breathing and circulation (ABC)
3. **To reduce absorption of phosphine gas**
   - Perform gastric lavage with 1:10000 $KMnO_4$ and activated charcoal
   - Antacids and liquid paraffin can also be used
4. **To enhance excretion of phosphine gas**
   - IV fluids—to maintain adequate hydration and renal perfusion
   - Dialysis—in case of renal failure
5. **Treatment of shock**
   - IV fluids
   - Hydrocortisone
   - Low dose dopamine
   - Extracorporeal membrane oxygenation (ECMO)

6. **Treatment of metabolic acidosis**
   - IV sodium bicarbonate ($NaHCO_3$)
   - If fails to correct metabolic acidosis, then hemodialysis is done
7. **Treatment of arrhythmias and toxicity**
   - IV **$MgSO_4$** is used to correct hypomagnesemia and arrhythmias
   - Anti-arrhythmic agents.

PM Findings

1. Garlic odor from mouth and nostrils
2. Blood tinged froth from mouth and nostrils
3. Stomach—hemorrhage and ulcerations
4. Lungs—congested and edematous
5. All other viscera—congested and edematous.

15. Classify irritant poisons. Describe the clinical features of acute arsenic poisoning along with laboratory investigation. Add a note on the differences between arsenic poisoning simulating natural disease condition. (Sher-i-Kashmir Institute, Srinagar supple, 2019)

Describe the mechanism of action, signs, symptoms, management and postmortem findings in case of acute arsenic poisoning. (Adesh, Bathinda 2018)

Ans:

Classification of Irritant Poisons

Refer to long question no. 14.

For difference between arsenic poisoning and natural disease—refer to difference no. 5.

MOA—arsenic affects cellular respiration by binding to the PDH enzyme in mitochondria

- Inhibits the process of oxidative phosphorylation
- Reduced cellular ATPs
- Apoptosis of cells

Signs and Symptoms

GIT	Gastroenteric form of acute poisoning **(in sequence)** 1. Metallic taste, **burning pain in throat,** intense thirst, garlic odor in breadth 2. **Vomiting:** Profuse, projectile, dark brown in colour 3. **Purging:** Initially stools are bloody, but later becomes *rice watery* (as seen in cholera) 4. **Tenesmus,** pain around anus 5. Colicky abdominal pain
CVS	Hypotension, ARDS, week pulse, sunken eyes, arrhythmias
Renal	Painful micturition, oliguria and uremia
Skin	Delayed loss of hair, skin eruptions
Liver	Fatty degeneration

Lab Investigations

1. Urine: Excretion of >50 μg/L in 24 hrs urine is indicative of poisoning
2. Blood: 0.9 μg/dL
3. Hairs: 75 μg% of arsenic
4. Nails: 100 μg% of arsenic

Treatment

1. Maintain airway, breathing and circulation (ABC)
2. Perform gastric lavage with 1:5000 $KMnO_4$ to enhance elimination
3. Chelation therapy with BAL
   - Antidote of choice
   - Given IM only
   - Dose of BAL in case of severe cases is 3 mg/kg at

4 hourly	For first 2 days
6 hourly	For next 4 days
12 hourly	For next 6 days until full recovery

4. Whole bowel irrigation
5. Purgatives can be used to remove the unabsorbed poison from the body
6. IV fluids, sodium bicarbonate—to correct shock
7. Hemodialysis can be done.

PM Findings

External	Internal
1. Sunken eyeballs 2. Rigor mortis appears early 3. Delayed putrefaction 4. Emaciated look due to dehydration	1. Ulceration of mouth, pharynx and esophagous 2. Stomach • Mucosa: Swollen and edematous • **Red velvety appearance** 3. Lungs: Congested and edematous 4. Liver: Congested and edematous 5. Other viscera: Congested and edematous 6. Heart: Subendocardial petechial hemorrhages

16. A 34-year-old police officer with no previous relevant medical history suffers from crampy abdominal pain, intermittent nausea, occasional vomiting, and persistent diarrhea for several weeks in conjunction with muscular weakness to his lower legs and exfoliative rash on palmar surface of both hands and planter of both feet. (Pondicherry 2016)

a. What is the cause of this man's apparent gastroenteritis and why?
b. What are the other usual signs and symptoms?
c. What studies should be obtained when considering the diagnosis?
d. Which treatment modalities are used for this?
e. What is the medico-legal importance?
f. As a treating physician, what is your role in such case?

Mention briefly the symptoms, signs and management of a case of chronic arsenical salt poisoning due to consumption of water of well/tube well contaminated with arsenic salts present in the earth. (West Bengal University 2019) (VNS, Gujarat 2017)

Write clinical features and diagnosis tests of a case of chronic arsenic poisoning. How will you manage a case of acute arsenic poisoning? (Rajasthan University 2016)

Ans:

a. The cause of man's apparent gastroenteritis could be **Chronic Arsenic poisoning.**

b. **Clinical features (signs and symptoms)**

GIT	Nausea, vomiting, diarrhea, abdominal cramps
Skin	• **Rain drop pigmentation** • Bilateral **hyperkeratosis of palms and soles**
Hair	Alopecia, golden hair
Nails	**Aldrich-Mees line**—transverse white lines
Bone	• Bone marrow depression • Pancytopenia
Nerves	• Affects sensory nerves (mainly) • Peripheral neuropathy in glove and stocking pattern (i.e. numbness of hands and feet), polyneuritis, anesthesia.
Blood vessels	Vasospasm and thrombosis leading to development of **gangrene/Black Foot disease**

c. **Diagnosis**

1. **NAA** (Neutron Activation Analysis)
2. **AAS** (Atomic Absorption Spectrometry)
3. Take samples from the hair, nails and bone, soil (arsenic is imbibed from the surrounding soil after death)

Refer to long question no. 15 for other investigations.

d. **Treatment**

1. Remove the patient from source of exposure
2. BAL in usual doses
3. Vitamin B complex, mineral supplements
4. Symptomatic treatment

Management of a case of acute arsenic poisoning: Refer to long question no. 15.

e. **Medico-legal aspects**

1. **Homicide** was common because it is cheap, colorless, odourless, tasteless, easily obtainable, symptoms simulate those of cholera and onset of symptoms are gradual.
2. **Suicide** is rare.
3. **Accidental** death may be due to admixture with articles of food, or from its improper medicinal use.
4. Chronic poisoning results from drinking well water containing arsenic.

5. It is applied on abortion sticks to procure abortion.
6. It may be used as cattle poison.

f. **Duties of a doctor with regards to poisoning:** First of all, we should treat the patient. *For legal duties refer to long question no. 1.*

17. Classify poisons. Describe the signs, symptoms and treatment of a case of opium poisoning. (North Eastern Hill University, Shillong Supple 2018)

Ans:

Classification of Poisons

Refer to long question no. 2.

Signs and symptoms of opium poisoning can be classified into 3 stages: Triad of respiratory depression, pinpoint pupils and impairment of sensorium is characteristic of opium poisoning.

1. **Stage of Excitement:** Euphoria, feeling of well-being, freedom from anxiety, talkativeness and laughter. Hallucinations, flushed face, red eyes and rapid heart rate.
2. **Stage of Stupor:** Headache, nausea, vomiting, weakness, heaviness in limbs, giddiness, drowsiness, diminished sensibility and feeling of sleepiness. Pupils are contracted, and face and lips are cyanosed.
3. **Stage of Narcosis/Coma:** Patient passes into deep coma. Muscles are flaccid and relaxed, absent reflexes, congested conjunctiva, secretions are suspended except perspiration. Non-reacting, pinpoint pupils, hypotension, hypothermia, weak and feeble pulse, slow and steatorous respiration, coma.

   (Mnemonic—**ESpN**)

Treatment

1. Support vitals through respirator and other emergency procedures (ABC).
2. Stomach wash with 1:5000 $KMnO_4$.
3. Activated charcoal—method of choice for decontamination following ingestion.
4. Enema with 30 g of sodium sulphate twice daily.
5. Whole-bowel irrigation in body packers.
6. **Naloxone** (dose of 0.4–2 mg IV/IM) repeated every 2–3 min, if no response occurs.

18. What is hooch tragedy? Write the signs, symptoms and management of methyl alcohol poisoning. (North Eastern Hill University, Shillong Supple 2017)

Discuss the clinical findings, management and medico-legal aspect of methyl alcohol poisoning. (Adesh, Bathinda Supple 2017, 2016) (North Eastern Hill University, Shillong supple 2016) (Delhi University, 2018)

Ans:

Hooch Tragedy

It is accidental consumption of liquor containing methyl alcohol by lower socioeconomic classes. Hooch is spurious alcoholic preparation. Outbreak of hooch tragedies especially in the villages and slum areas are common because the adulterated liquors are inexpensive and potent.

Signs and Symptoms (Clinical Findings)

GIT	Nausea, vomiting, cramps in abdomen, alcohol odor, dehydration.
Eyes	Pupils: Fixed and dilated. Photophobia, blurred or misty vision *(**snowfield vision**)*, scotoma, decreased light perception, diminution of visual fields causing *blindness due to optic neuritis and atrophy.*
CNS	Headache, dizziness, vertigo, restlessness, muscular weakness, hypothermia, delirium, amnesia, convulsion (terminal event), coma.
RS	Dyspnea, cyanosis, respiratory depression.
Renal	Acidosis, strongly acidic urine, scant urine.

Treatment

1. **Gastric lavage** is done with sodium bicarbonate solution to prevent absorption.
2. Sodium bicarbonate in 250 ml of water, 4 hourly orally to treat acidosis.
3. **Ethanol is given as competitive antagonist:** Dose 0.8–1 ml/kg orally of 95% ethanol in 200 ml of orange juice or 10 ml/ kg IV of 10% ethanol in D5W over 30 min.
4. **Antidote is 4-methylpyrazole (fomepizole):** Competitive inhibitor of alcohol dehydrogenase. It blocks the formation of formaldehyde and formic acid.
5. Calcium folinate IV, thiamine and pyridoxine may be given.
6. Eyes should be kept covered to protect them from light.
7. Hemodialysis in case of severe poisoning.
8. Symptomatic treatment.

19. Classify poison. Describe the signs, symptoms, complications, treatment and postmortem appearances of sulphuric acid. (Andhra Pradesh Supple, 2016)

Ans:

Classification of Poison

Refer to long question no. 1.

SULPHURIC ACID POISONING

Signs and Symptoms

1. Oropharyngeal burns (blackening) and pain in throat and epigastrium
2. Nausea and vomiting
3. Violent cough, dyspnea and glottic edema
4. Teeth become chalky white
5. Intense thirst, scanty urine
6. Swollen lips and tongue
7. Abdomen: Tender and distended
8. Constipation and tenesmus

Complications

1. Neurogenic shock
2. Perforation of stomach
3. Peritonitis
4. Septicemia
5. Septic shock
6. Glottic edema and asphyxia
7. Esophageal stricture
8. Renal failure

Treatment

1. Maintain airway, breathing and circulation (ABC)
2. In case of glottic edema—tracheostomy is recommended
3. Correct circulatory shock—by IV fluids, glucose
4. Gastric lavage is contraindicated
5. Milk/water should be given immediately to neutralize the acid
6. Avoid sodium bicarbonate
7. Start with steroids—to prevent inflammation and long-term complications
8. IV antibiotics—in case of perforation
9. Painkillers like morphine—to reduce pain
10. Symptomatic treatment
11. In case of skin burns—wash with large amount of water.

PM findings

External	Internal
• Erosion of skin, angles of mouth and lips • Chalky white appearance of teeth	• Corrosion of trachea and larynx • Blackish charring of stomach and thinning of stomach mucosa • Perforation of stomach • Toxic swelling of kidneys and liver

20. Classify poisons. Discuss the general principles of treatment of a case of poisoning. (BFUHS, Punjab 2015) (VNS, Gujarat 2016)

Ans:

Classification of Poison

Refer to long question no. 1.

General Principles of Treatment in Case of Poisoning (Treatment of Unknown Poisoning)

- **Immediate resuscitation of the patient and maintain**

A—Airway	Chin lift, suctioning of secretions to clear airway
B—Breathing	O_2 supply by bag and mask ventilation, ventilators, ET tube
C—Circulation	Measure BP, pulse, continuous ECG monitoring
D—Disability/CNS Depression	Corrected by drugs and IV fluids

- **Removal of unabsorbed poison**

Injected poison	1. Remove the sting in case of bee, wasp 2. Apply tourniquet or ice locally 3. Treat allergy and anaphylaxis
Contact poison	1. Remove clothes 2. Wash the affected area with soap and water
Inhaled poison	1. Remove the patient into fresh air 2. Start O_2 supplementation
Ingested poison	Gastric lavage with water/$KMnO_4$/activated charcoal is done to remove the unabsorbed poison from stomach with the help of Ewald tube or Boas tube.

- **Administration of antidotes:** Refer to short question no. 12.
- **Removal of poison by excretion:** Refer to long question no. 3.

21. Classify poisons. Discuss clinical features, management and autopsy findings in a case of phenol poisoning. What viscera will you preserve in such a case? (Delhi University 2015)

Ans:

Classification of Poisons

Refer to long question no. 2.

Signs and Symptoms

Acute Phenol Poisoning—also called **Carbolism**

Systemic effects

1. Eyes—Pupils constricted
2. Skin is cold and clammy
3. GIT—Burning and tingling sensation, and later on anesthesia. Diarrhea, pain in abdomen, but vomiting is rare.
4. CNS—CNS depression (like headache, giddiness)
5. Kidneys—Renal failure
6. RS—Laryngeal edema and pulmonary edema
7. CVS—Pulse is rapid, feeble and irregular. Unconsciousness and coma.
8. **Carboluria**—after 36–48 hrs of ingestion of carbolic acid, the urine is scanty and suppressed with greenish hue.

Local effects: Damage to nerve endings → Tingling sensation → Numbness → Painless white eschar

PM Findings

External	Internal
• Corrosion of mouth, tongue and chin • Smell of phenol at the mouth	• Stomach—hardening of stomach mucosa giving rise to **brown leathery stomach** • Kidneys—hemorrhagic nephritis

Management of Phenol Poisoning

1. Maintain airway, breathing and circulation (ABC)
2. **Gastric lavage** with water containing charcoal, olive oil (only corrosive acid poisoning in which gastric lavage is indicated)
3. Normal saline containing sodium bicarbonate IV
4. In case of renal failure: Hemodialysis is performed.

Viscera to be Preserved in the Case

Refer to short note no. 18.

22. A 19-year-old female presents to your emergency department after ingesting poison following a fight with her boyfriend. She was found unconscious near lavatory. She was brought to emergency. On examination, her lips were swollen, she had respiratory alkalosis and metabolic acidosis. The treating physician collected the urine for the laboratory investigations, during which the urine turned green on exposure to air. The patient died on 6th day during treatment. She was subjected to postmortem examination next day. No previous suicide attempts or history of depression. (Pondicherry 2019)

a. What substance or poison did the patient ingest?
b. What is the mechanism for the color change of urine?
c. What are the routine viscera will you collect and preserve the same for chemical analysis?
d. As a treating physician, what is your role in such case of suspected poisoning?

Ans:

a. She may have ingested **phenol (carbolic acid).**
b. Mechanism for color change—refer to long question no. 21.
c. Routine viscera collected and persevered for chemical analysis—refer to Short No. 18.
d. Duties of a doctor with regards to poisoning: First of all, we should treat the patient. For legal duties refer to long question no. 1.

23. Classify poisons according to signs and symptoms which they produce. Discuss about ideal homicidal poison. (Pondicherry 2015) (VNS, Gujarat 2017)

Ans:

Signs/symptoms	Causative agents
Hypothermia	Ethanol, opioids, barbiturates, sedatives, hypnotics, CO, benzodiazepines (BZDs)
Hyperpyrexia	Amphetamines, atropine, cocaine, salicylates, strychnine, marking nut, dhatura, cocaine, aspirin
Miosis	Opioids, phenol, OPC, carbamates, ethanol, nicotine, barbiturates, BZDs
Mydriasis	Dhatura, atropine, cannabis, strychnine, HCN, anticholinergics, amphetamine, cocaine, methanol
Diarrhea	Arsenic, boric acid
Hematemesis	Corrosives, salicylates
Hypotension	Narcotics, barbiturates, antidepressants, cyanide, CO, H_2S, arsenic
Hypertension	Antihistaminics, amphetamines, LSD, cocaine
Brachypnea	Alcohol, barbiturates, narcotics, elapid venom, strychnine, sedatives
Tachypnea	Methanol, cocaine, salicylates, CO, cyanide, amphetamine
Coma	Antihistamines, barbiturates, BZDs, ethanol, opioids, CO, cyanide, OPC, lead, antidepressants.
Seizures	Amphetamines, antidepressants, cocaine, withdrawal from alcohol

Ideal Homicidal Poison

Definition: The poison because of its characteristics favour the accused in committing homicide.

Criteria for an Ideal Homicidal Poison

1. Should be easily available (cost immaterial)
2. Should be colorless, odorless and tasteless
3. Can be easily administered with food, drink without arousing any suspicion
4. Symptoms should mimic natural disease process
5. Should be highly toxic
6. Signs and symptoms should appear late giving enough time for the culprit to escape
7. Should not produce any specific signs and symptoms
8. Should not be detected by routine tests
9. Should not produce any specific PM findings
10. No proper antidote should be available
11. Will be destroyed in body easily

Example

1. Thallium: Most ideal homicidal poison
2. Arsenic: Most common homicidal poison
3. Others: Insulin, aconite, etc.

SHORT NOTES

1. Classify neurotoxic poisons with examples of one poison in each sub-category. (Sher-i-Kashmir Institute, Srinagar 2020)

Ans:

Neurotoxic Poisons

These are the poisons which act mainly on the CNS.

1. Cerebral	2. Spinal	3. Peripheral
• Somniferous—Opioids • Inebriants—Alcohol, ether • Deliriants—Dhatura, Cocaine	• Strychnine (Nux vomica) • Gelsemium	• Curare • Hemlock

(Mnemonic—**SID**)

2. Duties of a doctor in case of poisoning (Jammu and Kashmir 2017) (Sher-i-Kashmir Institute, Srinagar supple 2017) (West Bengal University 2017) (North Eastern Hill University, Shillong 2016) (Rajasthan University 2016) (Andhra Pradesh University 2016)

Ans: Refer to long question no. 1

3. Barbiturate blisters (West Bengal University supple 2019) (VNS, Gujarat supple 2018)

Ans:

- These are tense subepidermal blisters found on the skin which occurs due to barbiturate poisoning.
- Blisters contain clear serous fluid that on rupture leaves a red, raw surface which dries to a brown parchment like area.
- These are found most commonly on friction areas such as axilla, buttocks, inner aspect of knee, etc.
- Sometimes may be mistaken for burns by hot water bottle.

4. Whole bowel irrigation (West Bengal University supple 2019)

Ans:

1. It is a method of removal of absorbed poison from GIT by excretion.
2. In this method, PEG (polyethylene glyocol) solution is given via NG tube at a rate of 2 liters/min.
3. While performing this, patient has to sit on the toilet seat.
4. This method can flush out our entire GIT within 5 hours.
5. **Criteria for its use:**
   a. When activated charcoal is not able to adsorb the ingested poison (or)
   b. When enteric coated drugs have been ingested (or)
   c. When some drug is ingested by body packers for illegal transport.

5. Toxalbumin (Adesh, Bathinda supple 2020) (VNS, Gujarat 2016, 2017)

Ans:

- Toxalbumin (also called **Phytotoxin**) is a toxic plant protein which is present in plants like Abrus *(rati)*, Castor, Croton, etc.
- It inhibits protein synthesis by inactivating ribosomes
- Structure of toxalbumin is similar to those of bacterial toxins (cholera, diphtheria, botulinium and tetanus)
- Toxalbumins are antigenic in nature and cause agglutination of RBCs leading to hemolysis
- **Examples:** Ricin, Abrin, Crotin, etc.
- **MLI:** As they are also cytotoxic and vasculotoxic, physiological and toxic properties are similar to Viper snake venom.

6. Gastric Lavage (University of Health Sciences, Rohtak supple 2020) (Sher-i-Kashmir Institute, Srinagar supple 2018) (BFUHS, Punjab supple 2016) (Rajiv Gandhi University, Bengaluru 2015)

Ans:

- Gastric lavage is a method used for removal of unabsorbed poison from stomach (also called stomach wash).
- Most effective—if done within 3 hrs of ingestion of poison
- **Tubes used** for gastric lavage

Ryle's tube	Children
Ewald/Boas tube	Most commonly used in adults

- **Agents used** for gastric lavage

In case of children	Normal saline
In case of adults	• Tap water • 1: 5000 $KMnO_4$ • 4% Tannic acid

- **Procedure**

Position of the patient	Left lateral position/Trendelenberg position (to reduce the chances of aspiration)
Insertion of tube	Till 50 cm mark (in case of adults) and 25 cm mark (in case of children)
Checking position of tube	Little air in a syringe is forced down the tube • Gurgling sounds heard through stethoscope placed over the stomach • Hissing sounds heard on other end—means tube has entered trachea
Pouring of fluid	• After confirmation of tip of tube, 250 ml of warm water is poured through the funnel • The first wash is preserved for chemical analysis

- **Contraindications of gastric lavage**

Absolute contraindications	Relative contraindications
Corrosive poisoning—as risk of perforation **(except carbolic acid poisoning)**	1. Convulsant poison (strychnine) 2. Comatose patient 3. Compromised unprotected airway 4. Kerosene/ volatile poisons 5. Esophageal varices

(Mnemonic: **Cs** as in "Contraindications")

7. Contraindications of gastric lavage (Sher-i-Kashmir Institute, Srinagar supple 2019) (VNS, Gujarat supple 2019) (Sai Tirupati University, Rajasthan 2019)

Ans:

Refer to short question no. 6.

8. Stomach wash tube (KHMS, Tamil Nadu Supple 2020)

Ans:

- It is also called Ewald tube or Boas tube.

Parts of the tube	
Material used	Made up of soft rubber
Length	1.5 Metres
Diameter	1 cm
Proximal end	Has funnel
Distal end	Is rounded with two lateral openings
Middle point	Suction bulb—to pump out stomach contents
Marking	At 50 cm from the lower end; mouth gag is present near it

- **MLI:** Used for removal of unabsorbed poison

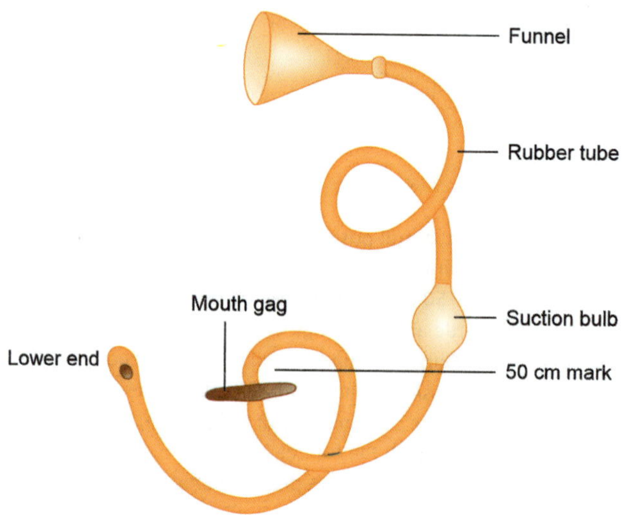

9. Factors affecting action of poison in the body. (Pondicherry 2017)

Ans:

The various factors affecting the action of poison in the body are:

1. **Quantity:** Toxic effects of drugs increase with increase in dosage of the drugs
2. **Form**

Physical state	On the basis of onset of action Gases and vapors > liquid form > solid form
Mechanical combination	Alteration in the action of poison when combined mechanically with inert substance, e.g. corrosive when mixed with water act as irritant

3. **Mode of administration**

Order of rapidity of action-

Inhaled in gaseous/vapour form > IV > IM > SC/ID > application to wound > ingestion > introduction to natural orifices

4. **Condition of the patient**

Age	Toxic effects of poison are more in extremes of the age
State of health	Healthy person tolerates poison better than the diseased
Tolerance	A dose of a poison which is toxic for someone may not be so in other which is because of the development of tolerance, e.g. alcohol, amphetamines, barbiturates
Idiosyncrasy	Even a small dose of the substance leads to toxic effects which is due to hypersensitivity towards the drug, e.g. penicillin, cocaine, mushroom
State of stomach	Presence of food in stomach delays the action of poison
Sleep and intoxication	Action of poison gets delayed: • If person goes to sleep soon after its intake (or) • If person takes poison in intoxicated state

10. Mention agents causing miosis. (Sher-i-Kashmir Institute, Srinagar supple 2019)

Ans:

Miosis is constriction of pupils. The agents causing miosis are:

Opioids (opium, morphine, heroine)
Organophosphates
Carbamates
Caffeine
Phenol
Pilocarpine
Barbiturates
Benzodiazepines
Neostigmine
Physostigmine

(Mnemonic—**OCP & BNP**)

11. Ideal suicidal poison. (Sher-i-Kashmir Institute, Srinagar supple 2015)

Ans:

Definition

The poison characteristics which are in favor of person committing suicide.

Criteria for an Ideal Suicidal Poison

1. It should be cheap and easily available
2. It should have a pleasant taste
3. It must be odorless
4. Can be easily mixed with food or drink
5. It should be highly toxic
6. It should produce painless death

Examples: Cyanide, Barbiturates, OPC, Alphos

12. Antidotes (Sher-i-Kashmir Institute, Srinagar supple 2018, supple 2017) (BFUHS, Punjab 2017) (Sardar Patel University, Gujarat 2018) (Jammu and Kashmir University 2017) (KHMS, Tamil Nadu 2017) (Uttarakhand University supple 2016) (VNS, Gujarat 2017)

Ans:

Definition

Antidotes are substances that act specifically to counteract the action or poisonous effects of a toxic agent.

The various types of antidotes are:

1. **Physical antidotes**	They neutralise the poison either by its mechanical action or by preventing its absorption. • Activated charcoal: It acts by adsorbing the poison on its surface; dose—1 g/kg body wt. • Demulcents: Forms a protective layer over the gastric mucosa, thus preventing absorption of poison, e.g. aluminium hydroxide, magnesium hydroxide, milk
2. **Chemical antidotes**	They neutralise the poisons by reacting with it and forming a harmless compound. • $KMnO_4$ (1:5000) oxidises the poison and reduces itself (losing pink color). Effective against most of the alkaloids (opioids, barbiturates) • Tannic acid—used in lead, mercury, zinc poisoning • Albumin—used in mercury chloride and copper poisoning • Tincture Iodine—used in lead, mercury poisoning
3. **Physiological/pharmacological antidotes**	Antidotes act on the target cell and produce pharmacological effects exactly opposite to the action to those produced by poison, e.g. atropine for OPC poisoning
4. **Chelating agents**	They inactivate the metallic ions by forming a complex with the metallic poison which is soluble in water and excreted through urine, e.g. BAL, EDTA, Desferrioxamine, Penicillamine, etc.

13. Universal antidote (Pondicherry supple 2017) (Delhi University 2015) (Rajiv Gandhi University, Bengaluru 2015) (VNS, Gujarat supple 2018, 2019)

Ans:
- It was earlier used when the exact nature of the poison consumed was not known.
- It is a mixture of 3 antidotes (2 physical and 1 chemical antidotes) in a specific ratio.

Activated charcoal	2	Adsorbs alkaloids
Tannic acid	1	Precipitates alkaloids, glycosides and metals
Magnesium hydroxide	1	Neutralizes acid

(Mnemonic—**ATM**)

- It is ineffective and not used nowadays.

14. Chemical antidotes (Sardar Patel University, Gujarat supple 2018)

Ans:
Refer to short question no. 12.

15. Chelating Agents (Rajiv Gandhi University, Bengaluru 2020) (BFUHS, Punjab supple 2019) (Rajasthan University 2018) (AIIMS, Patna 2017) (Himachal Pradesh 2017) (University of Health Sciences, Rohtak 2017) (Uttarakhand University 2016) (GMC, Chandigarh 2015)

Ans:
1. Chelating agents are specific antidotes against **heavy metal poisoning**.
2. These chelating agents have free sulfhydryl (–SH) groups which compete with the thiol groups of enzymes for binding with heavy metals to form a stable metal—chelate complex. The formed complex is then excreted from the body through urine.
3. They thus prevent the union of the metal with the –SH group of the respiratory enzyme system.

Some examples of chelating agents are:

a. **BAL** is used in (mnemonic-BAL CM) bismuth, arsenic, lead, copper, mercury and other heavy metal poisoning. It is given IM. *Contraindicated* in liver damage, G-6-PD deficient individuals, and cadmium and iron poisoning. BAL has two unsaturated –SH groups which combine with the metal and prevents the union of the metal with the –SH group of the respiratory enzyme system.
   - **Dose:** 10% solution in oil, 3–5 mg/kg IM 4 hourly for 2 days, 6 hourly on 3rd day and then 12 hourly for next 10 days.
   - **Side effects:** Nausea, vomiting, headache and hypertension.

b. **EDTA** is useful in lead, copper, cobalt, cadmium, iron and nickel poisoning; better than BAL for treatment of arsenic and mercury poisoning. It is given IV; contraindicated in renal failure.

c. **Penicillamine** is used for treatment of copper, lead and mercury poisoning. It is given orally.

d. **Desferrioxamine** is useful in acute iron poisoning. It is given IV. (Mnemonic—Ferric/Fe^{3+})

16. BAL is not injected by intravenous route (West Bengal University 2019)

Ans:

BAL is given by deep IM route not by IV route as the preparation contains oil which can cause fat/oil embolism. BAL is available in ampoules in combination with benzyl benzoate (20%) in peanut oil.

17. BAL antidote (Rajasthan University 2015)

Ans: Refer to short question no. 15.

18. Viscera preservation for chemical analysis in case of suspected poisoning after PM examination (Sher-i-Kashmir Institute, Srinagar supple 2019, 2017, 2015) (Jammu and Kashmir 2017) (Uttarakhand University 2017) (Rajiv Gandhi University, Bengaluru 2015)

Ans:

a. Viscera preservation (in routine)

Bottle 1	Stomach along its contents and upper part of small intestine (30 cm) along with its contents
Bottle 2	Liver—300 gm along with gall bladder Kidneys—half of each kidney
Bottle 3 (vial)	Blood—10 ml
Bottle 4	Urine—100 ml
Bottle 5	Sample of the preservative

b. Additional viscera preservation (in certain poisoning)

Brain	Cerebral poison
Heart	Aconite
CSF	Alcohol
Bile (Mnemonic—**GOBI**)	**G**—Glutathione **O**—Opium **Bi**—Barbiturates (as secreted in **Bi**le)
Hair, nails, bone	Metallic poisons
Spinal cord	Strychnine

c. Preservatives used

Saturated solution of NaCl	1. Most commonly used 2. C/I in corrosive poisoning (except carbolic acid)
Rectified Spirit	1. Best preservative 2. Used in corrosive poisoning 3. C/I in carbolic acid poisoning
Formalin	For histopathological examination
Sodium fluoride (NaF) (Mnemonic—**COCA**)	**CO**—Cocaine, **C**—Cyanide **A**—Alcohol

19. Vitriolage (North Eastern Hill University, Shillong supple 2020) (Adesh, Bathinda 2018) (Sher-i-Kashmir supple 2018, supple 2017) (KHMS, Tamil Nadu supple 2019) (Delhi University 2018) (Uttarakhand University 2017) (BFUHS, Punjab 2016) (Rajiv Gandhi University, Bengaluru 2015)

Ans:

Definition

Vitriolage is defined as throwing of any corrosive agent (acid or alkali) on another person with an intention of injuring him or for the purpose of disfiguring him out of jealousy

1. **Substances used for vitriolage:** Sulphuric acid, nitric acid, carbolic acid, caustic soda, marking nut juice
2. **Characteristics of burns**
   - Discoloration and staining of the skin and clothing (brown-black in sulphuric acid, and yellow in nitric acid).
   - Trickle marks
   - Scar tissue causes contractures.
3. **Treatment**

For skin burns	For eye burns
a. Wash the affected area with plenty of water and soap	a. Wash eyes with plenty of water
b. Apply thick paste of MgO over the skin	b. Topical anesthetic drop
c. Apply antibiotics over the raw surface	

4. **MLI:** It leads to Grievous hurt (Sec. **320 IPC**) by causing:
   - Permanent disfigurement of face (6th clause)
   - Permanent privation of sight of either eye (2nd clause)

Punishment

Section	Punishment
Sec. 326 A IPC	10 years to life imprisonment ± Fine
Sec. 326 B IPC	5–7 years of imprisonment ± Fine

20. Clinical manifestations and treatment of phenol poisoning (BFUHS, Punjab 2019)

Ans: Refer to long question no. 21.

21. Carboluria (AIIMS, Patna 2019, 2017) (Sardar Patel University, Gujarat 2019, supple 2019) (BFUHS, Punjab supple 2018) (Sher-i-Kashmir Institute, Srinagar supple 2015) (Uttarakhand University 2015)

Ans:

It is seen in **acute carbolic acid poisoning/phenol poisoning** after 36–48 hrs of ingestion of carbolic acid.

Mechanism

- After absorption through GIT, it is metabolised in the liver giving rise to the toxic metabolites of Phenol, i.e. **P**yrocatechol, **H**ydroquinone (mnemonic—**Ph**enol)
- These metabolites are then excreted into urine, which gets further oxidised on exposure to air giving rise to Green colour urine.
- So, the urine is scanty and suppressed with greenish hue—called Carboluria.

22. PM findings in case of sulphuric acid poisoning. (Rajasthan University 2018)

Ans: Refer to long question no. 19.

23. Internal findings at autopsy in case of inorganic acid poisoning. (Sardar Patel University, Gujarat 2016)

Ans:

Common inorganic acids include sulphuric acid, nitric acid and hydrochloric acid

Internal findings at autopsy in case of inorganic acid poisoning are:

Sulphuric acid	Nitric acid	Hydrochloric acid
• Erosion of skin, angles of mouth, lips with **blackening** • Corrosion of the trachea and larynx • Blackish charring of the stomach, peppery feel • Stomach perforation • Peritonitis	• **Yellow discoloration of skin** • Corrosion of skin • Congestion of larynx and trachea • Stomach wall is soft, friable and ulcerated	• **Brownish parchmentization** • Inflammation and edema of respiratory passages • Stomach contains brownish fluid

24. Drug automatism. (Adesh, Bathinda supple 2017) (VNS, Gujarat 2018)

1. **Definition drug automatism:** It is taking of a drug (usually barbiturates) repeatedly, forgetting each time that one has already taken the dose, because of mental confusion. This can lead to a cumulative overdose.
2. The drug-automatism hypothesis implies a medication-induced absence of intentionality for self-poisoning and a relative amnesia for repeated or single overdosage.
3. **Cause:** The patient develops a state of amnesia after ingestion of one or several doses of drug, and in the automatism state, takes additional doses of drug in order to get to sleep without any intention to commit suicide and without realizing it.
4. **MLI:** Such deaths should be considered "accidental" and not suicidal.

25. PM findings in case of chronic arsenic poisoning. (Uttarakhand University 2016)

Ans: Refer to long question no. 16

26. Chronic Mercury Poisoning/Hydragyrism (Sher-i-Kashmir Institute, Srinagar 2020) (Adesh. Bathinda supple 2020) (Uttarakhand University 2018) (Andhra Pradesh 2015) (Pondicherry supple 2017) (Delhi University 2017) (VNS, Gujarat 2016, 2017)

Ans: Chronic poisoning occurs due to:

a. Continuous accidental absorption by workers.
b. Excessive therapeutic use.
c. Recovery from a large dose.
d. If an ointment is used as an external application for a long time.

Specific Signs Seen in Case of Chronic Mercury Poisoning

A. Due to Inorganic Mercury Poisoning

1. **Mercuria Lentis**	a. It occurs due to exposure to *mercury vapors* b. Brownish deposit of mercury on anterior lens capsule c. On slit lamp examination: Malt brown reflex
2. **Acrodynia or pink disease**	a. It is seen mostly in case of children b. C/F: Hands and feet become puffy, pinkish and painful with peeling of skin, excessive salivation or perspiration
3. **Intentional Tremors**	a. It is also known as Danbury's tremors or Hatter's shake or Glass blower's shake or Mercurial tremors b. Classical feature of chronic mercury poisoning c. Tremors start from hands → lips and tongue → arms and legs
4. **Mercury Erythism**	a. It refers to the *neuropsychiatric manifestations* seen in case of chronic mercury poisoning. b. Also called Mad Hatters c. C/F: Insomnia, anxiety, depression, shyness, blushing, embarrassment, hallucinations, loss of memory, etc.

(Mnemonic—**LATE**)

B. Due to Organic Mercury Poisoning

Minamata disease	• Occurs due to consumption of contaminated fish • C/F: Disturbances in hand coordination, gait and speech, chewing and swallowing difficulties, visual blurring, tremors, seizures, rigidity

Management

1. Remove the patient from source of exposure
2. Chelation therapy—BAL, penicillamine
3. Oral hygiene
4. Demulcents

MLI:

1. Accidental ingestion may occur from broken thermometers
2. Metallic mercury is used in dentistry
3. Mercury chloride is used for criminal abortion
4. Suicidal and homicidal poisoning is rare.

27. Hatters shake (Sher-i-Kashmir Institute, Srinagar supple 2019, supple 2015)

Ans:

- It is also known as **Danbury's tremors** or **intentional tremors** or **glass blower's shake** or **Mercurial tremors**
- It is a classical feature of chronic inorganic mercury poisoning
- Common in workers in hat making, glass blowing factories
- **Characteristics of tremors**
  Tremors start from **hands → lips and tongue → arms and legs**
  Associated with shabby and shaky handwriting, stammering and hesitation inspeech, **finally,** the person is not able to write legibly or dress himself or walk properly
- The most severe form is called **Concussion Mercurialis,** where no activity is possible.

28. Mercury Erythism (Rajasthan University 2018) (Adesh, Bathinda supple 2017)

Ans:

Refer to short question no. 26.

29. Metal Fume Fever (West Bengal University 2019) (Adesh, Bathinda 2017)

Ans:

Definition: Metal fume fever is a self-limiting acute febrile illness occurs due to inhalation of metal oxide fumes.

1. Also called **smelter's shakes, brass chills or Monday morning fever**.
2. **Metals involved:** It is caused by acute exposure **zinc oxide** fumes, copper, magnesium, nickel, mercury, lead, etc when heated above their melting point.
3. **Seen in:** Workers involved in welding, melting or flame cutting galvanized metal or in brass industries
4. **S/s:** Flu-like symptoms (headache, fever, chills, cough, dyspnea, cyanosis, myalgia, salivation, sweating and tachycardia) start within 4–8 hrs after exposure of fumes. Finally, the symptoms subside within 24–36 hrs.
5. **Treatment**
   a. Oxygen supplementation
   b. Bronchodilators
   c. Symptomatic treatment.

30. Phossy Jaw/ Lucifer's Jaw. (Adesh, Bathinda supple 2019) (Rajasthan University 2018) (Uttarakhand University supple 2016) (North Eastern Hill University, Shillong 2017) (VNS, Gujarat 2017)

Ans:

Definition: Phossy jaw is a type of osteomyelitis of the lower jaw near the decayed tooth seen in case of chronic phosphorous poisoning

1. It is also called **glass jaw.**

2. **Cause:** Exposure to vapors of phosphorous for a long period of time
3. **Clinical features:**

Constitutional symptoms	Specific Lesion (in order of sequence)
a. Nausea	a. At first, there's complaint of **Toothache**
b. Vomiting	b. Followed by swelling of jaw
c. Anorexia	c. Multiple sinuses, discharging foul smelling pus with loosening of teeth and necrosis of gum **(Osteomyelitis)**
d. Pain abdomen	d. Finally, **osteonecrosis of mandible** develops.
e. Joint pain	
f. Loss of weight	

4. **Treatment**
   a. Regular mouthwash
   b. Surgical excision of the affected bone

31. Treatment of HCN Poisoning. (Rajasthan University 2018)

Ans: Refer to long question no. 12.

32. Plumbism (Sardar Patel University 2019, supple 2019) (Rajiv Gandhi University, Bengaluru 2019, 2015) (Pondicherry 2017) (GMC, Chandigarh 2015) (Sher-i-Kashmir Institute, Srinagar supple 2015)

Ans: Chronic lead poisoning is called plumbism.

Clinical Features

1. **Anemia:** There is anemia with karyorrhexis and dyserythropoiesis (*punctate basophilia, reticulocytosis, poikilocytosis, anisocytosis)*, nucleated red cells and increase in mononuclear cells in peripheral blood.
2. **Burtonian line:** A stippled *blue line* is seen on the upper gum due to subepithelial deposit of lead sulphide (by the H_2S formed from decomposed protein) at the junction of dirty or carious teeth.
3. **Colic** and **Constipation:** Colic involves both large and small intestines, ureters and blood vessels. Pain is spasmodic, paroxysmal, occurs at night and may be very severe. Constipation usually precedes colic.
4. **Lead palsy (Drops):** Common in adults than in children, and males are particularly affected. It occurs due to degeneration of nerves and atrophy of muscles. The extensor muscles of wrist *(wrist drop) and* anterior tibial *(foot drop)* are affected.
5. **Lead Encephalopathy:** Involvement of brain function, commonly in children is present in all cases. *Symptoms* include changes in personality, restlessness, hyperkinetic and aggressive behavior, fatigability, mental dullness, learning disorders, refusal to play, etc.
6. **Effects on reproductive system:** It may cause sterility in both male and female patients. In males, there may be loss of libido and impotence. In females, there may be inFertility, menstrual irregularities.

7. **Retinal stippling** is noticed by ophthalmoscope with presence of grayish glistening lead particles in the early phase of chronic lead poisoning.
8. **Lead osteopathy:** In children and young adults, lead is deposited beyond the epiphysis of growing long bones which may lead to their abnormal development.
9. **Effects on circulatory system:** It causes vascular constriction leading to hypertension and arteriolar degeneration.
10. **Effect on kidneys:** *Acute nephropathy* in form of *Fanconi's syndrome*. *Chronic nephropathy* causes hypertension and hyperuricemia.

(Mnemonic—**ABCDEF**)

Laboratory Tests

i. Microcytic, hypochromic anemia may be seen.
ii. Punctate basophilia: >200 cells/cu mm.
iii. Blood lead levels >70 μg/dL (severe toxicity) [10 μg/dL (cut-off level)].
iv. Urine lead level >80 μg/dL (in 24 h sample).
v. Coproporphyrin in urine >15 μg/dL.
vi. δ-amino levulinic acid in urine > 5 mg/L.
vii. *X-ray:* Radio-opaque bands or **'lead lines'** at the metaphyseal plate of long bones are seen in children.

Treatment

1. Remove the patient from the source of exposure.
2. Potassium or sodium iodide 1–2 g TDS orally
3. Sodium bicarbonate 20–30 g in 4 or 5 divided doses orally.
4. $MgSO_4$ or sodium sulfate 8–12 g orally.
5. **$CaNa_2EDTA$** IV in usual doses.
6. **BAL:** Chelator of choice in case of renal impairment.
7. Give iron, calcium, magnesium and zinc, and vitamins.

33. Brutonian line (Delhi University 2018) (Rajiv Gandhi University, Bengaluru 2015) (Andhra Pradesh 2015) (VNS, Gujarat supple 2018)

Ans:

1. Burtonian line is seen in chronic lead poisoning.
2. A stippled *blue line* on the upper gum is seen in most cases.
3. Cause: Due to subepithelial deposit of granules at the junction of teeth, especially near dirty or carious teeth of the upper jaw due to formation of lead sulphide by the H_2S formed from decomposed protein in the mouth.
4. A similar blue line may be seen in cases of poisoning with other heavy metals like mercury, iron, copper, etc.

34. Blood Picture in Chronic Lead poisoning (West Bengal University supple 2017)

Anemia and Basophilic Stippling occurring in Chronic lead poisoning (West Bengal University 2017) (VNS, Gujarat 2018)

Ans:

In chronic lead poisoning, there is anemia with karyorrhexis and dyserythropoiesis (*punctate basophilia, Cabot's rings, reticulocytosis, poikilocytosis, anisocytosis),* nucleated red cells and increase in mononuclear cells in peripheral blood and ringed sideroblasts in bone marrow. However, polymorphonuclear cells and platelets are decreased. RBC count comes down to 3.5 million/dL and hemoglobin level to 6.5 g%.

Cause of Anemia

a. Impairment in heme synthesis from protoporphyrin.
b. Increased fragility of RBCs due to loss of intracellular potassium.

Punctate Basophilia

1. Punctate basophilia/basophilic stippling is seen in chronic lead poisoning.
2. There is presence of dark blue colored pinhead sized spots in the cytoplasm of the RBCs representing aggregated ribosomes.
3. **Cause**—toxic action of lead on porphyrin metabolism.

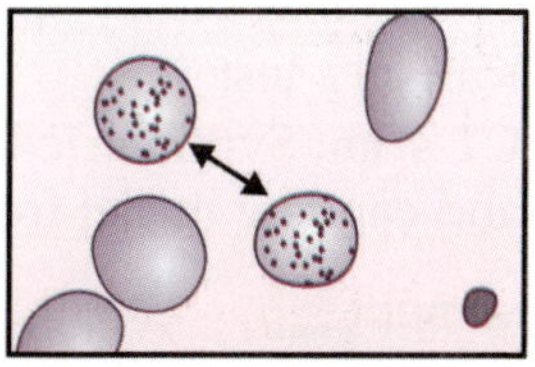

35. Dhatura Poisoning/ Ideal Roadside Poison/ Thorn apple poisoning (Rajasthan University 2018) (Sher-i-Kashmir Institute, Srinagar supple 2017) (Rajiv Gandhi University, Bengaluru 2015) (Sardar Patel University, Gujarat 2016)

Ans: Refer to long question no. 4.

36. Stupefying Agents. (GMC, Chandigarh 2015, 2016)

Ans:

Definition

- Substances which are used to daze a victim or putting the victim in state of drowsiness or unconsciousness.
- It is used by criminals for the purpose of robbery, kidnapping or rape during travel in bus, train and railway station.
- It is usually mixed with food or drink
- Poisons used as stupefying agents are Dhatura, Cannabis, and Chloral Hydrate.

37. Carbon Monoxide Poisoning (Uttarakhand University Supple 2018) (VNS, Gujarat 2019)

Ans:

Signs and Symptoms

Depends on the concentration of CO in the blood (COHb%)

Severity	COHb%	Symptoms
Mild	10–30	Mild headache to throbbing headache, irritability, buzzing in ears, breathlessness
Moderate	30–40	Severe headache, nausea, vomiting, dizziness, dim vision, impaired judgement, poor concentration
Severe	>40	**CNS**: Increasing confusion, hallucinations, convulsions, coma and death, staggering and incoordination **RS**: Rapid and irregular respiration **CVS**: Weak thready pulse, hypotension, arrhythmias
	>80	Rapid death from respiratory arrest

Lab Investigations

1. Conc. of COHb by spectroscopy
2. Kunkel's test
3. **CT scan:** Symmetric low density areas in the region of globus pallidus, putamen and caudate nuclei frequently seen within 12 hrs of CO exposure.

Treatment

1. Remove the patient from source of exposure
2. Maintain airway, breathing and circulation (ABC)
3. Oxygen is given by tight-fitting high-flow reservoir face mask or endotracheal tube.
4. Use of hyperbaric oxygen—to reduce neurological sequelae.
5. Gastric lavage—to prevent aspiration pneumonia
6. IV mannitol—to prevent cerebral edema
7. Antibiotics and supportive treatment.

PM Findings

External	Internal
1. **Cherry red discolouration of PM staining**	1. **Lungs:** Edema and congestion
2. Fine froth at nostrils and mouth'	2. **Heart:** Petechial hemorrhage
3. Skin blisters over bony pressure areas (buttocks, calves, wrist)	3. **CNS:** Edema and congestion

MLI:

a. Accidental cases are common in India from cooking gas leakage, and incomplete combustion of wood, charcoal or coal in ill-ventilated rooms.
b. Common method of suicidal poisoning in the West.
c. Homicide is uncommon.
d. Masochistic sexual asphyxia may be due to CO.

38. Treatment of CO poisoning (Pondicherry 2017)

Ans: Refer to short question no. 37.

39. Explain the treatment of Cyanide Poisoning (Rajiv Gandhi University, Bengaluru 2019) (Rajasthan University 2016)

Ans: Refer to short question no. 12.

40. Suis (AIIMS Patna 2016) (VNS, Gujarat 2019, supple 2019)

Ans:

1. **Suis** are small needles prepared from rati.
2. **Preparation of suis**—seeds of *Abrus precatorius (rati)* are crushed into powdered form, mixed with Dhatura, Opium, onion, water and made into a paste which is then shaped into sharp needles or spikes about 2.5 cm long and then allowed to dry.

Clinical Features of Poisoning with Suis

Local features	Systemic features
1. The wounds caused by two suis resembles viperine snakebite (fangs in snakebite) 2. At site of injection—painful edema, inflammation, necrosis with oozing of blood	1. Weakness 2. Faintness 3. Vertigo 4. Anorexia 5. Drowsiness 6. Coma

Treatment

1. Suis should be dissected out
2. IV fluids
3. Symptomatic treatment.

MLI:

1. Used as abortifacient
2. Used as cattle poison
3. Used as arrow poison
4. For homicidal purposes—by keeping two suis needles in between two fingers of hand with pointed needles facing ventral aspect of the hand. These are then struck with force into the flesh of other person resembling **Viper snake bites.**

41. Marking nut (Sher-i-Kashmir Institute, Srinagar supple 2018)

Ans:

1. It is also called "bhilawa" or "oriental cashew nut". Scientific name is *Semecarpus Anacardium*
2. It is an organic irritant poison.

3. Active principles
   i. Semecarpol
   ii. Bhilawanol
4. **Signs and symptoms**

Local lesions	Systemic features
Artificial bruise	• Vomiting
• When juice of marking nut is applied on the skin	• Diarrhoea
• Lesions are raised, blackish, painful and itchy blisters	• Hypotension
• On scratching—similar lesions seen on the tips of fingers	• Tachycardia

5. **Fatal dose:** 5–8 seeds
6. **Treatment**
   i. Wash the area with soap and water—in case of contact with skin
   ii. Demulscents
   iii. Activated charcoal
   iv. IV fluids—to correct hypotension
   v. Symptomatic management
7. **MLI**
   i. Used as abortifacient
   ii. Juice is used to produce **artificial bruises**
   iii. Juice is thrown on face—used as vitriolage
   iv. Used by washerman (dhobis)—to mark identification number on clothes.

42. Clinical features of opium/morphine poisoning (Adesh, Bathinda supple 2020) (VNS, Gujarat 2016, supple 2018)

Ans: Refer to long question no. 17.

43. Treatment of opium poisoning (Sardar Patel University, Gujarat supple 2018)

Ans: Refer to long question no. 17.

44. Brown sugar (West Bengal University supple 2019)

Ans:
1. It is semi-synthetic preparation of opium
2. Most dangerous and popular among drug of addiction
3. It is 2–4 times more toxic than morphine
4. **Routes of administration**
   a. Sniffing
   b. Smoking
   c. Dragon chasing
   d. Skin popping—subcutaneous injection
   e. Intravenous injections

5. **Signs and symptoms** (in order of presentation)
   i. Stage of excitement
   ii. Stage of euphoria
   iii. Feeling of well-being
   iv. Hallucinations and intense pleasure
   v. Drowsiness and stupor
6. **Treatment**
   i. Maintain airway, breathing and circulation (ABC)
   ii. Perform gastric lavage with $KMnO_4$
   iii. Naloxone IV is given in acute poisoning—act as antidote
   iv. Symptomatic treatment
   v. Methadone—to prevent withdrawal symptoms and to drug addicts to reduce euphoria.

45. Body packers (Adesh, Bathinda 2017, supple 2019) (Rajiv Gandhi University, Bengaluru 2019) (Rajasthan University 2017) (Pondicherry 2016, supple 2017) (VNS, Gujarat 2018, supple 2019)

Ans:
1. **Definition of body packers:** The person who swallows illicit/ illegal drugs for the purpose of smuggling across countries by ingesting or inserting them into body cavities.
2. They are also called **Mule, Courier.**
3. For smuggling, drugs of high quality are packed commonly in condoms, foils, balloons. After reaching destination, smuggler takes laxatives, defecates and then retrieves the packets from feces to deliver them to drug dealers.
4. The body packers are usually detected and arrested at the airports and sent for the custody.
5. In case of suspicion—**detection** by:
   a. Physical examination of body cavities like rectum, vagina
   b. Abdominal X-ray and CT scan
6. **MLI:**
   i. Risk of toxicity in case drug packets rupture
   ii. Acute intestinal obstruction

46. Delirium tremens (Rajasthan University 2018) (Uttarakhand University supple 2016) (BFUHS, Punjab 2015) (GMC, Chandigarh 2015) (Sher-i-Kashmir Institute, Srinagar supple 2015)

Ans:
1. **Definition delirium tremens:** It is defined as acute episode of delirium which is seen 2–4 days after sudden withdrawal of alcohol in chronic alcoholics.
2. Most severe alcohol withdrawal syndrome.

3. **Causes**
   a. Sudden withdrawal of alcohol
   b. On excessive intake of alcohol
   c. Shock after receiving severe trauma, e.g. fracture of bone
   d. Acute infection like pneumonia
4. **Signs and symptoms**
   i. Clouding of consciousness with disorientation to time, place and person
   ii. Hallucinations—visual, auditory and tactile hallucinations
   iii. Tremors of face, tongue and hands
   iv. Tendency to commit suicide
   v. Autonomic disturbances and hyperactivity of CNS
5. **Treatment**
   i. Diazepam—for sedation
   ii. Oral multi-B vitamins and thiamine
   iii. Haloperidol—can be added
   iv. Symptomatic treatment
6. **MLI:** If a person commits any crime in delirium tremens, he is not held responsible for his criminal acts as he is mentally unsound, as per Sec. **84 IPC.**

47. Food Poisoning (Sher-i-Kashmir Institute, Srinagar 2020)

Ans:

1. **Definition:** Illnesses which result from ingestion of food containing bacterial or non-bacterial products including viruses, toxins present within the food itself. But the term is usually used for acute gastroenteritis due to the bacterial infection of food or drink.
2. **Causes**
   a. Poisoning due to bacteria and toxins.
   b. Poisons of vegetable origin: *Lathyrus sativus*, poisonous mushrooms and *Argemone mexicana*.
   c. *Poisons of animal origin:* Poisonous fish and mussel.
   d. *Chemical:* Intentionally or accidentally added, products of food processing.
3. **Bacterial food poisoning** results from the ingestion of contaminated food, uncooked food or imperfectly cooked food. It is divided into two groups:
   i. **Infection type** results from multiplication of pathogenic organisms within body contained in the food. Organisms belong mainly to the *Salmonella* group.
   S/s: Sudden onset of nausea, vomiting, abdominal pain and foul smelling watery diarrhea stained with blood and/or mucus.
   ii. **Toxin type** results from ingestion of preformed toxins (*exotoxins*) from bacterial proliferation in canned or preserved food, e.g. enterotoxin of *Staphylococci, Clostridium perfringens or Bacillus cereus.*
   S/s: Salivation, diarrhea, nausea, abdominal cramps and vomiting.
4. **Treatment**
   a. Gastric lavage and purgatives are given.
   b. Glucose-saline infusion should be given to promote elimination of the toxins from the system.
   c. Antibiotics are given depending upon the causative organism.

5. **Postmortem findings**
   i. GIT: Mucosa swollen and congested with minute ulcers
   ii. Liver: Fatty degeneration
   iii. Causative organism can be isolated from the blood and viscera.

48. Truth Serum (Adesh, Bathinda 2019)

1. Barbiturates are used for narco-analysis as *'truth serum'* or *'truth drug'*.
2. Narco-analysis is a scientific procedure to obtain information from an individual in a natural sleep-like state.
3. The individual is put to trance-like state and loses all his inhibitions by administering *amytal sodium or sodium thiopental* in 2.5–5% solution, slow IV.
4. The dose is dependent on the person's sex, age, health and physical condition. A wrong dose can result in a person going into a coma or even death.
5. A person is able to lie by using his imagination. The subject's imagination is neutralized by using the drug. In this state, it becomes difficult for him to lie, and his answers would be restricted to facts he is already aware of.

49. Drunkenness (Adesh, Bathinda supple 2019, supple 2018) (Rajiv Gandhi University, Bengaluru 2015) (VNS, Gujarat supple 2018)

Ans:

1. **Definition:** Drunkenness is a consequence of drinking intoxicating liquors to such extent so as to reduce his capacity for rational action and conduct and can be dangerous to himself or to others.
2. **Exclusion of injuries and pathological conditions:** Head injury, hypoglycemia, diabetic coma, uremia, overdose of insulin, barbiturates, antihistamines, cocaine, morphine, and CO poisoning.
3. **Clinical examination**
   a. **Preliminary data** such as name, age, sex, address, time of examination, two identification marks and person escorting the patient should be noted.
   b. **Consent:** Under Sec. 53 (1) CrPC, an accused can be examined by a doctor at the request of the police, even without his consent and by use of force, if necessary.
   c. **History:** The history of relevant events should be obtained from the person while observing him.
   d. **General appearance:** Manner of dressing—properly dressed or not, and soiling of clothes. Posture—whether over-erect and over smart, can stand steady or not, and can stand without support or not.
   e. **General examination:** Scalp inspected and palpated for evidence of any head injury.
   f. **Specific physical examination**
      i. **Gait** is observed for any unsteadiness, staggering, bumping into people or furniture. Gait on turning (normal, unsteady, stumbling) is also noted.
      ii. **Orientation and memory:** Ask him about incidents which have occurred few hours prior to examination to check his memory. Ask him about the date, time and place where he is at present.

iii. **Behavior:** Whether noisy, jovial, boastful, rude, emotional, talkative, excited or uncontrollable.
iv. **Face:** Whether normal, flushed or pale. Redness of the face is indicative of alcohol intake.
v. **Speech:** Whether normal, thick and slurred, stuttering, confused, unintelligible, offensive or over precise.
vi. **Tongue:** Whether dry, moist and clean or furred. Dry tongue is seen in thirst, and waning phase of BAC.
vii. **Signs of vomiting and salivation:** Vomitus may be on clothes. Salivation and drooling may be found in the severely intoxicated.
viii. **Smell of alcohol:** Strong, moderate, faint or none. The smell of the breath may confirm that alcohol has been taken and the type of drink.
ix. **Handwriting:** The person can be asked to sign his name and compared with his driving license. Drawing simple patterns, such as triangle and diamond may be preferable, if the person is illiterate.
x. **Eyes:** Examine the eyes, noting the conjunctiva (normal or congested), pupillary size (normal, equal, unequal, mydriasis or miosis), response to light (normal, delayed or non-reacting), visual fields and acuity (reading the time on a clock across a room), and the presence of nystagmus (coarse, fine, continuous or absent). In drunkenness, there is drooping and swollen eyelids, congestion of conjunctiva and nystagmus may be seen, and convergence test is negative.
xi. **Tests to determine in-coordination:** Watch the patient unbutton his shirt, dressing, undressing or handling objects like picking up a pen. Carry out *standardized field impairment tests (FITs)* to check muscle coordination. These consist of Romberg test, Walk and Turn test, One Leg Stand test and Finger Nose test.
xii. **Knee reflexes** are elicited to check whether normal, exaggerated or depressed. Reflexes are equally depressed in intoxication.

Opinion

The opinion can be drafted with any one of the following statements:
i. He/she has not consumed alcohol.
ii. He/she has consumed alcohol, but is not under the influence of it.
iii. He/she has consumed alcohol and is under its influence.

50. Preservation of blood sample in case of drunkenness (West Bengal University supple 2017)

Ans:

The Blood Alcohol Concentration (BAC) is the most useful measure, as there is rapid equilibration across the blood–brain barrier; BAC reflects the concentration of alcohol currently affecting the brain.

Blood Sample Preservation

1. Soap and water (instead of spirit swab) is used to clean the site to be venepunctured.
2. The blood is collected from antecubital or femoral vein using a disposable syringe.

3. Blood container should be tightly stoppered to prevent loss of alcohol by evaporation, and labeled with name, date, time of taking the specimen and signature of the medical officer.

51. Magnan Syndrome (Uttarakhand University supple 2016)

Ans:

1. It is also called **Cocaine Bugs/Formication**
2. It is a type of tactile hallucination in which the person feels crawling or creeping of an insect on or under the skin giving rise to itching sensation
3. Presence of excessive scratching marks on the skin
4. Seen in:
   i. Cocaine addicts
   ii. Methamphetamines intoxication
5. **Treatment**
   - Stop the drug
   - Supportive treatment

52. Run amok (Adesh, Bathinda supple 2018) (BFUHS, Punjab supple 2018) (Uttarakhand University supple 2016) (Rajasthan University 2015) (VNS, Gujarat 2018)

Ans:

1. **Definition run amok:** It is defined as an acute psychotic disorder which occurs due to consumption of cannabis.
2. **Cause:**
   i. Sudden consumption of cannabis
   ii. Chronic consumption of cannabis
3. It comprises 3 phases (in sequence)
   i. Phase of depression
   ii. Phase of homicidal mania/impulse murder
   iii. Phase of depression

   Soon after intake, the person develops phase of depression which is then followed by killing a person against whom he has real rivalry or imaginary because of **Delusion of Persecution** and then kills anyone who comes in his way until the homicidal tendency stops.

   And finally after this phase, the person again enters the phase of depression in which either he commits suicide or surrender himself to the police.
4. **MLI:**
   1. As per Section **85 IPC:** The person will not be responsible for his acts in case of involuntary intoxication.
   2. As per Section **86 IPC:** The person will be held responsible for all his acts in case of voluntary intoxication.

53. Methyl alcohol Poisoning (Uttarakhand University supple 2018, 2016) (Delhi University 2015) (Rajasthan University 2015) (Sai Tirupati University, Rajasthan 2019)

Ans: Refer to long question no. 18.

54. Treatment of Methanol poisoning/ Methyl alcohol poisoning (Sardar Patel University, Gujarat 2020, 2019, supple 2019) (Adesh, Bathinda supple 2019) (KHMS, Tamil Nadu 2018)

Ans: Refer to long question no. 18.

55. Management of OPC poisoning (Adesh, Bathinda supple 2018, supple 2017) (Sardar Patel University, Gujarat 2018, supple 2015) (Jammu and Kashmir 2017) (VNS, Gujarat supple 2019)

Ans: Refer to long question no. 6.

56. Atropinization (AIIMS, Patna 2019, 2017)

Ans:

1. Atropine acts as an antidote for OPC and Carbamate poisoning
2. **MOA:** Atropine acts by blocking Muscarinic receptors, and no action on Nicotinic receptors, therefore reversing Muscarinic manifestations but no effect on Nicotinic manifestations
3. It occurs because of the repeated dose of atropine
4. **Signs of atropinization**
   a. Mydriasis—most common sign
   b. Heart rate—more than 100 beats/min (Tachycardia)
   c. Decreased oropharyngeal and bronchial secretions
      - Most specific or consistent sign
      - Considered as therapeutic endpoint
5. **Dose required for atropinization:** 2–4 mg IV repeatedly after every 5–10 min till secretions is reduced, then maintenance dose to maintain this effect for next 24 hrs.

57. Management of Aluminium Phosphide poisoning (Pondicherry 2019) (Sardar Patel University, Gujarat 2019) (Adesh, Bathinda 2018) (Sher-i-Kashmir Institute, Srinagar supple 2018) (VNS, Gujarat 2016)

Ans: Refer to long question no. 14.

58. McEwan sign (AIIMS Patna 2018) (VNS, Gujarat 2019)

Ans:

1. **McEwan's sign:** In alcohol intoxication, during the stage of coma, the pupils are contracted, but on stimulation of the person, e.g., by pinching or slapping causes them to dilate with slow return.
2. This is rarely seen.

59. Signs and Symptoms of Strychnine Poisoning (Adesh, Bathinda supple 2018)

Ans: A *'conscious'* seizure is the characteristic of strychnine poisoning.

Signs and Symptoms

1. Bitter taste.
2. Stiffness of neck and face.
3. Restlessness, increased acuity of perception, muscular twitchings.
4. Cyanosed face, eyeballs are prominent and staring, pupils are dilated. Mouth is filled with bloodstained froth.
5. **Convulsions:** Any sensory stimulus (light, pain, touch) may produce violent seizures. Initially, clonic but eventually become tonic, and affect all the muscles at the same time.
   - **Risus sardonicus** results from raising of patient's eyebrows, bulging of eyes and contraction of facial muscles in which the corners of the mouth are drawn back leading to a grin.
   - Convulsions are most marked in anti-gravity muscles resulting in hyperextension **(opisthotonus)**.
   - During convulsions, the patient remains conscious and aware of surroundings. In between convulsions, muscles are completely relaxed and breathing is resumed.
   - After 5–15 min, on the slightest impulse, another convulsion occurs with increased intensity.
   - Death occurs within 4–5 convulsions as the patient cannot breathe.

60. Desribe various positional changes in strychnine poisoning. (Sardar Patel University, Gujarat supple 2015)

Ans:

1. **Opisthotonus:** Contraction of the paravertebral muscles on back of trunk resulting in arch shape of back. Legs are extended, head is bent backwards and arms are flexed over the chest and hands clenched with heels touching the ground.
2. **Emprosthotonus** due to spasm of abdominal muscles, body may bend forwards (bending in front of emperor).
3. **Pleurosthotonus:** Body may bend to sides (bending along the pleura).

61. Treatment of strychnine poisoning (Sardar Patel University, Gujarat 2018)

Ans:

Control Convulsions

1. Keep patient in dark room, noise free room as any sort of sensory stimulus can start the convulsions
2. Start with diazepam IV followed by phenobarbital IV to control convulsions
3. If not effective—start muscle relaxants
4. Last resort—general anaesthetic agents (if all other measures fail)

After Controlling Convulsions

1. Gastric lavage with 1:5000 $KMnO_4$ and activated charcoal (cautiously)
2. Forced alkali diuresis—to enhance excretion of strychnine in urine
3. Symptomatic treatment.

62. Snakebite (Sher-i-Kashmir Institute, Srinagar supple 2017) (AIIMS Patna 2016) (BFUHS, Punjab supple 2016)

Neurotoxic snakebite (BFUHS, Punjab 2017)

Ans: Refer to long question no. 9.

63. Treatment of snakebite (SGRD, Amritsar 2019) (Uttarakhand University supple 2017) (Adesh, Bathinda supple 2017)

Ans: Refer to long question no. 9.

64. Polyvalent Antisnake venom used in India (West Bengal University supple 2017) (Sardar Patel University, Gujarat supple 2015)

Ans:

Polyvalent Antivenom

1. It neutralizes the venoms of several different species of snakes, usually the most prevalent in a particular geographical area.
2. It is less potent, less immunogenic and less effective than monovalent, and has more adverse effects (caused particularly by non-neutralized part of the polyvalent ASV).
3. In India, polyvalent ASV is raised in horses using the venoms of the four most important venomous species (cobra, krait, Russell's viper and saw-scaled viper).
4. Antivenom is indicated for patients with clinical manifestations with moderate to severe envenomation.
5. *Dose:* Freeze-dried (lyophilized) antivenom serum is dissolved in water. About 80–100 mL serum should be diluted in 200–500 mL of isotonic saline and given slow IV.
6. The recommended initial dose of ASV is 8–10 vials administered slowly via IV route over a period of 1 h.

65. Various forms of Cannabis Indica (Adesh, Bathinda 2017) (Sai Tirupati Univesity, Rajasthan 2019)

Ans:

Various Preparations of Cannabis

1. **Bhang** is the mildest of cannabis preparations (2–5% of active principle). It consists of dried cannabis leaves that are ground to a fine paste and taken as beverage.
2. **Majum:** Sweetmeat made with bhang.
3. **Ganja:** Obtained from flowering tops of female plant. Moderately potent (5–8%). It is mixed with tobacco and smoked in hukka/pipe.
4. **Hashish** is highly potent, concentrated cannabis resin that has been collected, dried and pressed into bricks.
5. **Charas** is a resinous exudate and handmade form of hashish. It is potent (10–20%) and is mixed with tobacco and smoked in hukka/pipe.
6. **Marijuana** refers to tobacco-like preparations of dried leaves and flowers. It is usually smoked, although it is occasionally baked into foods such as brownies or brewed as tea for drinking.

66. Classify Pesticides. Discuss signs and symptoms of OPC poisoning. (Jammu and Kashmir 2017)

Ans: Refer to long question no. 6.

67. Describe alcohol intoxication. (Sher-i-Kashmir Institute, Srinagar supple 2017) (Uttarakhand University 2017)

Ans:

Definition: It is a condition associated with drinking of too much of alcohol in a short interval of time. This may result in poisoning. The following signs and symptoms may be seen:

1. **Stage of excitement** *(Blood level: 50–150 mg%)*

   Euphoria, unrestrained behavior, alteration of time and space perception, might disclose secrets, show increased confidence, lack self-control, lowering of visual acuity, poor concentration and attention, and impaired judgment.
2. **Stage of in-coordination** *(Blood level: 150–250 mg%)*

   Person may be cheerful/irritable/sleepy—depending on the dominant impulses released. Nausea and vomiting, clumsiness, in-coordination of fine movements, and alterations in speech and fine. Flushed face, rapid pulse. Sense of touch, taste, smell and hearing are diminished, prolonged reaction time, hypothermia, breath smells of alcohol. Pupils are dilated and react sluggishly to light.
3. **Stage of coma** *(Blood level >250 mg%)*

   Thick and slurred speech, incoordination, rapid pulse, hypothermia, amnesia, diplopia, pupils are contracted. Patient passes into coma with steatorous breathing.

Fatal dose: 150–250 ml of absolute alcohol consumed in 1 h (BAC >300 mg/dl).

Treatment

1. Maintain airway, breathing and circulation (ABC).
2. Patient is kept warm, and made to lie on the side to minimize risk of aspiration.
3. In comatose and extremely intoxicated patient, endotracheal intubation and ventilator is useful.
4. Gastric lavage with alkaline solution within 2 h of ingestion.
5. Normal saline with 10% glucose and 15 units of insulin or 50% dextrose (50 in 100 ml) is given IV.
6. Thiamine 100 mg in 500 ml glucose solution IV. Multivitamins with folate and magnesium may be added to it.
7. Hemodialysis may be used.
8. In case of aggressive behavior, sedation may be given.

68. Differential diagnosis of opium poisoning. (Adesh, Bathinda supple 2019, 2017)

Ans:

Differential Diagnosis of Opium Poisoning

1. **Intracranial hemorrhage:** Stroke and brain trauma.
2. **Poisoning:** Alcohol, barbiturates, benzodiazepine, carbolic acid, CO and OPC.

3. **Metabolic conditions:** Diabetic and uremic coma.
4. **CNS infections:** Meningitis, encephalitis, encephalopathy and cerebral malaria.
5. **Others:** Epileptic and hysterical coma, and heat stroke.

DIFFERENTIATIONS

1. Poisonous and non-poisonous snakebite (Sardar Patel University, Gujarat 2020) (Sher-i-Kashmir Institute supple 2017) (GMC, Chandigarh 2015)

	Poisonous snakebite	Non-poisonous snakebite
Fang marks	Bite leaves two fang marks	Leave a semicircular set of teeth marks
Bite site	Discoloration, swelling, cellulitis and hemorrhage	Redness and slight swelling
Treatment	Wound care, antisnake venom, tetanus	Wound care, tetanus

	Poisonous snake	Non-poisonous snake
Head scales	Small	Large
Belly scales	Large and cover the entire breadth of belly	Small, and do not cover the entire breadth
Fangs	Long and canalized	Short and solid
Tail	Compressed	Not so
Habits	Nocturnal	—do—

2. Russell viper and cobra (Andhra Pradesh, supple 2016)

	Russell Viper	Cobra
Venom	Vasculotoxic	Neurotoxic
Pupils	Vertical	Circular
Reproduction	Viviparous	Oviparous
Head	Large, triangular, covered by small scales	Small, covered by large scales
Body	Short, stout	Long, Cylindrical
Tail	Tapering	Round
Fangs	Long, mobile, canalised	Short, fixed, grooved
Maxillary bone	Only fangs	Fangs and other teeth

3. Dhatura and chilli seeds (BFUHS, Punjab supple 2020) (Adesh, Bathinda supple 2019, 2016) (Rajasthan University 2017)

	Dhatura seeds	Chilli seeds
Size	Large	Small
Appearance	Kidney-shaped	Round
Color	Dark brown	Yellow
Taste	Bitter	Pungent
Smell	Odorless	Pungent
Convex border	Double edged	Single edged
Cut section	Embryo curved outwards	Embryo curved inwards

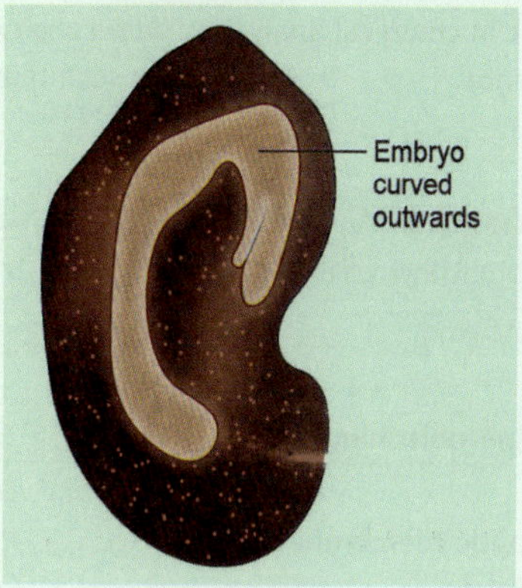

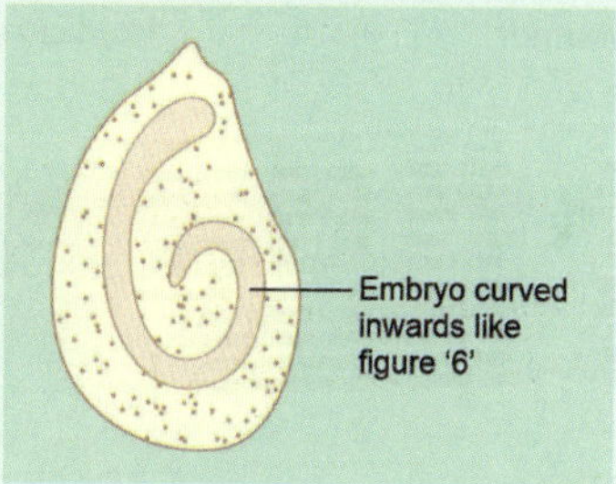

4. Ideal homicidal and ideal suicidal poisoning (Adesh, Bathinda supple 2016)

	Ideal homicidal poisoning	Ideal suicidal poisoning
Symptoms	Should mimic natural death	Should cause easy, painless, quick death
Characteristics	Colorless, odorless, tasteless	Does not matter
Onset of signs and symptoms	Should be slow (to avoid suspicion)	Should be very quick
Toxicity	Highly toxic	Highly toxic
PM changes	There should be no PM signs of its poisoning	Does not matter
Detectability	Should not be detected on chemical tests	Does not matter
Example	Arsenic, insulin, thallium	Opium, OPC, alphos, barbiturates

5. **Arsenic poison and cholera** (Adesh, Bathinda 2019) (BFUHS, Punjab 2015, supple 2019) (AIIMS Patna 2015) (Uttarakhand University 2015) (Delhi university 2015) (Sardar Patel University, Gujarat 2015, Supple 2015)

	Arsenic poison	**Cholera**
Symptoms (in order of appearance)	1. Pain in throat 2. Vomiting 3. Purging	1. Purging 2. Vomiting 3. Pain in throat
Vomitus	Contains mucus, bile and blood	Watery without mucus and bile
Stools	Rice watery; ± blood	Rice watery without blood
Tenesmus and anal pain	Present	Absent
Voice changes	Absent	Present
Lab investigation	Presence of arsenic in chemical analysis	*Vibrio cholera* present
Manner	Homicidal > accidental	No such thing

6. **Strychnine poisoning and tetanus** (BFUHS, Punjab 2019) (KHMS, Tamil Nadu 2015) (Uttarakhand University 2017). (Rajasthan University 2017) (Rajiv Gandhi University, Bengaluru 2015)

	Strychnine poisoning	**Tetanus**
Onset of symptoms	Sudden	Gradual
Site of action	Postsynaptic membrane	Presynaptic membrane
Convulsions	Generalised	Localised
Lock jaw	No preference	Seen predominantly
Fatal period	<2 hrs	>24 hrs
State in between convulsions	Relaxed	Rigid
Lab diagnosis	Strychnine can be found	*Clostridium tetani* found in lab culture